NEIL M. GUNN:

The Man and the Writer

A

NEIL M. GUNN

NEIL M. GUNN:
The Man and the Writer

Edited by
Alexander Scott
&
Douglas Gifford

WILLIAM BLACKWOOD
Edinburgh and London
1973

Published by William Blackwood & Sons Ltd, 32 Thistle Street, Edinburgh EH2 1HA, with the assistance of the Scottish Arts Council.

Introduction © Alexander Scott and Douglas Gifford, 1973

Selection © William Blackwood & Sons Ltd, 1973

Printed at the Press of the Publisher

ISBN: 0 85158 115 3

CONTENTS

(*Between pages 216 and 217 and 248 and 249 there are a
number of portraits of Neil M. Gunn, of his wife and
contemporary writers, and of his landscape.*)

Introduction

This collection of biographical, critical and bibliographical essays is published in honour of the eightieth birthday of Scotland's greatest living novelist, Neil Miller Gunn, whose splendid career in fiction spanned the years from 1926, and whose work remains a living influence both inside and outside his native country among writers and readers of every generation.

The editors are grateful to all the contributors to the collection for their readiness to join in this tribute to a man and a writer for whom they have the highest admiration and the deepest affection. We are grateful to the Scottish Arts Council and to its Literature Committee under the chairmanship of Neil Paterson, as well as its Assistant Director, Trevor Royle, for their interest and aid at all stages of the work. To Professor Francis Hart we owe a particular debt for his dedicated researches into Gunn's life and fiction. The novelist's brother John Gunn has been a constant source of assistance and encouragement throughout the project; for the fine photographs included in the volume we thank him and the novelist, as well as the Glasgow Art Gallery and Museum who allowed the painting 'Authors in Session' to be reproduced. We are also extremely grateful to David Fletcher of Messrs Blackwood for his devoted work on behalf of the book.

To Neil Gunn himself we owe more thanks than can be indicated in this brief foreword. We hope that the book speaks for itself. All the essays contained in it have been written for the occasion.

Alexander Scott
Douglas Gifford

TRIBUTE

The Burning Harp

A story for the eightieth birthday of Neil Gunn

GEORGE MACKAY BROWN

Two nights before Yule in the year 1155 a farmer called Olaf and his wife Asleif and all their household were sitting at supper in their house at Duncansby in Caithness, when a kitchen girl looked up and said that there was a fire in the thatch. They all looked up; the roof was burning. Then Anna a dairy girl pointed; the window was all flame and smoke. "We should leave the house now," said Olaf. "We are not going to die of cold, that much is sure," said his wife Asleif. The door was two red crackling posts and a crazy yellow curtain.

"I think we are having visitors for Yule," said an old ploughman who was sitting with an ale-horn in the corner. "I am too old for such boisterous guests. I think I will go to bed." While the women ran from wall to wall yelling the old ploughman stretched himself out on a bench and seemed to go to sleep. Olaf and Asleif kissed each other in the centre of the room. "I am glad of one thing," said Olaf, "our son Swegn is out fishing in the Pentland Firth."

The whole gable end of the house burst into flames.

Outside there was snow on the ground and beyond the burning house it was very dark. A dozen men one by one threw their torches into the rooted blaze. They took out their daggers and axes in case anyone should try to escape from the fire. A thousand sparks flew about like bees and died in the white midden and the ditch that was one long blue shadow.

A man called Ragnar said, " There are innocent ones inside, servants and children. We have no quarrel with them. They should be let out."

Oliver threw a bucket of water over the door. He shouted, " Servants of Olaf, and any children, you are to come out now."

A few girls ran out into the night with glaring eyes and rushed past the besiegers and were lost in the darkness beyond. A boy came out. He turned and looked back at the fire once, then he ran laughing after the servants, rising and falling in the snow, wild with excitement.

" I don't think we should have done that," said Nord. " These servants will tell the story of the burning all over Caithness. You know how women exaggerate. People here and there will think poorly of us for this night's work. That boy will grow up and remember the burning."

Now that the girls were out of the house all was much quieter inside. Even the tumult of the flames was stilled a little. In the silence they heard the sound of a voice praying.

" Valt the priest is inside," said Oliver. " I had forgotten that he might be here at this time of year. We would not be very popular with the bishop or the monks if Valt were to die. Throw another bucket of water at the door."

Father Valt came out with a scorched cross between his fingers. There was soot in his beard. He said to Oliver and the other besiegers, " God pity you, my poor children." Then he turned and absolved the dead and the dying inside, and walked away slowly towards the church at the shore.

" We didn't get much gratitude out of that priest," said
Nord. " In my opinion it was a mistake to let a man like
that go. With Father Valt it will be hellfire for all us
burners from now until the day he is able to preach no more.
We will have no comfort at all, standing in his kirk."

They heard a few faint harpstrokes through the snorings
and belchings of flame.

" It is my opinion," said Ragnar, " that there is a poet
inside."

" Well," said Nord, " what is a poet more than a miller
or a fisherman or a blacksmith? "

" From the sound of the harp," said Oliver, " from the
way it is being played, it seems to me that the poet in there
is none other than Niall from Dunbeath."

" Well," said Nord, " and what about it? What is
Niall more than other string-pluckers, Angus say, or Keld,
or Harald? "

" Nord," said Oliver, " you are very thick in the head.
I would keep my mouth shut. Niall is the poet who made
the ballad of the silver shoals in the west. He also sang
about the boy and the fishing-boat—if I am not mistaken that
was the first story he told. He was the one too who made
us aware of the mysterious well of wisdom. He made that
great song about the salmon."

" It would be a pity indeed, I suppose," said Nord, " if
the harp of a man like that was to be reduced to a cinder."

" Nobody in Scotland sings with such purity and
sweetness as Niall," said Oliver. " We would be shamed for
ever if we stopped such a mouth with ashes. The world,
we are told, will end in this way, some day soon, in ice and
fire and darkness. But how can a harp stroke given to the
wind ever perish, even though there are no men left on earth?

The gods will hear that music with joy for ever."

So another bucket of water was thrown over the threshold and the name of the poet Niall was called into the red-and-black dapple inside. Presently an old serene man carrying a harp walked from the burning house into the snow. He seemed not to see the lurid faces all about the door. Honoured, he sought the starlit darkness beyond the lessening circles of flame.

BIOGRAPHICAL

Neil M. Gunn : A Brief Memoir

FRANCIS RUSSELL HART

My friendship with Neil Gunn, an insignificant part of his later life, began eleven years ago in academic literary correspondence, progressed to biennial visits between 1965 and 1971, and has far outlived its academic origins to become, for me and my wife, a precious comradeship with one whom Alex Reid, an older and closer friend, calls, ' not only " a great writer " but a truly wise man, with a wisdom that is based always on his personal experience, is built into the structure of his very being, and comes out in his every action and even his most witty and whimsical remarks '. I shall make no effort to conceal my love and gratitude in what follows.

What follows is drawn from personal as well as published sources: the autobiographical books and essays, facts and phrases from Neil's letters, rough notes of our three or four dispersed weeks of talk, and several helpful letters of reminiscence from some of Neil's old friends and close kin responding to my pleas for help. I have benefited as well from essays by John Pick, George Bruce and Alex Reid, and from talks with Neil's brothers, his sister-in-law and his kind friend, Mrs Ena Macleod of Perth.

Finally, this is indeed a ' memoir ' based only on personal and collective memories, all fallible. It is written far from public records, and should be taken accordingly as a first essay—nothing more.

Neil Gunn has often described his native Caithness in

fiction. *Morning Tide* shows the home on the high street, built of stone by his father, the byre behind, the rented pasture, the village, and the small harbour below. *Highland River* preserves the reality of Dunbeath Water throughout its symbolic quest for springs. *Sun Circle* recreates the prehistoric shore and strath, the broch near Chapel Hill, the moor where Gael and Viking battled while a small older race lurked inland. *The Silver Darlings* evokes a nineteenth-century past when the whole Moray Firth teemed with the herring fisheries. *The Grey Coast*, the first of the novels (1926), shows Neil's unmistakable eye for landscape and ' other landscape ', trained on the ' intricately sculptured cliffs ', the ' geos and stacks and contorted strata ', that are ' more typical of Caithness than all else '. It is difficult to visualise Caithness other than through the binocular lenses of Neil's pervasive dualism. For, ' of all places, such a grey strip of crofting coast, flanked seaward by great cliffs, cliffs " flawed " as in a half-sardonic humour of their Creator to permit of the fishing creek, was surely of this duality of the mind, whereby the colourless, normal life becomes at once a record of the stolidly obvious and of the dreamlike unknown '. But the literal image is primary, the task of the memoirist is matter-of-fact, and Neil's own healthy respect for fact must be his monitor. History for Neil in school was ' very poor ', being chiefly the chronicle of English dates; history for the Scot, being ' full of facts, most of them ugly ', is not to be trusted. Nevertheless, the givens of experience come first, and no one, not even novelists, must violate them.

Neil's ' literal ' image of Caithness belongs to an essay done for Scott Moncrieff's *Scottish Country* (1935). Turning from Sutherland's grandeur, he has us ' walk out upon

Caithness, and at once experience an austerity in the flat clean windswept lands ', know ' a movement of the spirit that finds in the austerity, because strength is there also, a final serenity ', unique among Scottish landscapes. Here is Neil Gunn's unmistakable keynote: ' the wind of time has searched out even the flaws here and cleansed them '. It echoes as well on the white beach of John o' Groats, ' not the poet's dove-grey sand, but the crushed shells of whiteness from which all the sticky humours have been withdrawn . . . typical of this clean-swept county '. The effect of light on the wide Caithness moor catches the mind likewise in a timelessness ' more intimate than life and death '. But finally, Caithness is the sea. Coming from Sutherland, ' alluring, beckoning, heedless, feminine ', one finds the Caithness coast ' something simple, elemental, masculine ', and a kind of masculine life grew there. ' A fine breed of men, too, these Caithness fishermen, daring, self-reliant, rarely hypocritical or sanctimonious, game for whatever life offered in the sea-storm or in the public-house, and God-fearing over all. . . . Few of the mean " safe " qualities found time to sprout.'

Their life—the wonder story of the Moray Firth, the hectic blaze of the herring fisheries—was still a living memory when Neil was born. In 1840 Wick had 428 native boats and 337 strange ones at the fishing, and the minister complained that Wick drank up 500 gallons of whisky in a day. Down the east coast from Wick—twenty miles or more through Ulbster, Lybster, and Latheronwheel to Dunbeath—and on to Berriedale and Helmsdale the industry kept a life alive, with a great thirst, but not without its pieties. Neil takes this vignette from living memory: ' the crews of hundreds upon hundreds of boats at sea on a quiet evening, after their nets had been shot, taking up, one after another, one of the Psalms of David, until it seemed the sea itself sang and the cliffs and cottages were held in wonder '. Neil's youngest brother, born in 1901, was in time to remember the fulness of the older life at Dunbeath: ' Every day was as full as the meat of an egg.' He was home, too, to see emigrations pick up when work dropped off in the early years of the century. By 1911, seventy Lybster men and boys brought only 536 crans of herring, and by the 1930s, Neil reports, in small places like Dunbeath or Lybster, ' only four or five motor boats pursued the old calling '.

I walked by his side one grey July day in 1965 down the deserted quay, toward the breakwater of *Morning Tide*, past the old salmon house in the hillside. One old man worked where the nets were repaired, beyond him a row of ruined stone cottages, back up the beach more of the same. " When I was a boy," said Neil, looking east over the empty harbour, " there was enormous life there. The harbour would be solid with boats. But herring fishing died out at the beginning of this century, and now the atomics at Dounreay, where the men go daily by bus to work, have killed the harbour." There was no bitterness in his voice. There never is. But the bitterness had to be worked out in early novels, *The Grey Coast, The Lost Glen*, and the message of *Off in a Boat* is none the less severe for its evenness of tone: ' from the independence of crofting and sea-fishing or other natural industry to the dependence on tourism and sport is a regrettable descent '.

Sentimental guidebooks of the turn of the century, oblivious to such facts, find Dunbeath, ' Hill of the Birches ', the prettiest town in the ' shire ', with a ' Swiss-like appearance' and a strath famous with picnickers. Here Neil was born on 8th November 1891, the seventh of nine surviving children. James, the oldest brother, remained an excise officer in Scotland during his lifetime. Three others— including the older brother of *The Atom of Delight* and *Morning Tide*—Donald, David and Benjamin, emigrated to Canada, and all three died in or as a result of the First World War. Of the two sisters, Jessie and Mary, both older than Neil, one married a doctor and settled in Dalry, in Galloway, while the other married John George Sutherland, head of the police at Invergordon. After Neil in the late '90s came John, now retired H.M. Chief Inspector of Schools, and in 1901 Alex, retired schoolmaster of Castletown. The father died in 1916; the mother in 1926. Both parents are buried in Latheron Parish cemetery. Afterwards the Sutherlands provided a family home in the north. It was Sutherland who told Neil that Chapel Hill above Dunbeath had been called 'The Hill of Peace' and thus helped to conceive *Sun Circle*. To Sutherland, *Butcher's Broom* is dedicated.

Neil repeatedly insists, "I never made up anything extraordinary in my novels: invention is too easy." So I have asked him often for the real-life ancestries, however oblique, of his characters. No, none of the fathers in the novels reflected his own. "They were all 'outside' for me. Some of the west coast fathers, however—I heard of them—were often tyrants." The heroic skipper of *Morning Tide* was obviously an exception. Neil heard of his father's skill later from an old Dunbeath man who had seen him put a boat just bought from the Duke of Sutherland through her paces in the bay to the cheers of the local boys. And old Malcolm Macleod, of Bernera, fisherman father of

Neil's friend Dr Peter Macleod, turned out to be one of his father's Gaelic-speaking crew. He sailed each year from Lewis to Ullapool and walked across Scotland to Dunbeath. Neil met old Malcolm at the time when he was collecting materials for *The Silver Darlings*, and it is no accident that this is the book dedicated ' to the memory of my father '. The Freudian critic could picnic amply on the disappearance there of the ' real father ' and the curious three-cornered combat of boy, bereft young mother, and would-be stepfather, heroic but intimidating fishing captain. But I know what Neil's response would be to such ingenuity, for as we walked a bit past the Dalcraig gate down the shore road near Kessock one summer afternoon, we saw a young bull leaping and galloping in the sloping field—and Neil said, " The Freudian would say it was sex, but it may be just the flies! "

" If his mother was the earth, his father was the sea. In fact he could hardly think of his father without thinking of the sea." The father, John Gunn reports, was a wonderfully quick witty man who had been at school in Dunbeath in the 1850s even though it wasn't compulsory until the 1870s. He makes brief, quiet appearances in *The Atom of Delight* as the brave, kindly figure coming home up the steps from the harbour, the father of *Morning Tide*. Although a figure of authority, he gave no thrashings. The gamekeeper was more awesome. The schoolmaster's thrashings were a force in nature to be reckoned with. The minister— ' whitebearded, tall, erect, square-shouldered figure in the pulpit—archetype surely of the patriarchs ', was ' the son of a poor crofter, and as a lad had walked his 250-odd miles to Edinburgh University (starting out with a stone of oatmeal on his back), and, at the end of the session, had walked them back '. Neil recalls never being ' inside ' of religious orthodoxy. Were his parents orthodox? " They were very broad-minded people," John Gunn recalled, " but they had to live in the community." " My father," Neil recalls, " would take down the book every Sunday and read chapters, and we would all take turns, and it was a game to see who got the shortest verse. I remember "—the word rolls out and his face lights with glee—" I managed once to get ' and Jesus wept ', and read it *triumphantly*, and my father looked at me as if to say, ' That's not the tone to use.' But that was all."

" On my mother's side," Neil teased once, " I'm afraid we had a professor in America. She was a Miller. She runs into the Stewarts, all rather brainy people." John recalls George Stewart, head of a medical faculty somewhere in the western United States, coming home to visit during Mrs Gunn's last painful years. *Atom* gives the image of ' his mother's grave face ' and notes that ' she had to use a stern voice at times '. Just as Neil has no memory of thrashings from his father, so he ' has no memory of having been kissed by his mother '. Yet she was ' at the centre of the world '. ' Where she was everything else was about her, naturally each in its own right and pleased to be there.' Here is the germ or echo of those solitudes of mother and son that give the novels some of their most resonant moments: *Morning Tide, Butcher's Broom, The Silver Darlings*, and of course the nativity scene of *Bloodhunt*. On a more ideological level, there is the playful rejoinder (in *Atom*) to Freud's patriarchialism—' matriarchy preceded patriarchy and the first gods were female '; the notion that ' the drama of the father horde is a man-made drama for men, and all that follows from it may be expected to be bloody in a terrible and terribly dull way '; the insistence, in *Butcher's Broom* and elsewhere, that the reality behind ' history ' is a legendary continuity of ' innumerable women whose suffering and endurance were like little black knots holding the web of history together '.

The remembered family of *Atom* also includes the ' long brotherly sequence ', with repeated references to a single unnamed older brother, a kindly monitor four or five years older, and a younger brother, the model for the boy sent to the beach in *Morning Tide*. Young Art, the later hero of two novels, was inspired instead by Neil's nephew Hamish, who once in a shop saw a toy engine he very much wanted, for four and sixpence. " Could you possibly led me have it," he asked, looking up at the clerk, " for sixpence as an extreme obligement? " But anyone blessed in recent years with the sight of Neil, John and Alex together knows what a careful, whimsical devotion brotherhood for Neil has been; the destructive perversion of brotherhood in *Bloodhunt* and the affirmative image of brotherhood in *The Key of The Chest* assume new power in a biographical perspective.

Dunbeath as a larger community evidently prompted other characters, but I can report only two. Old Hector is " a composite of two or three old men whom I knew as a little boy "; one thinks of the old road man who kept the moor road above Dunbeath Strath in repair. And Tom, the freethinking protagonist of *The Serpent*, has a Dunbeath ancestor:

> When I was a boy there was a man who had gone to Glasgow to work, then returned, opened a cycle shop, hired cycles, did many kinds of repairs *and* was a free-thinker. A quiet but persistent man, with a sense of

humour. Sporadic talks about most things, including Socialism and no doubt religion, though I was too young to be more than vague about it. He is not Tom of the book, though the seed of the conception may have been there. But I should say that in most communities in the Highlands there would have been then one Sceptic at least. . . . I was a very small boy with an elder brother and two others when we saw a serpent (as we called the adder) pouring through a clump of heather. I think that was the first one I had ever seen.

But the boy Neil most vividly—essentially—recalls is the boy alone, ' the boy of the strath ', the ' prehistoric boy in a modern strath ', ' the nut-cracking young savage on his river stone '. The strath was the ideal size for a small boy up to ten or twelve. It was three miles up and three miles back, up the river lined with birches, with rowans, alders and oaks. Surprised rabbits scurried off; a couple of peewits screamed, a curlew joined in; from the hazel tree at the pool a chaffinch gave an angry *spink! spink!*, and from the hillside above, a willow wren's song came tumbling down. Varieties of nuts were there to be cracked with stones from the river, and blaeberries, pods of wild violet, wild bees' honey. Finally there was the challenge of the salmon pool, ' the brown tinge in the hill water that went black in the depths '. Such is the image left by *Atom*, and it need only be echoed here as the *local* of that essential impulse: the boy Neil breaking away, star-runner of the local games, from the stone house, away from the men round the fire, the byre up back, the family cow's grazing, the family chores and rhythms and ties—' I'm off! I'm away! and sheer into the freedom of the strath the boy flew! ' And beyond the strath.

Less than thirteen years in a boyhood place, and the

shock of departure closed the circle of myth. Childhood, says Nabokov, always has this mythic integrity. But Neil's departure was no exile. His sister, who married the doctor and settled in Dalry in Kirkcudbright, had no children of her own and her invitation to live with them was exhilarating. Moreover, " With brothers in Canada, cousins in Australia, an uncle in New Zealand and another in New York "—and even a brainy Stewart in the western United States—" we were in touch with the whole wide world and felt so even in remote Caithness." The two years in Galloway are briefly recalled in *Atom.* Formal schooling ended, and a private tutor took over and imparted a love for poetry on walks ' up the Earlston way '. His voice trembled when he read Tennyson. The headmaster of the local Latin school also provided temporary aid, as well as fishing expeditions. And Neil, for whom, at school in Dunbeath, ' arithmetical reasoning ' had been the ' strength ', discovered he must work up Euclid on his own, and surreptitiously did so. The results soon spoke exceedingly well for the educational method. There were tests to be taken.

For at ' about fifteen ', the essential impulse came again. " Och, I just wanted to get off—away—by myself, and I heard about the Civil Service Examination." He heard, in fact, that he had a fifteen-to-one chance for a four-year boy-clerkship, took his parsing and geometrical skills uncoached to Edinburgh, came out of the exam high on the passing list and was posted off to London with a few emergency pounds in a Gladstone bag. His job five and a half days a week was ' hard writing ', at full speed, on warrants, acknowledgements, envelopes for bundles of bank books in the Post Office Savings Bank branch at

Shepherd's Bush, beyond Bayswater and Notting Hill, a long ride on the twopenny tube or horse bus, longer on a borrowed bicycle or late-night walk, west of Westminster and London. He remembers this job as the only hard work he ever did! His wages were fifteen shillings a week, with a yearly increment of a shilling a week. His digs, soon shared with two other Scots boys, cost twelve shillings. This was exotic, drab Edwardian London, for the stranger aged fifteen to sixteen from ' the strath, the corrie, the dizzy cliffs '.

It was a brave, athletic stranger, who evidently relished the spectacle. Neil speaks of it still with excitement. " I saw a side of London life—prostitutes on street corners and the rest—which was," he told me, " really astounding to a fifteen-year-old from Dunbeath and Galloway. I recall going by bus with this fellow Reid [*Atom* calls him ' Will '] I had digs with in Shepherd's Bush—to the sixpenny seats in the gallery to see Gilbert and Sullivan. Reid was very fond of Gilbert and Sullivan." They missed the last bus home. There was a visit to the Tivoli to see Harry Lauder, a Sunday morning in Petticoat Lane watching for pick-pockets, or in Kensington Gardens, or listening to the atheist speakers near Marble Arch. In the office, governed by an elderly pompous Civil Servant with flower in buttonhole and flawless crease in pinstripe trousers, there was a bold confrontation with a senior boy over places in the section football team. " The debate became heated," says Neil, " and one of the fellahs said if I said that sort of thing again he'd have me out in the cloakroom to settle it, and I told him I was quite prepared to go out in the cloak-room just then." It was settled, Neil had his place in the team, and this led in turn to a place as left back or occasion-ally centre forward in a west London team. Saturday afternoons ' the boy caught his tram and for twopence was hurled along Uxbridge Road to green fields in the west '. Introduction to that foreign game cricket, on the other hand, was momentary—a moment terrifying if triumphant facing that ' Lucifer of the sunlight ', the fast bowler. The bold runner of Dunbeath was still there, but silver birches, as incongruous as shy cockneys, had no business growing so far from the strath as Hampstead Heath.

The boy who did not take to cricket took, on the other hand, ' to Socialism as a duckling to water '. In a letter replying to queries about *The Serpent*, Neil associated Tom's city experience with his own late teen years. ' Now I was a teenager in both London and Edinburgh . . . and knew all the arguments (Huxley, Darwin, Haeckel and what have you). . . . Anyway, that kind of atmosphere. And though my reading was very limited, basic statements of doctrine &c. were whizzing around among us, or a good few of us. And I did read for my own information quite a bit of academic pol. econ.' The idols are recalled elsewhere: ' Haeckel and Huxley did have an effect on our early teens, and to this day I can repeat the lengthy advice to the seeker after truth to beware of the Idols of the Tribe.' On the poetic side, he could repeat half of Omar's *Rubá'iyát* from memory. And the Tennysonian tutor of Dalry had been replaced by the digs-mate Reid: " Reid," recalled Neil, " was very strong on Tennyson." " You were pretty strong on Tennyson yourself," interposed his brother John. " Yes," said Neil, " but Reid would lie on the bed reciting ' Airy Fairy Lilian '." Later literary gods were evident too. He recalls reading Pater's *Renaissance* several times when young. He recalls the excitement in London over Shaw and Wells, " true and startling innovators ", and on the other side of the ideological fence he read Chesterton and Belloc. London survives in memory as robust and exciting days, and it is no wonder that *The Atom of Delight* gives five climactic chapters to these two years, when the boy aged fifteen to seventeen suddenly knew the dual consciousness of the autonomous self, with its accompanying freedom and delight.

The chance to go back to the north led first to Edinburgh, where the boy clerk did his remaining two years on ' the income tax side '. " I lived," he recalls, " with medical students in digs near the Meadows, a nice old lady (like my housekeeper Isobel at Dalcraig) taking care of us. . . . I'm afraid we were rather wild." The recollected Edinburgh of the novels suggests a recklessness, an anxiety, a social malaise and peril, that the seventeen-year-old clerk, faced with a strenuous exam at the end of his final two years, may have felt. In *The Lost Glen*, *The Key of the Chest* and *The Drinking Well*, whose middle section gives Neil's fullest evocation of Edinburgh, city careers end prematurely. I mention these merely to note the sort of social and personal anxiety Neil might well have felt in his brief late adolescence in Edinburgh. Two specific recollections at least suggest a first exposure to social stratification of the sort his Highland community knew nothing of. He went to visit his mother's ' brainy ' relatives the Stewarts and played chess and discussed religion. And he recalls going with one of the medical students he shared digs with, doing his midwifery course, to attend a birth in the Edinburgh slums. A similar visit in the company of John MacNair Reid later in Glasgow was conflated with this into a nightmarish episode in *Wild Geese Overhead*.

After passing the higher exam for permanency, Neil

set his sights on the Customs and Excise Service, as only that service offered posts throughout the Highlands. He went through six weeks of training, and began a period of temporary assignments at various stations all over the Western Highlands. It was a period he remembers with strong nostalgia as his ' ten years of wandering ' (1911-21), a time of coming to know the Highlands and Islands intimately and coming to know people and incidents (many through his old-age pension investigations) which appear transformed in his books. He remembers himself in these years of freedom ' as a boy '. His sister and her husband had moved from Galloway to Glenelg, on the Sound of Sleat, across from Skye, and he recalls several visits there. The association (in 1937) of the new ferry at Kylerhea with the thought of Boswell and Johnson (Hugh Kingsmill and Hesketh Pearson had visited Neil in Inverness on *their* Highland jaunt a few weeks before) recalls, " As a lad I had many a time pulled my row-boat smartly into the current and then lain back to be floated away towards Glenelg. There was a Christmas memory, too, of carrying a pushbike on my back up the hillside through the snow and down the steep slopes to the shores of Loch Duig. But what sticks in the mind most persistently is a boyhood day spent on the moor beyond the stiff climb from Kylerhea." On the moor road winding towards Broadford, Neil spent " a whole summer day . . . guddling yellow trout, looking over the silent moors, seeing no living soul ", a " day of such curious and intimate loneliness, so withdrawn from all practical ways of being and thought, that I can afford to wonder if it happened to me in this life, or indeed if it happened at all ". Other moments, less alone, were less unearthly. " I had gone across to Raasay with a girl in a row-boat, leaving another couple on shore, and on the way back a growing wind very nearly beat us."

His temporary assignments took him farther into the Hebrides. Recalling the quieter, slower life, his memory finds an essential image on Benbecula:

> a picture of great waves on its western strand, a herd girl sheltering against a stook of corn, wild geese on a stubble field, in a grey day of small rain. What virtue there is in that picture I cannot tell, but it has already much of the force of legend. . . . It is the mood of human comradeship, quiet and simple, but strong. It is the smile that acknowledges Fate—and no more.

But the same memory fixes on the odd old English major—" if he was really a major I called him a colonel; if he was really a colonel I called him a major "—in the Benbecula hotel, who asked him once, in a late night debate on Omar, " Did you ever hear the beating of a distant drum? " The old major, Neil wrote me, did indeed keep a trunk of retired embassy candles in his little room. ' And even if he did not set the hotel on fire, he did light all those candles, and I remember going to sleep with a smile for the thought of the place going up in flames and the hope that I might wake up in time if it did.' He is translated now into *The Other Landscape*, and perhaps belongs in the company of another endearing fool who rises vaguely from the same period, the fellow-inspector who travelled with Neil, an Englishman who loved the Highlands so much he never went home. His mannerisms and his hopelessly inept spaniel led somehow to Cocklebuster of *The Well at the World's End*, " one character I fully visualised ", said Neil with delight. " I loved Cocklebuster."

The First World War made a strange episode in these

years. Neil had at least four brothers in the war. John Gunn recalls that all three from Canada were casualties— one on the battlefield, one in surgery, one back in British Columbia as an indirect result. The fourth was John himself, who joined the artillery after his father's death and was temporarily blinded in the first German gas attack— the story is told in *Highland River*. Neil recalls of the excise inspectors: " We were ordered to Stirling, then, for the physical exam, but told we wouldn't be called up, and if we enlisted we would lose our place. I remember the sergeant chap who did the measuring—he measured me and then called out ' SIX FEET! '. But I had four brothers fighting, and so I decided I had better stay, and though I was only a boy I was in charge of shipping and routing ships around minefields—I had been specially trained for work with shipping and mines on the west coast—away from the Minch, which had a German submarine we knew. I got telegrams with instructions from the Admiralty, and sent reports back of all I could learn." His station was at Kinlochleven, site of an aluminium plant; he lived for a time in a tent on a hillside near the pier. On occasion he would join Captain MacDougal, the harbourmaster, on the road to Kentallen, " to meet a foreigner and pilot her up the narrows. . . . I used sometimes to take the wheel and respond, ' Steady it is, sir,' for I got to know the seaway to Kinlochleven almost as well as the pilot himself ". The summer afternoon in " one of the long sea-fiords of Argyll " when he decided on the spur of the moment to try to beat the sunset shadow up the three thousand feet, seeing near midnight a herd of stags come over the brow of heather near the top, may belong here. And then there was the man from Tiree, the retired crofter-sailor in charge of loading at the Kinlochleven pier, reprimanded by his foreman for disobeying an order he considered recklessly unsafe. "He came straight over to the harbourmaster and myself who were his friends. His English at such a moment was naturally uncertain. But I remember the culminating sentence: 'I could have broken the pugger in three halves.'" One who has heard Neil's hilarious re-enactment comes upon the story in *Off in a Boat* with delight.

Near the end of the war even those specially trained were ordered to France. Neil went to say good-bye to his mother at Dunbeath. She looked at him and said, "Don't you think we have given enough?"

He had just got back to Inverness when the war ended. His assignments then took him on temporary duty to various distilleries, "being in charge of a distillery, perhaps, keeping accounts and checking to make sure none was sold without the duty being paid". Of the excise officer's job, he says, "Long experience has created an almost perfect system of supervision, interfering so little with practical operations and supplying such figures of liability or accountancy as distillers unhesitatingly accept, that normally the relations between the excise official and the distiller are pleasant and charged with mutual respect." Naturally, as Neil tells it, there was little work for the holiday substitute officer to do. "I'd replace Maurice Walsh, for instance," he told me, "for three weeks—and I'd write ahead and say, 'Look here! I'm coming to replace you. Kindly see that the books and all are in perfect order so that there is absolutely no work to be done.'" Walsh depicts their life in these years in his first novel, *The Key Above the Door*. The narrator Tom King in

B

Morayshire is joined by one Neil Quinn out of Ireland and Alistair Munro from Sutherland. Munro it is who is a ' rascally Heilan'man from the borders of Caithness ', whom ' the pools of the Dunbeath River knew . . . but too well '. But it is Neil Quinn whose friend is the daughter of a Dingwall house, a ' golden-haired Norse maiden '. And it is Neil Quinn who writes from Skye describing Neil Gunn's favourite ' duty ':

> I shall be here for a full month and shall be able to house you royally. The distillery officer is on leave, and I am doing duty for him. He has loaned me his house, his garden patch, and his motor-boat, so that I—and you— may not suffer as we deserve in the small house they call an inn, where the staple diet is salt herring, fresh whiting, and the flavour of peat. I cook ham and eggs to perfection; the mutton is the best in the islands; and rod and gun yield luxuries galore.

The culinary luxuries Neil Quinn prophesies Neil Gunn lovingly recalls in 1959 in an American magazine:

> The most memorable dish I ever ate was cooked in the Isle of Skye by Maurice Walsh and myself, before either of us started writing fiction. Here are the ingredients: one red grouse, two rabbits, butter and onions. While I prepared the rabbits, Maurice undressed the grouse. . . . We had a conscience about that grouse. I had got permission to fish and shoot rabbits but not to shoot grouse, for the grouse shooting had been let. Yet that bird had got up the previous evening in such a way that we thought it wounded. Like good sportsmen, we put it out of its agony. Then we learned it had not been wounded. So, next day, to soothe our consciences on the way back, we dropped into a place where we got two drams of Talisker whisky, twelve years old, out of a sherry hogshead.

Walsh's account of the same recipe may be found in chapter fifteen of *The Key Above the Door*.

There are many warm reminiscences of nights with Walsh and others in these years, salmon fishing, telling ghost stories in a ruined castle, sleeping in the heather, coming home at dawn, and Neil says of them urgently, " This sort of close companionship won't disappear in a hurry." There came the time, of course, when Walsh's country, Ireland, became independent, and he had to decide whether to remain or to take advantage of the choice offered Irish Civil Servants to go home. His wife Toshon had spent her whole life in Morayshire. " I had to help them decide what they should do," Neil told me, " and I told Toshon that I could only advise Maurice to do what his conscience told him to do, what he thought was right. And I told Toshon not to worry, that she'd get to know Ireland and feel quite at home there. Which she finally did, and spent the rest of her life in Ireland. I used to go over to visit them there every summer." When, in 1965, my wife and I drove over the Sutherland-Caithness border, Neil remembered how Walsh had stopped at the Kerry border, got out, shook hands solemnly, and said: " I welcome you to my county." There are good stories of the visits of the Gunns to the Walshes in Kerry, of Neil's growing fondness for Ireland, and rumours, too, of how this other exciseman turned novelist, who liked to boom out " I write RO-MANCE ", had trouble with his plots and sought and bought the help of the rascally Heilan'man from the pools of Dunbeath River.

By then the ten years of wandering had ended, and Neil Quinn's Dingwall friend, the ' golden-haired Norse maiden ', had entered the picture. Neil was sitting with Walsh and others in a distillery one idle summer day, being teased about the imminent news of his first fixed assignment. One darkly prophesied he would be sent to Wigan in Lancashire—and the letter came, and he was. " So I wrote Daisy," says Neil, " and she went down there and we were married in Lancashire—hastily, so that we could have the final six weeks on the lease of my predecessor's house." They were married in 1921, and Daisy died in 1963. Neil's and Daisy's mutual devotion is legendary.

Daisy was Jessie Frew. Her father was Provost of Dingwall, had a shop in the town, and she was the only one of the family to stay home from college and help her father. Her mother was related to Wilkie the painter. George Bruce told me that T. S. Eliot, who visited the Gunns, spoke of Neil as a fine novelist but was especially fond of " his lovely wife, Daisy ". Alex Reid recalls " an adorable as well as a most beautiful woman ". Another old friend remembers Daisy's long golden hair, which took half an hour to plait and made her look like a Burne-Jones painting. " How lovely and quiet she was," remarked Neil once, " and emotionally projected." She had two stories that she told. Once, visiting in Perth. she overheard two ladies say, " That's Mrs Neil Gunn. Isn't it a pity she dyes her hair! " And once at a dinner she heard a very formal lady with a long cigarette holder comment on the subject at hand: " I don't know much about sex, but I know a *little*." Such were Daisy's stories.

Her quiet, devoted role in Neil's life is implicit in her unobtrusive appearances in his books: ' the Crew ' of *Off in a Boat*, ' the Gardener ' of *Highland Pack*, and I would add the image of Primavera, Jenny, the heroine daft on flowers, in *Wild Geese Overhead*; but most notably, Fand, the patient whimsical wife of *The Well at the World's End*.

My query about this sent Neil to check 'his' copy. (It was actually Daisy's. She made him give her a copy of each book, knowing that otherwise he would never remember to keep one for himself.) His reply follows (13th July 1964):

> it began with an inscription on the first blank page: "This is Fand's own copy, from her husband N.M.G." . . . Anyway, I began to read—and (I hardly expected this) read on. For it described right off our setting out for a spell at one of our remote places, called the 'Picts' Houses' (an actual place, on the map), coming to a cottage, being directed to a well and so on, all as it actually happened. Then the vehicle that wasn't there—I still remember how desperately I looked for a passing-place. Then, having arrived, my attack on a salmon and Fand standing so awkward and gauche on the slippery stone with no boulder in her hands. . . . Last thing we did when the sun was setting was climb a near hill, see the silver sea that the sun left behind, listen in stillness to a hill bird, then wander back, and while Fand made the bed (the seats folded for the purpose) I'd fetch some water from the nearest hill burn for the dram, which was a good dram and sat quietly on the sill of the car window as the gloaming deepened.

This was just one of many later trips in the car fitted out for sleeping. Their favourite was the long circular drive west and by Achnasheen and Loch Maree; they spent many nights in the car above the shore of Gruinard Bay, then returned east to Dingwall. The companionship was complete. He noted once, in our drives, the place where he had lost his water jug, and whenever they passed the place he would jokingly promise to go back and look for it. She would observe, " You're a complete idiot," and he would respond, " And you're an utter ass."

The most memorable image of Daisy, however, was written in a letter at the time of her death by her husband, with all his marvellous gift for the commemoration of wonder—and I hope he will not mind a brief excerpt:

> her courage shed its normal golden light to the end, & the surgeon wrote to me, afterwards, about the wonder of it. There was a quiet still pool of goodness in her & it turns to light (as it always did) when I think about it; inside but at the same time outside, under the sky, with colour & gaiety in it. She loved flowers & made them grow everywhere & blossom. We were married over 42 years, & to look back is to see us wandering over the Highlands, sleeping in our car in lonely spots, in our boat among the Western Isles, times & homes & most of human experience.

All of this was yet to come in Wigan in 1921. In less than a year Neil applied for and got a transfer to a station in Lybster, a few miles north of Dunbeath. This, in fact, was the homecoming (after almost twenty years), and while Neil places his beginnings as a writer in Inverness, it is tempting to associate them with the regular revisits to Dunbeath, which were now possible. They would spend the morning and afternoon with Neil's mother, then retire to 'some remote corner', or an 'outpost 14 miles in the heart of our highest hills where the " back ran out " ', for fishing, for a climb to witness the sun rise from the top of Morven, and on one occasion a quest for the likely source of his Highland river. They had a camp site, too, near the cottage of a shepherd, where they visited for a milk supply, blether with the shepherd and (after drams) the shepherd's piping. 'From the shepherd,' writes my kind and modest authority, ' he learned much of his sheep knowledge, from the local fishermen of Dunbeath much of his sea knowledge. For hours he would sit with a select few listening to their tales of storms, calms, and great catches, of days of prosperity and adversity and of the grim uncertainty of the sea.' The Lybster station closed, and the Gunns were assigned to Inverness, where they would live for more than a decade, and where Neil would combine his duties as an excise officer with the early writing that established his reputation and the quiet activities that made him an influential force in Highland Nationalist politics.

Recognition as a writer had come much earlier. Authoritative hearsay has it in Neil's last session at school before leaving Dunbeath. The seldom imaginative essay subjects assigned included ' A Sea Storm '. I quote from my authority:

> Came the day of retribution. Taking his stance mid floor with exam papers in left hand the teacher in no uncertain voice told the class what he thought of their misuse of tenses, poor spelling etc etc and then gave out the marks (possible 25). Mary McKay 21, Jean Sinclair 20, George Sutherland 20 until finally only two papers were left. John McKay 5. " Take it home, John. Frame it and nail it to the wall where you and all may see. Neil Gunn—come out to the floor. Your choice, and you were the only one in the class to choose it, was ' The Sea Storm '. $24\frac{1}{2}$ marks out of 25. Boy, that is the highest mark I have ever given for an essay. You are a credit to your teacher, your school, and your parents." Forthwith he read the essay to the class, then taking Neil by the shoulder led him through the other classrooms reading the essay in each one.

The prize-winning writer was thus in public view a quarter-century before a short story called ' The Sea ' won a contest and was expanded into a triumphant second novel, *Morning Tide*. Numerous other short stories prepared the way.

Neil sent his first story to *Pan* magazine—which switched to become a fiction magazine in the early '20s—under an assumed name: he used two in those years, McPhee and McNeill. I have been unable so far to trace the magazine, but the short story collection, *Hidden Doors* (1929), does not mention *Pan*. He was stunned to receive a reply asking if he would accept twelve guineas for the story. Then he began sending stories under his own name to *The Cornhill*, which paid more. The first appears in *The Cornhill*, June 1924 (' The Sleeping Bins '), and it published three more stories—one in 1925, one in 1926, one in 1927. The acknowledgements in *Hidden Doors* also mention *The Dublin Magazine*, *The Scottish Nation*, *The Northern Review*, and *The Scots Magazine*.

The contest winner had also been busy in the Kinloch-leven days. Neil identifies his first publication as the boisterous, jolting sonnet, out of Omar-Tennyson-Keats, signed Nial Guinne, and adorning page one of the (first) May 1918 issue of a little magazine called *The Apple-Tree*, published by and for members of The Aspirants' Fellowship (Hon. Sec., Esther Hyman, Clapham Road, London). The issue is taken up largely with the report of the Prize Competition. The Committee reports Mr N. M. Gunn to be one of ' the only two competitors of outstanding merit ', laments that his short story ' The Divining Rod ' while brilliant, humorous, and subtle ' could by no stretch of imagination be called a story ', and quotes his replies to questions such as, ' What is the artistic value of red geraniums? ' ' What is the moral significance of Garden

Cities?' 'What are the precise relative values of frivolity and
dignity?' and ' What place has a kitten in the general scheme
of things?' The reply to the last is priceless early Gunn:
' Women talk, lions stalk, and the gods thunder to gain
their ends: a kitten plays endlessly as an end in itself.
Consider man " at a loose end ": any loose end is good
enough for a kitten. The cosmic significance of it! ' The
prize went to Mr N. M. Gunn, The Pier, Kinlochleven,
Argyll, who also won a guinea for an ' almost Chesterton-
ian ' comparison of Chesterton and O. Henry, and remarks
on Wilde, Meredith, James, Shaw, Stevenson, Walpole,
Barrie, Wells and Galsworthy. The Committee regretted
only that neither he nor Mr Wellsted Miller ' seems
to have grasped fully the nature of the sonnet '.

So the Stickit Sonneteer settled in Inverness in the
mid-1920s and, in his spare time, became a novelist. *The
Grey Coast*, his first, published by Cape in 1926, Neil says
little about, other than that he must have been trying to
' get rid of something ' when he wrote it, and that he
could not bear the thought of re-reading it. A long letter
of my own (August 1965) forced him back to it: ' perhaps
one of the reasons for my reluctance to re-read, is the
intensity and complexity which are split open and seem
too much now, if not then. It is not easy for me to read
it over easily or lightly. As if there is a too muchness that
embarrasses ' (23rd August 1965). I asked him once, on a
sunny first sight of green Caithness, how he ever saw it as a
grey coast, and he explained, " It was a vision I saw of it
one spring, darkly stone walled, and grey for miles and miles.
In that book I suppose I was doing something intense and
narrow instead of giving it the broad stroke." One
flamboyant northern littérateur remarked of the book:

B 2

' this Gunn is a one-novel man ', and perhaps such bleak intensity gave that impression. The same uncharitable novelist was also alleged to have said that Neil wrote *Morning Tide* four years later merely for the Book Society choice it won.

Neil never ceases to marvel at that choice. George Blake and Faber had taken over the Porpoise Press, and Neil sent him *Morning Tide*, then thought the likelihood of London approval so absurd that he wrote to have it back,

> for, you see, here was a book concerned with five or six people, living traditionally in the remotest part of the Highlands, speaking as they normally spoke, a plotless book, dealing with two or three days in the life of a local boy, and with the climax in the first chapter. Enough to make a fellow squirm, what? But dear old George did not send it back. . . . And Faber took it! And then, my dear fellow, the London Book Society " chose " it as their book of the month. And George sent the simple author a telegram, followed by a note that he could expect to make at least £1,000. (1st March 1970)

Indeed, Blake or Frank Morley, another Faber partner, got wind of the choice after a first printing of fifteen hundred copies had been done and dated in late 1930, talked Cape out of reprinting rights to *The Grey Coast*, held up the issue, and prepared for the much larger issue of 1931 (hence the bibliographical puzzle). Neil keenly enjoys other people's financial cleverness, delights in his good luck at having a banker friend persuade him to invest his first £200 for *Morning Tide*, and recalls that the royalties from the book paid off the house in Inverness (Larachan).

I wrote Neil in 1961 about my recent arrival (as a New

Englander) in Virginia and about my sense of the complexities of the Southern view of cultural union, which I
likened to the viewpoint of the Highlander. His reply
(8th September 1961) concerned his third novel, *The Lost
Glen* (1932)—which he ordinarily has no memory of
whatsoever: " Ah yes. *The Lost Glen*. Do you know, I
don't remember that book at all? I haven't opened it since
it was published." His publishers wanted another *Morning
Tide*, but " I never wanted to follow in the same thing
twice ". I quote from the 1961 letter:

> my publishers were hopeful that my next would carry
> on the good work. Instead of which they were presented
> with a novel that had so much of the inner attitude of
> the South to the North in Scotland (and vice versa)
> as paralleled by your remarks on the same directions in
> America (your Deep South to my Gaelic North). But
> one of the Faber directors, Frank V. Morley of U.S.A.
> (brother of the late Christopher) explained to others
> what was biting me in terms of the American parallel
> and did so with such deep feeling that I was positively
> " enlightened " on the spot. For him at least I was none
> the worse for getting something off my mind, even in a
> book of uncertain value.

Sun Circle (1933) is even vaguer in Neil's memory.
When on two occasions I have argued with him heatedly
that he has published twenty novels and not (as he insisted)
only nineteen, *Sun Circle* has been the forgotten book.
In a letter I associated its genesis with the prehistoric novels
of Naomi Mitchison, of whom he is greatly fond. But
he replied (2nd November 1966): ' Yes, I was impressed
by Naomi's CORN KING, which I must have read long after
publishing SUN CIRCLE, for which I had merely local lore

and/or legendary "memories".' But he reconstructed the conception vividly in a visit to Dunbeath: the nearness of early Christian Chapel Hill (or Hill of Peace, as J. G. Sutherland told him it had been called) and Pictish broch; his imagining of the Viking ships appearing in the little harbour of *Morning Tide*; his sustained fascination with what struck him most in Adamnan's *Life of Columba*, the extraordinary tolerance of the Picts in meeting the new peace of the Christians. The book became an epic paradigm of his views on ethnic conciliation and survival in history. But it evidently gave no more help to his stalled reputation than its predecessor.

Butcher's Broom (1934) had a similar genesis in local legend, though he used Macleod's *Gloomy Memories*. As we drove down the coast from Caithness in 1965, he pointed out near Helmsdale where the crofters, burned out, had come down from Strath Kildonan and made their crofts on the hills above the shore. Here, too, were the hills where Dark Mairi appeared and disappeared. I said to him later, " I've often wondered where such a remarkable study of primitive mentality could come from." He didn't hesitate: " I'll tell you exactly where it came from. I was at a *ceilidh* of a sort in Inverness one night. Women were doing waulking songs and so on, and I watched them, but there was a woman there who simply sat forward in her chair—she was in her sixties, but she had straight black hair that was pulled straight back from her forehead, and her cheekbones slanted straight down back below her ears, and a little smile on her face, and this woman's image simply stayed with me—and became Dark Mairi." Why had he written the book? Did it demand the sort of sustained research that went into *The Silver Darlings*?

" No. I'd always felt the *need* to write about the Clearances. I hated doing it. Most Highlanders hate bringing back that awful recollection, and are not even willing to talk about it." His mind, however, was filled with it when we talked in 1965, because of a recent reprinting. " Actually," he said, " there is very little of the Clearances in *Butcher's Broom*. The tragedy is the destruction of a way of life, and the book is more about what is destroyed." His impatience with novels on the Clearances is characteristic: in such a book one should *invent* nothing; the cruelty was sufficient in fact to require no invention—and he recalled the old fellow from Tiree, the loader at Kinlochleven, who saw his grandmother carried out of the burning house and heard the factor say, " Let the old bitch burn! "

Later in 1934 Neil received letters from J. Leslie Mitchell (' Lewis Grassic Gibbon '), whom he did not know, praising *Butcher's Broom*, saying Neil wrote the best English in Scotland, and asking him to contribute a volume to the ' Voice of Scotland ' series. " I told him," said Neil, " I hadn't written essays. Anyway, I didn't think much of it. I am afraid I was a bit unenthusiastic. It should have been better." But there are those who think *Whisky and Scotland* with its wealth of knowledge and ' spiritual ' whimsy, as well as its reflections on cultural nationalism at a difficult time, is quite good as it is and long overdue for reprinting.

No doubt Neil's patient publishers were less than pleased, awaiting their second *Morning Tide*, through three diverse sequels and now this special essay for another publisher. This, I suspect, was the time for one of the visits of the Faber partners to Inverness. Perhaps it was now, even, that T. S. Eliot joined them and found himself uncomfortably sharing a caravan for sleeping with the mountainous Frank Morley. At any rate, " Morley, Blake and so on came up, and they were unhappy about some book I'd just published. They told me about a Yorkshire novelist who had just done a novel on his river at home, and suggested I do a book on my own river. They wanted another *Morning Tide*." They got *Highland River* (1937), something extraordinarily different, even though, as Neil says in the dedication to his brother John, ' some of the characters seem to have strayed in from *Morning Tide* under different names '. But the exhilaration of the search for the springs of one's native river had been born even earlier. The story of Kenn, as boy become mathematician become war casualty, is generally associated with John Gunn's early life. And this lovely and intricate book, far from merely re-establishing the author of *Morning Tide*, struck out a new territory for Neil as a philosophical novelist. The book won the James Tait Black Prize, the modest author managed typically to finesse the acceptance speech by a pathetic phone call to Dover Wilson in Edinburgh, and the book's subsequent popularity is guessed from the fact that it sold twenty thousand copies in paperback during the Second World War. Long before this, however, Neil had left the Civil Service and Inverness.

The Inverness years of the exciseman-author had another quieter side. Neil's characteristic role in Scottish Nationalist politics goes unnoticed in contemporary sketches. More flamboyant and divisive literary Nationalists naturally make better copy. The staunch believer in consensus is less glamorous. Neil's own stance is seen in his praise for Tom Johnston: " So he propounded his idea thus: on nine out of ten things for the good of their country all Scots agree, but over the tenth they will cut one another's throats, *therefore* let us forget the tenth and come together on the nine." The reasons for his long admiration for John MacCormick, the moderate Nationalist leader, are the same: " There was in [MacCormick] no air of fanaticism, of an egoism reaching for its own satisfaction, but simply of an assurance that what mattered in our inheritance was of profound value." It is John MacCormick, in his own account of modern Scottish Nationalism, *The Flag in the Wind*, who recalls Neil's role.

Coming to Inverness for a meeting in 1929, MacCormick secured the help of Neil and of a young solicitor, Duncan McNeill, in organising a Highland branch of the National Party.

> Both of them were to become my life-long friends and to play a leading part in the national movement. . . . Within a few months they were able to report the establishment of a branch with over 500 members and money in the bank! . . . Neil Gunn's house in Inverness, Larachan it was called, became our unofficial head-quarters and no matter how late our return from distant parts we would find him waiting for us, eager for our report and ready to sit up talking with us till all hours.

As Civil Servant Neil could not speak publicly, and by inclination avoided the limelight. Some of his most hilarious stories are of the many speeches he has avoided making and of the very few he has not avoided. But, says MacCormick, ' behind the scenes he inspired us with his clear vision of the Scotland that should be '. So a group round MacCormick ' regarded Larachan more or less as their spiritual home ', and recalled long nights there where ' we constantly reaffirmed our faith, not in any narrow and bitter nationalism, but in the capacity of the Scottish people ' to provide a model of freedom and individual dignity in a technocratic mass world.

There came a time of stress and division. Neil recalls: " We were fighting against the Scottish curse of splinter groups "—or, as he put it in a letter to one of the more militant Nationalist leaders: ' Disruption or internal quarrelling has not only been Scotland's curse but has come too perilously near to being her death.' " There was another party starting up," Neil explained to me, " more conservative in economics—less Leftist—headed by men like Sir Alex MacEwen—for years Provost of Inverness—and the Duke of Montrose." MacCormick found MacEwen shy and reserved and ' would have found it difficult to talk freely to him had it not been for Neil Gunn who acted as intermediary and for whom the Provost had the highest admiration and affection '. None the less, the other group formed their own new party, and once more the conciliators needed Neil's quiet diplomacy. A joint meeting was planned in Glasgow (after the hammering out of *essential* Nationalist policy), but an effective and influential leader was needed to preside. Neil was sent to Cunninghame Graham's home on the Clyde. " He was sitting by the fire with another man," Neil recalls, " and he gestured me to a chair by the door. I sat there until he said, ' Are you by any chance related to Neil Gunn the writer? ' I told him I was he. He jumped up, shook hands, and showed me to his chair by the fire." Graham agreed to chair the meeting. Neil, caught in traffic, arrived late, and Graham took him out to an ante-chamber. " Now don't worry," he said, " everything will go smoothly. Here. Can you do this? " and he seized a straight chair and by his powerful wrists brought it up with its back parallel to the floor. Neil followed suit and did the same. Graham burst out: " Keir Hardie couldn't do that."

The later history of the S.N.P., to 1942 when MacCormick and his allies seceded and, as Neil puts it, " the purists and the poets took over ", has little place here. MacCormick himself remembers how Hitler in the mid-'30s gave ' nationalism ' a ' highly distasteful meaning ', and how the growth of Fascism joined separate movements in the hatred of a common enemy. John Pick wisely observes that politics could only thwart or exhaust Neil's search for the essential. Naomi Mitchison recalls: ' We argued tremendously about politics, for he could never have been an unprotesting member of any party.' No doubt Neil himself meant this when he said once, " I was an anarchist at the beginning and I'm a gentle anarchist now. I was always a natural anarchist."

The departure from Inverness in 1937 coincided with a general time of political terror. He wrote me once about dictators.

> I know them at once, whatever the colour or race. I begin to look out when I hear even the word " idealism ". In my youth I stood far Left—& hopeful, later, of the Russian experiment. But the purges of '37-'38 in Russia set me researching, though I could find little of authentic account, even in London. . . . It was not the political aspect that troubled me, but the psychological— the applied psychology, so to speak, that could produce such extraordinary " confessions " from the Old Guard. However, all that would take too long to tell now— including a visit to Munich in '39, where I was at a fancy-dress ball in the Europa Hotel (where Hitler & Chamberlain had met) shortly before war 2 broke out, & learned a lot, from Germans who could trust me, about the ways of dictators. (11th August 1964)

And, in a later letter (2nd July 1969): ' I was even a fellow traveller myself once upon a time. Now I am tame and sometimes even on The Way.' But long before this, the Anarchist was off and away from Inverness, his Civil Service job, his pension and the rest—committed with Daisy to the precarious life of the full-time writer.

The decision came before the great success of *Highland River* could be known. The news of the Black Prize came when the break was made and Neil and Daisy were ' off in a boat' down the west coast. One friend explains it this way: ' When Neil decided to give up his excise job and forego his pension in order to write he realised he had to leave Inverness. As his fame as a writer grew . . . he was besieged by the Scalp hunters & though he was trying to combine his distillery work in the morning & writing in the afternoons he found little peace.' Then, too, there were the political involvements. Whatever the chief motives, he recalls saying one day to Daisy, " Can you live on three pounds a week? " She said yes, and there followed the marvellous fugitive gesture—the breaking off and away—described lovingly in *Off in a Boat* (1938). " I bought the boat," Neil summed up once, " after a drunken night on Skye." And—let the book continue—' here was I, suddenly become the owner of a boat—with the prospect of three weeks' cruising! ' The three weeks stretched out, from the beginnings in a fine June to the arrival back at the head of the Caledonian Canal when ' the corn was turning to gold and the rowan berries were red '. But first the painter was to be cut.

' The only way to meet all these fantastic happenings, it seemed to me, was to be even more fantastic, and when a man came out of the blue and asked me if I was selling my house (the rumours of our going to sea must have been spreading!), I said yes.' The house was sold; the three-pound plan agreed to; and the following day the resignation was handed in to the chief of the Civil Service department, whose fatherly consternation was touching but to no avail. 'After these two days' action, our only abode was a boat in doubtful condition [a defective twenty-five-year-old Kelvin engine], and . . . if we had lost all visible means of support we had at least gained a little control of time.' The concerned literary world of Faber, *et al.*, would not, however, let the Gunns take to sea unequipped. "When I came back from Skye with the boat purchased," he told me once, "Harcourt Brace, Eliot, Morley and Blake were waiting for me. I told Daisy of my purchase. We took our guests on a pleasant and amusing excursion all round, talking of our planned cruise, and they promised suitable gifts for the boat. George Blake proposed an almanac for weather and tides, Frank Morley a small cannon for popping-off German submarines, but T. S. Eliot—Uncle Tom, we called him—being a poet, said he would give us a keg of rum."

Then suddenly all the thoughts and actions of that time were cleansed of their uncertainties, and a bright, free world opened before them both. Neil associates the moment with a tragic incident of their private lives. Daisy had been expecting a child, and an appalling household accident sent her to hospital and caused the still-birth of a son. They never spoke much of this, if at all, yet it had the profound effect of drawing them closer together. Life became more an affair of intuitions, of final understanding, than of words; and their uncertain thoughts about the future, now in 1937, were brought to a focus. Only the old boat was left, but the boat took them down the west coast, and never had its seas and inlets seemed so vivid, so wonderful. " Maybe the future is only a beginning," he said. Her smile steadied on his face, then wandered out over the sea.

Abrupt, whimsical gesture that it was, the trip represented many things. It meant recovering the image of the west and many aroused memories of the wandering years. It meant, too, recalling that innocent Scotland with the mature political-economic vision of the seasoned National-ist—for *Off in a Boat* has its share of commentary on fisheries, landlordism, crofting, reforestation and the rest. It anticipates in impulse, as well, the travel quest of a much later book: it seeks not just the sea that joins all nations, but the well, too, of man's primordial ' superstitions '— the well of essential delight, the water of life, which is never dry. The trip served as a renewal for the writer: ' Small things or incidents . . . were continuously surprising us, and gave the sheer living of life a vivid interest. It even quickened local history, usually so dull a subject, till its human movement took on dramatic values, till the universal was seen in fact as an extension of the local.' It is no surprise to see in *Off in a Boat* the germs of novels— *Second Sight* to come shortly, the western parts of *The Silver Darlings*. But centrally on Neil's mind, cutting ties and taking off at a time when the world seemed headed for cataclysm, was the issue of ' escape '.

It is easy, of course, to dismiss the picture by calling it the escapist's dream. . . . Have we . . . grown afraid to escape, become dominated by the idea of a social duty that must keep our noses to the human grindstone, the grindstone that an ever-increasing mass hysteria keeps whirling with an ever-increasing madness of momentum? . . . Are we in social honour bound to increase this ghastly momentum by adding the thrust of our own forebodings and fears? or has a time come when it may be the better part of courage to withdraw sufficiently far from it to observe with some sense of proportion what exactly is taking place?

Neil's answer was plain. And the first novel written at Brae Farm, *Wild Geese Overhead* (1939), the story of a Glasgow newspaperman braving the scorn of his cynical colleagues to put a pastoral distance between himself and the growing murderousness of the modern city, buttresses the same position.

The Gunns rented a farmhouse near Brae, ' one half mile up a dirt track off the road between Dingwall and Strathpeffer—a lovely spot with no telephone and few buses on the high road '—so says an anonymous old friend. Another places the house ' on a steepish hillside in the crofting country between Dingwall and Strathpeffer. The croftland ran away into moors above '. Three miles away in Strathpeffer John Gunn, loyal Mate of *Off in a Boat* and hero of *Highland River*, was inspector of schools for the area. Strathpeffer sits at the foot of Ben Wyvis; the Rogie Falls are near by; and on the moor of the heights of Brae are five standing stones, remains of a sepulchral cairn, and near by the site of a hut circle, the Picts' Houses. The scene is well set in the Thoreauvian walks of *Highland Pack*. The delicate drawings of the whole countryside done by Neil's good friend Keith Henderson for the essays are also indispensable. The house is marked out by Jibydo the special cock chaffinch, who ' starts upon the ancient ash-tree by the north-east window, does a carefree swoop to the aged elm beyond the south-west window, and when he has exhausted his second urgency of song there, takes a double swoop to the old plum-tree in the vegetable garden at the back '. At the foot of the glen is (' as there ought to be ') a small town, whence the air-raid siren, the ' modern banshee', can be heard.   Up the hill road on the edge of the moor is the old crofter to be talked with: he can remember ' when there were seventeen houses along this hill road.   You can count the ruins there yourself, although many of them have been cleaned away '. The shops are three miles away.

The life and living of the full-time author at Brae required a persistence and versatility whose scope cannot be known until the bibliographical spade-work is done. We know he began soon with a series of ' notes on country life ' for J. B. Salmond's *The Scots Magazine* that later became *Highland Pack*, and that the same collection contains material published in *The Glasgow Herald*, the *S.M.T. Magazine* and *Chambers's Journal*. He remembers (in a letter of 29th March 1966) once ' doing a series of articles for the *Daily Record*, Glasgow, and keeping them lest I write the same article twice ', but is inclined to consider all such ' journalism ' *infra dig* for serious biographers. Short stories continued and were collected (1950) in *The White Hour*, and later he delighted in receiving almost as much as Maurice Walsh for stories sold to the American *Saturday Evening Post*, as well as half a dozen large post-war articles for *Holiday Magazine*. He had been trying plays in the '30s and this possibility, like much of the journalism, belongs to Glasgow and his friends there in journalism and the theatre. He had a three-act play, *The Ancient Fire*, produced in Glasgow. " Had I lived in Glasgow," he speculated, " I might have been successful in the theatre— not doing ordinary things, mind you, but wild new things.

But there are many technical details to know—I thought it was just a matter of writing a play. But you have to be close by—and I would have had to live in Glasgow."

He had at least one good friend and guide there in James Bridie (Dr O. H. Mavor). Since Bridie's autobiography, *One Way of Living*, written in 1938, does not mention Neil, I infer that they met during the Brae years. But the timing was right, for Bridie could be depended on for sensible advice on the bread-and-butter details of authorship. " I remember being in a pub once with Bridie," Neil recalled, " and we agreed that money was the reason for writing, and Bridie said a writer should be a craftsman— like a cobbler, able to fit shoes to anyone's feet. Bridie was, as the Irish say, a lovely man, a lovely man! My favourite of all that renaissance group. No pretensions at all. He would just tell you the truth, and you would never mind, whatever he said, whatever judgements he made." Only of Edwin Muir and of Naomi Mitchison, in the older Scottish literary generation, does Neil speak with equal warmth of affection.

Off in a Boat, proposed by Frank Morley, was published in the first year at Brae. It was followed by two novels already mentioned, *Wild Geese Overhead* and *Second Sight* (1940)—the former was George Blake's favourite. But the first ambitious effort at Brae—without the leisure it is inconceivable—was *The Silver Darlings* (1941). As Neil recalls it, many things for the book were simply thrown at him. His good friend Peter Anson of Morayshire proposed it, and on the basis of Anson's *Fishing Boats and Fisherfolk on the East Coast of Scotland* he began. At Helmsdale he found a ledger for 1815. An old Dunbeath man told him of the first four men from the district to sail through the

Pentland Firth to the western fishing, miss the Butt of Lewis and head past the Flannans till a large ship coming in directed them straight about. Visits to Peter and Ena Macleod in Stornoway provided talks with fishermen and local fishcurers. Peter Macleod's father, Malcolm, still fishing off Bernera, one of Neil's father's crew, was persuaded to take Neil on his semi-annual sail to the Flannans to deliver or return his lambs from the grazing there. Neil described it in three instalments for *Chambers's*; they are incorporated into the closing sections of *Highland Pack*, and they provide the precipice episode of the novel. Then he came upon a doctor's account of the plague's coming to Caithness, with prescriptions and all. He remembered, too, from earlier visits to Dunbeath, the story of the sailor with the silver clasp in his head, memento of fights with the press gang operating out of Helmsdale. Such in part was the provenance of *The Silver Darlings*.

Next, in 1942, came *Young Art and Old Hector*. He met Geddes of *Chambers's* at a party and Geddes asked, " Why don't you write a story for me? " Decorum proscribed any sexual overtones, which meant avoiding the middle-group. Neil hit upon the idea of the young boy and the old man. Art was patterned on a nephew full of marvellous questions, and Hector was an amalgam of two or three older men he had known in his own youth. The germs of the sketches came from a book of Gaelic proverbs. " And I could have gone on writing about the little boy and the old man for ever. Whenever I heard or remembered a Gaelic proverb, it led me to visualise a whole story, developing out of that proverb, and I could use Young Art and Old Hector. But as I got started, the thing just ran away with me, and I didn't bother to stop for the stories at all, but went on and finished the book." The story of the genesis of the sequel, *The Green Isle of the Great Deep* (1944), has been told elsewhere (see John Pick in this collection). Naomi Mitchison's challenge was accepted, and " I decided to put the boy and the old man in Naomi's kind of world, but carry it further than she would have carried it ".

Between the two came *The Serpent* (1943) which, together with *The Drinking Well* (1946) and *The Shadow* (1948), continued the effort begun with *Wild Geese Overhead* to find in the essential Highland experience a curative vision of the murderous modern world. Tom's hill in *The Serpent* and the environs of *The Shadow* both begin near Brae farm. As Neil wrote (Fall 1966):

> The place is " arranged a bit " though the hill behind the glen, that Tom climbed, is very like the hill and moor where Daisy and I spent wandering days when we stayed in that part of Ross-shire. I fished the small Skiach burn, while she hunted wild flowers or bathed in a pool. Blessed days. *Highland Pack* is made of such outings. And the farmhouse where we stayed is the farm house in *The Shadow*.

He reminisced further at Dalcraig once about the genesis of *The Shadow*. There was no actual woman behind the heroine of the book. He recalled the climbing roses with the wind in them that Daisy grew at Brae outside his window, and traced the moments of intense visualisation in the book to his own experiences at the time. It was he who leaned against the birch and pulled his hand away when he found it hot.

Of course, the essential place of a novel of Neil's is never to be confused with the locality of its conception. And some began elsewhere. The ' psychological thriller '

The Key of the Chest (1945) " I think I would have had," said Neil, " on the west side." *The Drinking Well* (1946) was set largely in the Grampians, on a big sheep farm between Newtonmore and Dalwhinnie. Neil knew the old farmer and his son, Ian, had stayed in the house, and borrowed the farm notebook for details of the shepherding. As for the legal office in Edinburgh: " When I wrote the book Robert Wotherspoon said *he* knew that law office well. I knew the legal fellows and knew what a legal office was like from my work there." The mysterious well of this novel and the later *The Well at the World's End* (1951) came from the same trip with Daisy which began " where we stayed in Dingwall ", but for exegesis Neil sent me to ' Connla's Well ' in Rolleston's *Myths and Legends of the Celtic Race*. Even after he left Brae, the setting persisted; *Bloodhunt* (1952), too, was ' set ' there. *The Lost Chart* (1949), of course, was a final imaginative return to Glasgow and the west. And interestingly, the last form of Neil's fictional search for the essential in the archaic—seen in *The Silver Bough* (1948) and *The Other Landscape* (1954)— demanded a return of *local* to the sea precipice, the dizzy cliffs and caves, of his earlier imagination. The point is that identifiable *local* matters less than ever, and books as differently ' localised ' as *The Lost Chart* and *Bloodhunt* share a single idea of essential place, generated by the apocalyptic mood of the late '40s and early '50s. He summed it up once, speaking of *Bloodhunt*:

> Yes—there's a thing about that book—something I had very much in mind, but it never really shows, because I didn't *write* it anywhere. When the old sailor finds the policeman's brother and decides to say nothing, and the girl has her baby in the barn—I thought that

the world after the bomb might well be like this—
with just a few pockets of life left, and the old man by
himself living on the fringes, being forced to decide
what *laws* are to be followed at such a time, and recog-
nizing that life must and will go on.

This, of course, was after Brae.

It is at Brae that we can best fix our image of Neil's
working life as a writer. " I wrote quite a lot of books
there," he recalled once. " Ah, yes, I was just like a chap
sitting down to do his day's chore." Once he started a
book, he always finished it. He made no full plans or
outlines in advance. He wrote for two or three hours each
morning in a big ledger, thinking he had done well enough
if he had just one thousand words. Working regularly at
this rate he would finish a book in five or six months.
Before stopping he would add notes in the margins of what
was to come next. Daisy would type from his manuscript,
and he would make a few corrections and send the typescript
off to be put directly into page proof. He marvelled at
Daisy's amazing ability to read his hand, and at a later
house-flitting he found the old ledgers so messy and obscure
that he made a bonfire of them all. Fortunately Daisy's
typescripts survive. One good friend and frequent visitor
describes the daily routine as follows:

> I think most of Neil's best writing was done in Brae—
> it was a challenge to him of course giving up a sure
> income & the war coming on & everyone sure that
> books & reading were doomed. How wrong they
> were! The usual routine when there were no visitors
> was that after breakfast, & perusing the letters & the
> daily paper, Neil sat down in a big armchair at the fire
> with a writing pad & pencil & wrote on his knee till
> lunchtime, always smoking of course. Daisy saw to

it that at his right hand side was a very large wide-mouth copper coal scuttle to catch the cigarette ash that tended to be flicked everywhere but the right place. Daisy brought him coffee at 11 & she retired to type the previous day's script. After lunch, they went for a walk up the hill at the back of the house through the crofts & sometimes Neil got a hare or a rabbit for the pot. The book "Highland Pack" is just a record of these rambles. I think most of Neil's reading was done in the evenings—all his philosophical & comparative religious study was done then.

Such was his manner of life for ' almost thirteen years '.

Others who knew him there have kindly shared their impressions. John Pick, novelist, editor, sensitive interpreter of Neil's later work and thought, had begun corresponding with Neil as a result of a fine essay of his on the novels. Pick and his wife settled near Ullapool in January 1946, and one day in early summer Neil appeared at the door.

He was tall, with resilient, greying hair and a strong-boned, vigorous, Viking face. His movements were easy and relaxed, his gestures few and fluent, his manner at once friendly and courteous. His courtesy was not mere politeness, but a quality of mind, profoundly natural and giving the impression of personal reserve unified with full acceptance of others. He neither pressed opinions nor avoided issues. He suffered fools with patience but was concerned with truth, and would not be content with less. My overall impression on that first occasion was of a man balanced easily on his own two feet, who would accept a new acquaintance as he found him, without prejudgement.

Neil's close friendship with the Picks continues, and Mrs Pick has a woman's eye for essential appearance that supplies an image we can all recognise:

> Grey hair springing from a high forehead, brown eyes,
> a long dimple on his chin. He always wore well-
> tailored lovat suits in Harris tweed and strong walking
> shoes. A walk was an essential part of the day. His
> enjoyment of his landscape was infectious. Afterwards
> he would fling himself into an armchair, his long limbs
> sprawling, his fine delicate hands pushing his hair back,
> and talk would begin. He was very gallant to women,
> especially when he felt he had been off at length on
> "men's talk" and would approach with a twinkle and
> the hint of a pas de bas and suggest "Well now, isn't
> it time for a dram?"

About 1948 the Gunns were forced to leave Brae.
They took what one friend calls 'a horrid house perched
on a cliff overhanging the shores of Cromarty Firth, on the
way to Invergordon, nothing separating the back of the
house from the Great North Road but a white wooden
fence'. She was amused when Daisy exclaimed, on looking
out to the Firth and seeing a man in a small rowing-boat
trying to spear flounders, "Who's that fishing in *our* sea?"
John Pick writes:

> The move to Kincraig was enforced, and wasn't a
> success. The house was pleasant and right on the shore
> of the Cromary Firth. You could watch the water and
> a young bloke incessantly fishing, from the windows,
> but it was also bang next to the road to Invergordon,
> on which heavy lorries were continuous passers-by.
> It was this which eventually drove them out.

Not too much writing could be done at Kincraig, and the
'horrid cliff hanger' was soon left behind when the Gunns
were 'off and away' to the lovely isolation of Cannich,

in Strath Glass, almost thirty miles south-west of Inverness, on the way up to Glen Affric, where Neil's friend Robert Wotherspoon had the shooting lodge. The Gunns bought Kerrow House, and Neil had his own fishing rights at last. "I bought a place with a salmon river, so that after being a poacher all my life," he said once, "I could watch out for other poachers."

Those who saw Neil at Kerrow House recall the essential fisherman. Here is George Bruce, for example:

> I recollect Neil, the tall, thin figure walking easily over the bridge, carrying a fishing rod, then picking his way over stones with an easy balance, to the river and then casting into it and at the same time taking in the whole scene. He said to me, smiling, "Man the hunter". But of course he was also man the philosopher, man the poet and the man who loved.

When my wife and I crossed the old bridge at Kerrow with Neil in the summer of 1965, he looked down at the alder-lined river and recalled "a most extraordinary, terrifying experience". An American 'movie magnate' was visiting—perhaps in the company of his new friend Neil Paterson—and the man, an inexperienced angler, had hooked a salmon. Neil Gunn netted the fish, only to find that it had vanished through a forgotten hole in the net. Kerrow House was a good place for retrospective netting, too, between 1950 and 1960, and the most important 'Kerrow' book was not a novel, but the autobiographical *The Atom of Delight* (1956).

The move to Kerrow in 1950 coincided with the appearance in England of a work uniquely significant for Neil's later life and thought, Ouspensky's *In Search of the Miraculous*, a book he discussed for Alex Reid's *Saltire* in 1959 and

for John Pick's *Point* ten years later. He found in it the
kind of essential search that he now saw throughout his
own work. He admired Ouspensky as a scientist concerned,
in an insistently empirical way, with modes of experience
which self-styled ' rationalists ' vaguely misname ' mystical '.
" My own psychology as a novelist," he remarked once,
" can be found in Ouspensky. I believe we are all born
with a personality which does not alter basically but may
atrophy." He associated the book with his own insistence
on a balance of intellect and feeling. " Only this and man's
primal faith in light," he said, " will ultimately keep the
finger off the trigger."

The impact of Ouspensky coincided in turn with a
growing respect for certain scientists, concerned with the
nuclear, the essential, the life-giving, who seemed to be
confirming experimentally very old intuitions about life
and light—and this at a time when literature had been
spoiled for Neil. " I think all this egotism business among
writers in my time," he said, " has just about killed my
interest in literature." The same decade at Kerrow brought
a similar encounter with the disciplines of the East, with
Japanese art and poetry, through the enthusiastic correspondence of Professor Nakamura in Japan. Once more, as
the 1958 *Saltire* articles attest, this was less the discovery
of something new than the delighted recognition, in a remote place, of something he had known and sought to
convey all along. But the difficult task of tracing Neil's
thought during the Kerrow years is not to be tried here by
this memoirist. It is a side of his life best known and closely
shared with John Pick and with Alex Reid at whose editorial
encouragement the *Saltire* articles were written.

The biographical point here is that his thought was

leading further from the novel, in the direction of the meditative essay. Novels still 'sold': Neil thinks of *The Well at the World's End* (1951) and *Bloodhunt* (1952) as among his financial successes, but *The Atom of Delight* (1956) was another story. 'The Book,' he wrote (8th September 1961), 'was almost completely ignored by reviewers and book buyers. So I decided it was time to stop writing books.' It took a year to become accustomed to the change, and he even thought once of trying a novel along *Atom* lines. Journalism continued; there were commentaries for documentary films; the articles for Reid's *Saltire* were sequels to *Atom*. *Atom* was remaindered without notification of the author, the old Faber partners were gone, most of the novels slipped out of print, and the isolation of Cannich suited the ambivalent sense of being 'forgotten' by the 'literary world'. Being 'nothing', he said once, gave him freedom—no commission appointments to be avoided, speeches not to be given, oxygen-starved formal dinners to be escaped. Cannich, says my correspondent, 'was inaccessible as they wished but when it came to illness, accident or such & a doctor 14 miles away cut off by snowdrifts I think they realised it was time to move'. In 1960 they bought Dalcraig, on a wooded hillock two miles west of the Kessock Ferry on the north shore road by the Beauly Firth, and here, in an ample high house with a fine garden, Neil had a striking combination—privacy, a sight of the mountains in the west, the east coast at hand and Inverness a few moments' crossing away.

The history of the '60s can be brief. They began and persisted as a time of serious illness for both Gunns. Daisy died in October 1963; Neil recovered slowly from major surgery, and found his energy again only sporadically.

But there were regular holidays and fishing trips with Alec and Gretta Gunn in Caithness, and trips to the sun farther afield—the Canaries, Majorca, Portugal—with good friends such as Neil Paterson and with his devoted brother John. The admiration and friendship of the brilliant young Highland historian, Ian Grimble, who had settled in Bettyhill, meant lively visits to the north coast and renewed contact with Highland political economy. It was a time of renewed recognition—the earlier articles by Pick and Reid, the admiring climax of Kurt Wittig's *The Scottish Tradition in Literature*. Edinburgh University had bestowed an honorary LL.D. in the '40s with little éclat, but now even ' foreign academics ' began to besiege and tire him, and younger Scottish authors needed and received his support. He and his books came to radio and television attention, in discussion and dramatisation, through the efforts of friends such as George Bruce, Alex Reid, Finlay MacDonald and Stewart Conn. His home county honoured him with a portrait by Stanley Cursiter (he did SPEAK! on that occasion). And most gratifying of all, the mail or the phone brought the occasional startling testimonial—from an engineer, a retired general, a farm woman in Strath Nairn, an Edinburgh schoolgirl—that his example had prompted a man's one sermon, or brought needed enlightenment, that *The Drinking Well* was some-one's household bible, that his books were ' the greatest '.

The signs have pleased him, and as he sat at Dalcraig in 1967 pondering a volume called *The Psychedelic Experience* and suspecting that all his books were about expanding consciousness, he warmed to the suggestion that a younger world, sickened by the egomanias of ideology, seemed genuinely edging toward his way. He is far beyond caring

c

for the erratic shams of literary ' greatness ', but he delights to hear that someone somewhere has caught the essential light or comradeship of his books. We chatted once about *The Lost Chart.* " Yes," he said, " I knew a girl who sang Gaelic songs, and her name was Helen, and I was sort of full of her at the time. Did you like that book? " Yes, I said, I did, for it was literally filled with *light.* "It makes me glad," he said, " to hear you talk that way—because what I really wanted to do—and perhaps do it anonymously even—was to add a little bit to the light."

After four years of increasingly informal correspondence, I first visited Neil at Dalcraig in the summer of 1965, when he was seventy-four and quite serene and I was thirty-eight and entering nervous academic middle age. Had I taken him at once on his own newly won terms, it might have been easier for us both, but I, alas, came with an academic-historical interest in his career and his development as a writer, and tended to force him, in his patient kindness, to dredge up the accidentals of which this essay is largely made. He on the other hand was working toward mastery of the peaceful disciplines of concentration and quite able to answer my demands for the cause-effect of literary biography with zen *koans* about wild geese. That this essay exists means that I distracted him tiresomely from the more essential Way he had found. But eventually he won. My notes fade away as the visits pass, and my own essential image of Neil has little to do with the history constructed here. As he has often said, apropos of attempts to explain Ouspensky's explanation, one cannot explain an experience to a person who has never had it. I will try with three images and say no more.

I found him after a nap in his lounge at Dalcraig in the

late summer twilight of 1965, gurgling with delight over
' Tight Lines and Other Loose Verses by Green Highlander '.
He was stretched full-length in his low chair, long legs
crossed, feet on the slide-proof cushion Daisy had made
him. His white hair was framed against the deepening
dusk outside, while bats wheeled over the garden and the
shore of the Beauly Firth. His loose reversible spectacles
tilted astonishingly, and he took them off occasionally to
rub, gently, his usable eye, the other having been damaged
in an accident ' umpteen years ' ago. He told with flawless
lucidity how whisky is made, and held high against the
light a bottle of old malt whisky, explaining its second fill
colour, and rubbing a drop on his hands to warm and inhale.
There was light everywhere.

We walked on a blowy day in November 1969 over the
long strenuous dunes on the lagoon at Vila Nova de
Milfontes to the sea beach of a very angry Atlantic, and
he sat down on a dune top, his face glowing with delight
at having made it all the way to the shore. We talked
about those he calls " the few great companionable chaps "
in literature. He had written me of *Siddhartha* once, ' it
was companionable. It was and is where some of us
belong. From the end of time, I can only say that that is
what literature is for, the literature that matters '. And now
on the dune near Milfontes he remembered, " There was
some fellow a few years ago who asked a lot of people to
write and say what they thought was the most important
thing in the world—and that fellow you mentioned
yesterday, E. M. Forster, who did the Indian novel I liked,
said, ' human relations '. And when you look back from
the end of your life, down the long corridors, that's all
there is in it." There was companionship everywhere.

One May evening in 1967 we took one of the brisk walks that punctuated my visits to Dalcraig, ten minutes along the shore road to the west and ten minutes back again. His talk was irrecoverable, exhilarating. It was about light and freedom, and he was zestfully certain in his knowledge of " what we are finally after ". I thought, as I had on other walks, that he seemed so taken up with states of being, with impressions of air and light, that he seemed scarcely aware of the particulars round us. But he knew his two sheldrakes. And as we shut the wide gate and wound slowly up the drive toward the house, he stopped suddenly still and whispered, " Hush! Listen—the corn-crake! " There was reality everywhere.

A Friendship

NEIL PATERSON

When I was a boy I met Neil Gunn in a book—*Morning Tide*—and he gave me something I have cherished ever since. It's hard to put a name to the thing he gave me, but I like to call it the atom of delight.

I was at school when I first read *Morning Tide*, and I am quite sure I didn't think of it then as a classic in the making. I certainly didn't think of it in terms of the Scottish Renaissance. I doubt if I even thought of it as literature. I simply read it, and recognised its magic, and enjoyed it. Enormously enjoyed it. I would like to stress the enjoyment one gets from Neil Gunn because I think that at a time like this, when we are celebrating him, we can be so busy isolating what is significant in his writing that we may sometimes lose sight of the joy in it, and this, for me, is the most precious thing of all.

I did not meet Neil until many years later. I had gone to Glen Affric to see something of the shooting of one of my films, and, learning that Neil lived close by, I armed myself with a bottle of whisky and ventured to call on him. Neil, a connoisseur of malt, cast a polite but quizzical eye on my indifferent blend, and I wouldn't be surprised to learn that he has the bottle in his cellar to this day. I think he forgave me some years later. Daisy did better. She forgave me on the spot. Despite the fact that she already had guests (John and Jean Pick) she insisted on my staying the night. She used to tease me afterwards that I came to the door, said, "My name is Neil Paterson. Here's a bottle of cooking whisky and I'm staying the night." And I used to say, "Well, if I hadn't there would have been so much gracious Highland manœuvring either to get me to stay or to get rid of me that we'd never have got to bed at all."

Myth upon myth, of course.

At that time they were living in Cannich in a fine country house surrounded by some acres of woodland. It was a splendid setting. Neil even had his own river within a stone's throw of his study. We cast lines on that river next morning, and Neil was almost immediately into a salmon which he played, tailed, and killed with precisely the degree of expertise you would expect to find in a man who has been taking salmon since he was five years old.

I don't remember when we next met, but it was soon, and Rose was there too, and thereafter it was often, and we were four.

My brief is to write a few words about Neil. Daisy is about Neil. So much so that while she was alive I could never think of one without thinking of the other; and I am still apt to.

Dear Daisy. She was beautiful. She was gentle, and she was proud. She knew things that other people did not know. She understood the mystery of being without ever bothering her high head about it. She was brave too, and she was practical. She was the crew of Neil's boat, and there were times when she took the wheel. She loved all growing things. When I saw her with flowers, which was often, I felt that there was a communion between her and them that was beyond my understanding. I only knew there was a rightness in what I saw, and that it was absolute.

Some years ago, when Neil was recovering from a major operation, Daisy would say to him occasionally, " Walk tall! " and he would immediately throw back his head and thrust out his chest in an exaggerated way. Just a little by-play between them, you might think, but it was also something more. There was so much pride in it—her invulnerable pride in him and for him, his proud response to it.

The Scottish Arts Council, in conjunction with Educational Films of Scotland, is in process of making a film on Neil, to be shown this year. During the filming Neil was far from well, but you will never guess that when you see him walking along the foreshore by his house. He is walking as tall as any man can walk, and I do not think it fanciful to say that Daisy was with him then.

Because Neil has lived for most of his life in relatively remote parts of the Highlands, there may be a mistaken idea among those who do not know him that he is something of a recluse. Nothing could be further from the truth. He loves to be with friends, and all sorts of improbable people are his friends. He is in his element at a *ceilidh*. I remember a party given in his honour at the White House in Guia—some thirty Spaniards—and how he charmed the shynesses away, and latterly joined enthusiastically in flamencos that he didn't know, and made the night memorable for us all because of his own special kind of fellowship.

There is nothing Neil likes more than what he calls a ploy. I don't know how he would define the word, but I have learned that it requires other people united with him in a common enterprise, that thereafter anything may happen and does, and that high spirits are always the order of the day. It was a ploy when Neil and Chris Grieve ' plotted ' the Scottish Renaissance, and when he became briefly involved in politics in the Scottish Nationalist cause. *Off in a Boat* was a grand ploy. It was a ploy, too, when he joined a consortium applying to the I.T.A. for a television station and found kindred spirits in John Grierson and Johnny Bannerman. The forays to Edinburgh and Glasgow and the Western Isles were ploys, and the visits to Ireland and Maurice Walsh, and our little Highland tours, and the long week-end at the Lodge in Glen Affric, and the fishing expedition with Alec on the Thurso, and our month in Gran Canaria, and the trips to the Mediterranean with John. All ploys, all of happy memory.

Even *Highland River* was in the nature of a ploy, because he wrote it largely as the result of a challenge from his publisher. It was his greatest ploy of all; he has told me that he might never have written the book if he hadn't had the challenge and felt his publisher's involvement.

In *Morning Tide* Neil pays what I think to be one of the most moving tributes a son has ever paid to his parents. Of the members of the family that are left I know only his brothers John and Alec. Neil, John, Alec—three strong, gentle men, so different and so very alike, ' common to them a hundred little invisible currents of the blood '. They do not require words—it is more than that—they do not permit words to communicate their understanding of each other; but that understanding is always there or thereabout, in the back of the odd phrase or occasionally in the tone of what is on the surface a casual remark. I have never seen brothers fixed in so close a relationship. One does not need to be perceptive to know that each would go to the stake for either of the others, although he would, of course, deny it all the way there.

It seems to me that this profound family loyalty, using family now in the widest sense, is at the root of Neil's being, and that much of his power as a writer stems from it. He has Adam's blood in his veins, and, unlike the rest of us, he knows it. Is it by feeling his own pulse that he gets these quite extraordinary instinctive intimations of the source of man's being? Or does he pluck them out of the air? I have seen him listening. He listens, and he hears. But even he himself often cannot put in words precisely what it is that he hears. How do you explain the deep note of existence?

I am not competent to write of Neil's interest in Zen-Buddhism. I simply know that he is deeply religious because he has such a wondrous sense of wonder. He had it as a little boy. As a man of eighty he has it still. And it is his unique quality as a writer and as a friend that he is able to share so much of this wonder with others, to isolate a glimmer of beauty or a particle of truth and to hold it out to you for a moment or two and marvel at it, and invite you to marvel with him.

I went to see Neil on his eightieth birthday. I hadn't seen him for some months, although I had spoken to him regularly on the telephone. I knew that he was not at his strongest, and I intended to stay only a few minutes. I got to the Black Isle just after lunch. Neil was in fine fettle. John was with him, and the floor around them was heaped with letters and telegrams of congratulation. Neil poured us a wee dram. (Willie Birnie's, of course.) Nobody pours whisky as Neil does. The act of pouring and the offering of the glass are themselves ritual celebrations. It is

C 2

almost unnecessary to drink the whisky, although we always do. We talked for half an hour, John leaving us every few minutes to take another telegram from the telephone. Neil was relaxed, physically at ease, marvelling at the interest his birthday had aroused, full of a kind of joy that is wholly innocent and wholly his, and, of course, contemplating ploys. He and Grierson had been invited to receive honorary degrees from the University of Stirling, and they were both to stay in Crieff with us for a day or two. But that was a long time off, in the summer. How about going back to Gran Canaria in the early spring? It would be good to see David Leacock again. And so on.

We had a cup of tea and a slice of splendid birthday cake, and I gave Neil a modest little flower plant that Rose had chosen for him, and got into my car and drove away.

It was the day of the first snow of the year, and there was sleet on the road all the way from Inverness to the Sma Glen. I thought of Neil on the way home. I thought of the things we had spoken about, and some that we hadn't. I thought of his courage, and of his constancy. I thought of the way he welcomes each day no matter what it may bring, and I thought of the way he looks at a glass and always says it is half full although he knows that it is also half empty. I thought of John's solicitude for him, so tender and so carefully concealed, and so well understood by them both. I thought of Neil's capacity for friendship and his inability to be other than loyal. I thought of the gentleness of his judgements. And I thought of the fun that's in him, the curious innocence of his joy, and the warmth that comes from him. I thought of him, and I was possessed of him, and I was proud.

It took almost five hours to get home. The road was

bad and the visibility poor. It should have been a tiring and a tiresome journey. It wasn't. I was completely at peace. Neil had done again what he has done for me so many times. He had given me something of himself. His message, maybe. The message that is in his books and in his life. I am not sure that I understand it all, but I know that all of it has to do with the dignity of man.

INDIVIDUAL WORKS

Early Tides : The First Novels

JOHN ROSS

I

Most readers of Neil Gunn's early fiction, if not all of them, read it because they have read and responded to some of his later work. One begins with what one has heard most about, or with what is most easily available, and when that has made its impact on the imagination and the emotions and the intellect one sets about the more difficult business of finding and reading the novels which are no longer in print, nor on the shelves of most libraries, nor ever to be found in the shops. To put the argument simply, one can assume that all of Gunn's readers are familiar with *Morning Tide, The Silver Darlings, Butcher's Broom* and *The Green Isle of the Great Deep* before they read *The Grey Coast* or *The Lost Glen.*

It seems, therefore, to be an unnecessary and even a misleading critical strategy to write or talk of the early fiction as if it were one's first taste of his work, as if one read it without hindsight, as if our experience of it conditioned our response to the later work, and not, as in fact happens, that it is the opposite that is true.

It is, of course, perfectly true that we can never read any one novel of Gunn's (nor of anyone else) as if it were our sole introduction to the world of his imagination, for we bring to our earliest reading of his work our own ideas or knowledge of the world which is the source of his material; for example, our own memories and evaluations of the Highland past. If the reader is not a Scot, his responses cannot help but be coloured by his archetypal construct of Scotland, or the Scotland of song and story, which is a very different thing, and is an arcane mystery to those of us who cannot share his spectator's view. For Scots, Highland or Lowland, who share in any way in our myths, legends, history or literature, Neil Gunn is using and creating constructs which tease our minds and move our emotions. Apart from their literary impact, qualifying it and heightening our response to it, *The Silver Darlings* and *Butcher's Broom* are still searing political tracts for those who care about the past and the future of the Highland counties.

But before the reader comes to too many conclusions, it should be said that I have no wish to maintain in any way an argument that Neil Gunn is a novelist whose work is only of local, parochial interest—an ethnic parallel to the examiner's hackneyed suggestion that only an Anglican can respond to George Herbert or that only a Catholic can read Dante. Apart from the way in which such arguments collapse from the weight of their inherent inanity, and the blunt opposition of the universal relevance of, say, *The Green Isle of the Great Deep*, it seems obvious that although the Clearances and the herring fisheries have had a local and a particular impact, the experiences of those who were cleared and of the fishing people were not very different from the experiences of others who found that economics, morals and culture did not cohere to their comfort or advantage in their own lives. The critically aware Highlander may bring to much of Gunn's work something akin to what his Irish equivalent brings to Joyce, but we, too, can read *Ulysses*. What all of us bring to Neil Gunn's early fiction is our growing awareness of the nature of Neil Gunn's imagination, gleaned from his later work, and this enlightens our approach, and simultaneously obfuscates it.

We bring hindsight, we bring knowledge, we bring minds which he has already trained to read his work, trained by reading his work. We cannot pretend to read the early fiction as something wholly self-contained, so we need not waste effort in the attempt. (On the other hand, since the early work is less widely read, less widely discussed, we are not the prisoners of a critical orthodoxy which would control our responses whether we accept or reject it.)

II

We find ourselves, then, reading *The Lost Glen* or *The Grey Coast* with pre-set expectations of certain values, concerns and ideas we have found in his fiction; we can 'place' their themes, events and characters in a wider context. The life of the coast is the life of other coasts, the northern shores of *The Silver Darlings*; the world of the glen is, on one level, the world of all the other glens. Similarly, the events of these novels remind us of events in later novels that we have already seen, though it is equally true that many events will also remind us of events in the work of earlier novelists. A sea-storm, involving drowning or the rescue of the fishermen, evokes not only other storms in Gunn's fiction but carries us back to the hard agony of the Mucklebackits. Love and hate, sex and impotence, the conflict between economics and humanity are not the sole preserve of Neil Gunn, nor are the High-landers, but all of these have a peculiar tone which we recognise.

This is most clear in relation to events; when Ewan MacLeod strangles Colonel Hicks at the end of *The Lost Glen* we are close to Will Montgomery fighting in the streets of Glasgow in Chapter VII of *Wild Geese Overhead*, in Ewan's mixed bloodlust and confusion of motive; neither character really knows why he is fighting, and both fight fiercely. When Maggie's Uncle Jeems goes poaching in *The Grey Coast*, we are with Kenn and Beel in *Highland River*, with Iain Cattanach in *The Drinking Well*, with Donald watching the salmon in ' Whistle for Bridge ' in *The White Hour*, even with Neil Gunn himself in ' The Boy and the Salmon ' in *The Atom of Delight*. It is true that there are differences: in *The Grey Coast* we see more of the details of how Jeems poaches, we are taught (or reminded) in great detail how to make snares, how to set them, and how to avoid being caught poaching, just as we are told much more about the minutiae of life on the coast; the novel omits no necessary detail in its description of life in general on the coast. We read how Maggie milks, how Jeems fills his pipe, how he gets Daun Tullach to fill it for him, cut his peats, work his land. Such detail is of a piece with the rest of the novel—with the explana-tions we are given for the way Canada figures in Ivor Cormack's imagination or literature in Allan Moffat's.

By way of contrast, in *The Lost Glen* the tone is more like Gunn's later fiction; he explains less, and what he does explain he does so obliquely. We have to discern for ourselves that Colonel Hicks is stupid and vicious, that Ewan's fault is a minor one in the eyes of anyone (except his uncle) who knows what happened, that the Ardbeg crofters have a very powerful case in terms of Highland populist morality if not in the courts. Colonel Hicks does not understand the land revolutionaries; Neil Gunn leaves it to the reader to disagree with the colonel and to discern the men's case:

> Yet a certain vague popular sympathy went out to the crofters who complained that they could not get sufficient soil on which to grow what at the best would but provide the bare essentials of existence. There was, however, a consideration that was vaguer even than the sympathy and yet took the shape of a claim to the land on the grounds that forefathers had cultivated it from time immemorial, or certainly from a time when under the tribal system the land had been held in common. In short, almost a claim that in the dark processes of history the land had been filched from them. (*The Lost Glen*, 139-40)

The feelings are vague, and we must make them concrete: not that Gunn gives us much of a chance to be obtuse, for only a few pages later we have an argument where the Blimpish colonel is put very firmly in his place by James Duffy, the visiting Union organiser.

The question of tonal differences and similarities between *The Grey Coast* and *The Lost Glen*, and between these and Gunn's other work deserves more lengthy consideration, but for the meantime I wish to concentrate on other aspects of Gunn's work of which this episode may remind us.

The argument between Duffy and Hicks is, after all, an event, and there are some events which we expect to happen in Gunn's fiction. In all his work there is a blend of events which can be classified as events which involve physical or emotional confrontation between characters, those in which the conflict is verbal, and those which occur in the mind of an individual, and I have already referred to some typical examples of these near the beginning of this section.

III

The colonel, as befits a stage villain, is too stupid to suffer from interesting internal conflicts, and Duffy is too minor a character; it is their argument, in which each case is misstated, and in which victory goes to the more confident, that makes us formulate our own discussion of the case for and against the crofters. In *The Grey Coast*, on the other hand, in a way which is more like the technique of *Butcher's Broom, Morning Tide* and *Highland River*, the terms of the discussions are made more explicit and the arguments are conducted with more rationality from the participants, just as the narratives of these later novels ask the reader to supply less information.

There is a discernible difference in the way in which Neil Gunn presents events in the two novels; and this difference is paralleled in the characters. In *The Grey Coast* the names of the characters emerge in the course of the fiction, and we have to wait to discover such basic data as Maggie's surname, that the schoolmaster's name is Allan Moffat, that Daun Tullach is Donald Tait who farms Tullach. And if Gunn allows such data to emerge as it does in life, he expects us to supply our own reasons why Donald should be Daun, and not a more common variant of the name—we are expected to recognise the characteris-

tically long-back ' a '. In the first chapter he uses the word
' enigmatic ' to describe Daun's perception of his relationship with Maggie, but the word can be applied with equal
justice to Gunn's relationship with his reader.

This is not to say that all is, or remains, obscure—by
the end of the novel the action has explained its own
perplexities, and when Gunn feels we need a solid anchor
of factual detail we get it. He names all the characters
eventually, lets us learn their ages, and even some of their
opinions; and when Ivor Cormack sails to the fishing in
Chapter XII we are inundated with facts. Three boats sail
from Balriach, the *Endeavour*, the *Sea Swallow* and *The
Dawn* (and it is punningly ironic that as Jeems, Maggie's
uncle, depends on Daun for his economic survival, so Ivor,
in love with Maggie, has to depend on *The Dawn* for his);
we are told that Ivor sails in *The Dawn*, that Sanny Ardbeg
is her second, and that Davie Mackay is her skipper. To
give us even more actuality, the falling wall and derelict
boats of the dying harbour are described, and *The Dawn's*
great brown mainsail. Such detail is to be compared with
the detailed description of poaching techniques for which
Gunn is justly admired: I would argue that it is in his
description of events which are slight in themselves, though
fascinating to a spectator, that Gunn anchors the more
elusive elements of his fiction.

IV

At the beginning of this essay I excluded from the
concept of Gunn's early fiction the novel *Morning Tide*
(1931), not because I thought it was late, but because the

adjective which most readily springs to mind when one thinks of *Morning Tide* is not ' early ' but ' major '. Now, after consideration of *The Grey Coast* and *The Lost Glen* it seems appropriate to think of *Morning Tide,* for it avoids the limitations of the other two novels and is more successful as fiction in communicating to the reader the peculiar wholeness of Highland culture.

It, too, is a novel of Highland life, of the connection between life and art, of the shadows of emigration and poverty, and of what remains when these have been expressed. Like them, it is on one level a narrative of events, a record of some salient experiences in the childhood of Hugh Macbeth, the son of a fisherman, growing up in a small Highland village. The precise date is irrelevant—it is enough to know that it is set in the past, and that no war is happening, so the village is reasonably isolated from the world outside, the world to which its children emigrate from time to time, and from which they sometimes return. Hugh's father, John Macbeth, skippers a fishing-boat, his brother Duncan has been drowned at sea when the *Fateful* went under ' battened down and with sails set ', his other brother Alan incurs his mother's displeasure by going to the fishing, and then brings loss on the family by his emigration to Australia; and Hugh has two sisters as well, Grace and Kirsty, whose lives introduce Hugh to the ways of men and women. At the end, with all his family away except Kirsty, he becomes aware of death as his mother almost dies, and after his rites of passage have been completed we leave Hugh to get on with his adult life.

Crude précis is no substitute for critical comment, but it is as well to present Hugh's situation and experience simply in order to point to the pattern of the action and the familiar structure found in *Morning Tide*, if to do nothing more than to demonstrate Hugh's averageness, or the averageness that is the setting for Hugh's uniqueness. For Hugh, whatever his situation, is not average—he is our viewpoint on this world, and as a sensitive observer who acts in our stead he is necessarily special, just as much as his character helps to solve the problems of communication which beset *The Lost Glen* and *The Grey Coast*. We have all been children, and we all share the experience of growing awareness of the adult world with Hugh; and Hugh develops his knowledge of the adult world of the Highland fishing village from inside its culture, so that we are inveigled into a sympathetic imagining of the village and its people. Hugh, the child, has to learn, and we learn with him, and Hugh is the natural audience for whatever information we need. Similarly, we move from the narration of readily imaginable events to an event which for all its centrality in Highland culture has had less crucial importance elsewhere, to the events of the third book which are simultaneously of local and universal significance, and *Morning Tide* brings our world and Hugh's together.

V

To begin at the beginning: we start with a boy on a beach, gathering bait for his father's lines, and the novel's opening starts with the first process of a fishing—first the bait, then the lines are baited, then the men sail, if lucky they catch fish, if lucky and skilful they bring home their catch, and the proceeds enable family life to go on, as the men clean their lines for the next sailing. And at once Hugh is given a place in the world, for he is working at something which will help to feed the family, not away playing football as he would like, but that too places him, for we know that just as he is part of his family he is also one of the village boys. Moreover, in gathering the bait, he falls in with Sandy Sutherland, who walks home with him making adult conversation, talking of bait and the last storm. Hugh can talk to Sandy, but he can fight with Rid Jock, he can notice Grace with Charlie Chisholm—he relates to all sorts of experience—and then he can go home and be a boy in his parents' house, eating his mother's cooking and listening to the family's talk. Already Hugh and the reader are learning about this world, so that when its great event comes it comes in its proper context of family history and social relationships; before the storm begins on the sea in Chapter V we have the warnings of a potential emotional storm in the sisters' jealousy for the farmer Chisholm and the painful exchange between Alan Macbeth and his mother over Alan going fishing for Geordie Macleod; their mother hates the sea that has taken her son Duncan, but Alan fancies Cathie Macleod, whose father is too ill to sail, so he sails in Geordie's place, out into the storm with the other men, who have no choice but to risk the sea.

"They had their lines baited," observed the Viking, almost gently. "They wouldn't want to let the bait rot for the second time." (*Morning Tide*, 87)*

The storm comes, and the rest of Book I is concerned

* The page numbers refer to the first edition.

with it and what it does to the people involved, in the boats and on the land. Kirsty puts it clearly to Hugh:

> " It would be a terrible thing if anything happened to Alan. Just the one night—the one night he had to come down. It would be a terrible thing—if it was fated.... And mother told him, too. If he was ... this one night."
>
> Hugh swallowed, his back teeth close shut.
>
> " It's so often the way," she finished. (*Morning Tide*, 73)

" It's so often the way ": the fatal expectation, the mixture of terror and resignation that is the distinctive response of the women of the fishing community to the sea sets the tone for the varieties of response to the storm; Hugh himself mixes fear and elation, though the elation and the pride are kept for the safe arrival of his father and brother.

There is no need to demonstrate Neil Gunn's ability to describe the storm; the people at the harbour, men at one side, women at the other, the comments of the old sailors, the breathtaking bravery of the men sailing home to death or safety, Alan's heroic rescue and his near-drowning are the stuff of many of Gunn's dramatic passages; but the climax, the safe return of Hugh's father, is a very powerful scene. At first, his boat is sighted:

> " By God, that's them! " cried one man, and he hit another man on the back with a loud whack.
>
> It was an incredible joke, the appearance of the boat. It was the greatest joke of all. Everybody laughed and stamped and shouted to everybody else. (*Morning Tide*, 103)

It is an incredible joke, and it calls for an incredible response; John Macbeth is at the tiller and although the boat looks doomed she must win through. The watchers discuss his chances, their knowledge of the ways of the sea and of the limits of human skill tempering their hopes, and they watch to see what will happen, till the moment when his daughter Kirsty greets her father's success with her cry of "He's managed it!" (110) There is no more to say; John Macbeth has managed to bring his boat safe into the harbour, and the event is so amazing there are no superlatives Kirsty can use, though Hugh is ecstatic. They are alive, Hugh and the reader are aware of the threat and the challenge of the sea, and Hugh goes on to more experiences taking us with him.

After the high point of the successful weathering of the storm, we move to the loss by emigration. The second book centres on Alan's impending departure for Australia, and Hugh's informal training to take his brother's place in the life of the village. We see Alan's place as a young man in his participation in the traditional ritual of the dividing of the catch, which is made suitably jocular by his father, while Hugh is getting on with his schooling. The rest of the book shows us Hugh being encouraged by Alan to take part in the ploys of the village youths, in particular Hugh's introduction to the social scene at Hector the roadman's, where the young men gather, and in going poaching on Alan's last expedition.

At Hector's there is talk and there is piping; Hugh hears the story of the *Fateful*, of Duncan's death, and we learn the quality of the bravery of the fishermen. Hector's story is a long story, and Chapter VI should be read in full, but something of its quality lies in Hector's moral:

" Never give in to the thing when it's coming at
you. And at the worst—at the worst—"
Alan leapt to his feet with a laugh.
" At the worst, battened down and with sails set—
sail her right under! " (167-8)

If you are going to hell, do it in style; and Alan, bound
for Australia, does it stylishly. They have a pibroch from
Hector, and set out for the river with the sounds of *Cha till
mi tuille* in their ears. On the river they have a great last
time—four salmon in three hours—with jokes about the
keeper and his strange accent: " What would MacAulay
say if he saw us now? ' You wass after the saamons you
puggers! ' " (179), and the practical joke of nailing the
tails to the keeper's door, but the ceremonies are observed
and they leave a half-fish on Hector's doorstep on their
way home. The high time is over, and the next day sees
the living death—Alan leaves for Australia amid the forced
cheerfulness of farewells, and then the old familiar sadness
sets in.

> Then a great slackness came upon the people. They
> stood in groups, moved listlessly, drifted away, talking
> all the time in easy tones. " Oh, they'll get on all right,
> the same lads! " They smiled. " Trust them for that! "
> But their smiles were weary, as though there was a final
> element in them of defeat. (203-4)

It is a defeat for the village to lose its sons, and the villagers
know it. Hugh can only cry his heart out when it is all
over, and he has tasted loss as at the end of the first book
he tasted victory.
As a child, Hugh had been proud of the seamanship of
his father, as an older boy he had sorrowed for the loss of

Alan; in the third book Hugh becomes a man himself, in
his response to his mother's illness and Kirsty's connection
with Charlie Chisholm. Hugh has his fears for Kirsty,
increased by his perception of a physical homology between
Kirsty and Peter Navook's idiot, infanticidal daughter,
fifty-year-old Margat whom he watches playing five-
stones like a girl, and they are almost justified when he
sees her with Chisholm: their love-making is interrupted
only by Bill making a noise, and Hugh has to fight Bill for
his sister's sake. Win or lose, Hugh has learned more
about sex. More important, in this book he learns about
death, and what death's approach means, as his mother
lies dying. That she survives the danger is good, but
Hugh has to pass through the valley of the shadow before
she recovers, the shadow of death and the shadow of
human inadequacy in the face of death. Neither Hugh
nor Kirsty is there when his mother takes a bad turn, and
the doctor is extremely dilatory in turning out for a woman
who is poor; and Hugh cannot bear to watch his mother
preparing to die.

Yet her preparation brings together her strong mind
and Highland religion, in a way which is typical and
moving. Kirsty is neither the first nor the last who has
to bring out the books for final consolation, and the consolation is a tough one for a tough person, ending on the
statement of the Forty-sixth Psalm, which is a Psalm of
affirmation rather than comfort, the only Psalm fit for the
deathbed of the wife of John Macbeth, the mother of
Duncan and Alan:

> When Kirsty had finished reading, her mother
> told her to turn to the Forty-sixth Psalm,

> *God is our refuge and our strength,*
> *in straits a present aid.*

As Kristy lifted up her voice in the old slow tune, Hugh could not bear the sharp tumult of his emotion. (273)

There is no need for Neil Gunn to specify the tune, for we all supply the tune we remember from childhood; nor is there any need for him to quote the cardinal verse, which follows the words quoted, for we supply them automatically:

> Therefore although the earth remove,
> We will not be afraid.

Hugh's mother is sailing herself right under, with her hatches battened and her sails set, and yet, like her husband, she wins through, smiles at Hugh's grilse, takes tea, and revives. Hugh, in delight, takes off ' across the fields of the dawn! ' (287)

Hugh has survived the rites of passage, and now his adult life is before him, rooted in a solid experiential base, much more solid and complete than this condensed account can hope to indicate. For Hugh, unlike Ivor and Maggie and Ewan, is at the same time at one with his civilisation and with its culture; the piping at Hector's is familiar and clear to him, but so is the nature of poetry, puzzled as he is by Walter Scott, and he knows not only the culture of story and tune but also the other folk-culture of the Highlands, the Bible and the Psalms, omitted as an item in the cultural scene in the other two novels, and thereby harming their claim to full authenticity. His mother's deathbed religion is one more detail, whose addition to the world of fiction brings it nearer to the real Highland world.

VI

The three novels have many things in common—the milieu, and many of its values. Australia as the place of emigration mirrors Canada, it is the equivalent of death:

> Kirsty shook her head with a sad smile.
> " It is likely none of us will ever see him again. My mother's brother—who has paid his passage—he never came back; and now never will come back. Alan also will work out there, taking years and years to gather money to start a place of his own. Then he will settle down and marry. He will die out there, and this old dun land will know him no more. It's sad." Her lips pressed tight. (*Morning Tide*, 129)

We find a similar attention to authenticating detail in the descriptions of actions and in the words of the characters— even to the gnomic sayings of : " It's in the Lord's hands " (80), or on a more humorous level: " Man, I'll spit in your eye and chok' you! " (151) We find the same values, the same cultural assumptions, with a greater coherence, even in the more obvious patterning of the novel, with its distinct formal design—one need do little more than look at the way the novel is divided into books and chapters to see this. Above all, *Morning Tide's* success lies in the way in which its moral is dramatised, in which the events explain themselves, in the fact that the narrator rarely has to tell the reader what any event or conversation signifies.

Ewan has to cut himself off from life—Ivor and Maggie have to take their chance—but Hugh has lived and will go on living.

VII

I began this argument by suggesting that our reading of the early fiction was almost always bound to be informed by our reading of the later fiction, and I hope that I have shown how someone who is familiar with Gunn's later work will find himself on familiar ground in *The Lost Glen* and *The Grey Coast*, and we can see that *Morning Tide*, in its centring on Hugh, the boy growing up, solves the fictional problems which beset the other two novels, the problems of how much the reader must be told, or how much he can be expected to accept or to find out about the real world on which the fictional one is modelled. That *The Lost Glen* and *The Grey Coast* are worth reading in themselves, not just as a context for *Morning Tide* or as a preface to Gunn's later work, but that they are as full of interest and delight as many other books of his, that their similarities to and differences from Gunn's other fiction makes them simultaneously familiar and surprising is an argument that I may offer but only the books themselves can prove; in the end, we must go back to the books themselves. About *Morning Tide* there can be no argument; like Hector's last tune, *Cha till mi tuille*, some of the sentiments may sadden, but what a tune!

Scottish Saga :
Sun Circle *and* Butcher's Broom

MARIE-HÉLÈNE RESCANIÈRES

The first time I read *Sun Circle*—although I was not sure of understanding the writer's intention and symbolism —I was under a spell. Analysing my feeling, I found I was most impressed by the quality of the prose. The book struck me as a refined 'long poem', bringing out the essence of the Scottish primeval element in relation to its surroundings. Then, coming back again to the novel, I realised that I had been deeply affected by Gunn's attempts at a thoroughly artistic and philosophical rendering of the birth of Scotland. This is the reason why I have always considered the book as a Scottish saga. The writer's attempt to give the Scots a philosophical romance about their own country justifies this term.

When reading it, the first thing that struck me was the absence of precise geographical bearings. Apart from what Gunn mentions in the outline, he never alludes to any real or even fictive place throughout the novel. Tower Glen appears to be the seat of the power around which the reader assumes various houses or hovels are built. When the lad Col takes his sister to the shielings the reader has a glimpse of the surrounding woods and moors. Now and then some allusions are made to other people living far away on the same land: the Koorich ('a pastoral people whose shepherds were sometimes encountered on the remote verges of the forest. They were reputed to be a wandering race and the strangest stories were told about their manner of life '); the Finnlags. But again Gunn does not precisely locate anything. His only commitment lies in the outline. The setting is somewhere in the ' moors and forests facing the islands of the Orcades '.

The same deliberate vagueness exists in the historical framework of the novel. Once again the reader has to come back to the outline to get the purely relative details.

> Before the Roman a conquering race had here built its wonder towers and struck southward for a kingdom. Through this summer day across the Eastern sea comes the ghostly echoing of master craftsmen hammering the smooth flanks of the longships of the vikings against yet another final invasion.

However, one accepts that this vagueness helps the book to wear its cloak of legend. Gunn narrates a tale which seems to have happened once upon a time in a remote past, in a remote northern place nearly at the end of the world. That is all the reader needs to know. Gunn is not interested in writing a detailed rendering of historical proceedings. He aims at unwinding the frame of mind of these ' primitive ' men. He wants to explain what happens from an anthropological point of view.

The main facts of the book concern the invasion of the Vikings and how a tribal-organised society faces the problem. Gunn constructs his tale round three particular moments: when the information about the invasion becomes known; the battle itself; and the consequences.

No one knows exactly what is brewing, but there is a feeling that something important is about to happen.

D

The Tower suddenly becomes the focal point of all activity and attention. Strangers are seen, others are expected. The Master (whom the reader has not been fully told of yet, although enough has been said to make us regard him as an important and indeed mythical figure) walks down to the Tower—which happens, we realise later, only at moments of supreme importance. And as the story proceeds, nothing is revealed except what has been overheard. All the unquestioned pieces of information will come from the Grove, the Master's abode, either from himself or through emissaries such as Aniel. After some hints the reader has guessed that a raid from the Vikings is expected, and, if they do come, yet another raid by local people, the Logenmen, is likely in consequence up in the shielings. Gunn then describes the way the population responds to the news. All the able-bodied men have been asked to leave their daily commitments to form a kind of army. But none of them seems to realise what they will have to face. Gunn describes them walking down and joking about their enemies as though they are going to an entertaining spectacle. One cannot help feeling they think that to fight is only a part of a game. No one—not even their chief, Drust—thinks they might be defeated. In spite of some realistic discussion and advice as to the most important things to protect—houses or flocks—Drust is confident that he can stop both raids one after the other: ' he would give the boatload of Northmen the surprise of their lives, smash them in bulk and individually, and that over, gather his men along the coast and intercept the Logenmen on their return, necessarily slow, with the herds '.

Nothing happens in the way Drust had thought it would. Gunn presents the battle quite objectively. He begins by stressing the differences between the opposing forces. The Vikings are ' trained and hardened warriors, experts with the shield, the sword and the axe '; their opponents are ' home-grown, crude-weaponed '. The former have the sense of war, ' the battle sense which made the eyes of the grizzled faces before them smile in cunning foreknowledge '; the latter have no ' thought of ambush or tactical concealment '. So Drust's people wait on the beach in the open; the thought of ambushing the Vikings does not occur to them, because, Gunn explains, they have ' a simple code of behaviour, so simple that had the Northmen landed and been greatly inferior in numbers, Drust would have felt it laid upon his honour to offer them terms rather than immediately destroy them '. And of course this simplicity will be fatal for them. In spite of their great enthusiasm for the battle (caused by Taran the Bard's war-cry, and the markings on the chief's body: ' the dark raven with outstretched wings between the shoulder blades, the three blue symbols, and the red circle in its boat beneath his heart '), their situation quickly becomes desperate. Against the cool, careful advance of the Vikings, the Ravens have only their simple desire to fight face to face. And their lack of iron weapons makes the result inevitable from the beginning. Twice Gunn portrays a Raven against a Viking and points out the inequality of a face-to-face encounter for the Ravens, and the warriors' smoothness of the Vikings: ' the clear eyes, the tempered adventurous spirit and the mastery of iron . . . that were already making a conqueror of the western world '.

The more the Ravens are defeated, the fiercer the battle turns. They are reduced to clutching and tearing.

Even Taran, although fighting is not the function of the Bard, raises his sword, unable to bear longer the slaughter which ' turns weed from brown to red '.

Then once the battle is lost and the enemies spreading, Gunn points out the two kinds of consequences they have to face. Most of their houses are burned and their flocks are killed. They need to reorganise themselves and protect the Tower, but all their leaders have been killed and they need a leader for that. ' Being an affectionate and peaceful people ' they do not seem to care about conquering and moving forward, because, Gunn thinks, ' they feel that by going forward they leave their true riches behind '. Any incentive will come from outside—and this is why their new ruler will be Haakon, the young chief of the Vikings, whom they have captured. He will be husband to Nessa, Drust's daughter. His being chosen will also bring peace and prevent any further raids from the Vikings. And in this manner Gunn presents the welding of the two peoples who gave birth to Scotland.

What makes the understanding of *Sun Circle* so difficult is Gunn's frequent shifts from an objective, descriptive level to a highly intellectual and lyrical one. The writer is not only interested in presenting a social clash; he wants to trace, as it were, the religious and ethical backgrounds of these men. In *Sun Circle* Gunn portrays a turning point; the ancient practices of the pagan religion are still prevalent at the time the story is set, suffering a kind of decline as they meet the new faith of Christianity, which seems to have been introduced by Silis, wife to Drust, who comes from a country farther south. She is pictured as the only fervent supporter of Molrua, the Christian priest. The older she grows, the more she wants her religion to overcome the ancient rites which she tends to despise. She has no doubt that Christianity is superior to the ancient faith. Christianity is a 'civilised' religion, the other is not. In *Sun Circle* Gunn imagines what remained of the old sun worship based on a universal doctrine regarding the two states of existence: the one in the visible world where the Sun-god reigns by day, and the other in the lower world into which he disappears at night. The Grove, an undefined place far away in the woods, is the abode of the Druid, the Master whom the bard or other priests visit. Gunn describes their old religious organisation and presents its important characters. Taran, the Bard whom everybody likes because of the 'great intelligence on his face', has a voice which can take so legendary a tone that no one dares interrupt him. Gilbrude, just under the Master, is portrayed as the old-fashioned priest who refuses change and sticks to the first, old, hard rules. He complains of the weakening of their organisation and wants to fight against 'the cancer that would in time wipe its tribes from the Sun'. Strongly against the Christians, he keeps reminding the Master of their increasing power which gnaws at their own cohesion. Probably because of this extreme tendency, Gilbrude is not popular among his own people. Young men like Aniel prefer the Master.

As Molrua calls him, the Master is 'the Druid', 'the wizard', 'the sorcerer'. His physical appearance already belongs to eternity or a timeless age and to nature itself.

> The small body was like a part of the bank, an outcrop of the ancient earth . . . the face was so old that its beginning was lost in the ages . . . the skin was the

colour and the texture of a sheepskin that drying in the sun had been forgotten.

This ageless person is worshipped with awe by his people. Regarded as a God, his words and decisions are obeyed without question. His knowledge is so wide and *intuitively* true that it excludes all doubt: 'for whatever the Master would do, would not only be right but would have the dreadful inevitability of rightness'. Hence the primary role of the Master—as Teacher. Rulers, Bards, priests all accepted his teaching at the Grove.

This explains why Molrua urges the people to make up their minds and choose. They cannot be Christians and yet follow the Druid. For him as for Gilbrude, no compromise is possible, whereas the Master, who might be considered as Gunn's spokesman, does not see the problem from such an angle.

So essentially the book is about a moment of choice and a balancing of past and present where Pict meets Viking and Druid meets Christian. And to show how difficult it is for Gunn's simple Picts to face up to these choices and new developments, Gunn weaves into the story the triangular relationship of Aniel (the Master's favourite pupil), and two women, fair, extrovert Nessa and dark, reticent Breeta. In a way the two girls stand for the two different poles between which Aniel, like his race, must choose.

At first each of the girls seems to stand for the same thing: both are Christian—although we realise that while Nessa is deeply convinced by her mother, Breeta has accepted Christianity as something more external to her.

Aniel's attraction to Nessa is mainly physical—and in a way this represents, even symbolises, the people's response to Christianity: a direct straightforward response to apparent simplicity, appealing in its 'modernity', but hardly involving the deepest self. Breeta means a lot more to him. She is the only one apart from the Master to whom he will show his drawings and pictures. At first Breeta seems rather upset by him, and she fears the way he moves her. She struggles within herself against any kind of surrender, but she cannot help but feel how close to each other they are. Gradually she gives in, rejecting all her outward layer of Christianity, and returns to the primeval sources of her own people. When she walks to the shielings with her brother, she lets the fire within her explode; she holds everybody spellbound, even Grannybeg —and there she is seen as a witch. There is something about her which made the Master choose her as the epitome of her people. On his way to the Tower he stops to watch her, 'a smile on his face'.

Counterpointing her people's defeat, Breeta's love surges within herself. The passages describing her and Aniel's happiness are among the most beautiful and lyrical in the book. The challenge between them has been so fierce that there is indeed something akin to the other primeval forces in the story of their love. Surrendering to Aniel, Breeta finds how much rooted to the earth she is. Many times Gunn portrays her trying to force herself down into the earth, either to release her tension or to seek comfort; like the sick Catrine at the beginning of *The Silver Darlings*, or like Dark Mairi in *Butcher's Broom*, she appears as 'an earth outcrop' to Aniel's brown stream. Like Mairi again, she finally sees herself as always 'concerned with happenings and not with thoughts'.

Out of their mutual surrender, they both emerge not

only purified but having achieved their personal wholeness. Aniel attempts to picture it for the Master:

> . . . two animals stretching themselves on a sunny bank, curling, lying still, stretching themselves again, scraping with their toes, dreaming watchfully, then hit by a wind of mirth, stirred by excessive ease, touching quickly, teasing, tickling, laughing, fighting, tossing, panting, and stretching again lazily, drowsily . . . this picture was the true picture of the loneliness of being abstracted from the world-in-common. And the loneliness of one was intensified and made complete by the loneliness of two. For one will often have a watchful malevolent loneliness, but two will be at the centre of the circle of perfection where thought had ceased and the moment achieves the eternal.

Although Nessa tries to tempt him a last time, Aniel realises that he cannot give in. She is not made for him. Breeta represents his final choice. This symbolises the achievement of the Master's teaching. He has conveyed more than a religion—he has profoundly influenced the individual ethics of Aniel. The importance he has lies not so much in his creed but within the effect he has on individuals themselves, *within* themselves. Aniel was often puzzled by the Master's talks, unsure of understanding his message. The only thing he could cling to was the image he had of the Master:

> a ghost withdrawing and going further into regions of stillness until he came to the centre . . . there he stood with eternity about him in a circle of light.

The Master is a symbol of clarity, ultimately an example to others, helping them to draw their own circles of light about themselves. The main thing is to 'see clearly', he teaches; once that stage has been reached, one no longer needs to worry about anything else.

> As the sun put a circle round the earth and all that it contained, so a man by his vision put a circle round himself. At the centre of this circle, his spirit sat and the centre of his spirit was a serenity for ever watchful. Sometimes the watchfulness gave an edged joy in holding at bay the demons and even the vengeful lesser Gods and sometimes it merged with the Sun's light into pure timeless joy.

There lies the explanation of the title and the ethical message of the book. For in describing this circle man fulfils the final law and his spirit is satisfied. The choice of any religion or philosophy then becomes secondary. Whatever the choice may be, man is at one with himself within his own circle. Finally, Aniel waits for Breeta to join him at the heart of his circle, and 'the earth beneath, the Sun above, and we the children of their union'. Gunn concludes: 'that is all we know and perhaps all we need to know to find the power that has serenity at its heart'.

Thus one sees that what really matters for Gunn is to reach this primeval integrity. One might object to this as a purely egotistical pursuit—but is it not the only truly satisfying and realistic issue?

My calling *Sun Circle* a saga would not be entirely justified if the style and the prose did not also fit the description. The entire book is pervaded by the close and vital connection of environment and persons:

D 2

the landscape local and particular in configuration acts reciprocally with the growth of inward vision.

At many points one could say that the book is a song written to the glory of Nature. On their way up to the shielings Breeta and Col are gradually released from their own cares; and when they hear the melody Leu is playing, they immediately recognise it as the musical representation of the scenery before them—' the evening falling as a cool transparent shadow from the sunken sun '—and they fall under its spell. Gunn excels in making the natural elements present in the reader's mind. He personifies and animates the moorland, and establishes a mute dialogue between it and Breeta. And colours change in their symphonic relations to people: grey can either be silver or green.

Indeed from the earth itself a voice is raised which is in tune with and echoed in the musician's notes:

> Out of the sounds of trees, the singing of birds, the speaking of quiet seas, the racing of light and shadow, out of the breasts of women, the fun of children, the swaying of strong men, he selected his notes and his rhythms and created new shapes all in tribute to the Gods.

Gunn makes this musical and poetical reverence of the earth pervade the novel to show that there one feels one's own roots and senses one's own end.

To see the originality—in its literal sense—of *Sun Circle*, one must look at *Butcher's Broom*, which may be considered as its sequel, and the ' end of an old song '. Gunn sets the story just before the Highland Clearances.

Here again he is not primarily interested in tackling the situation from a historical point of view. Concerned with the anthropological nature of his people, he portrays the concrete and spiritual life of a small community in a Kildonan village, and portrays the society the factors found when they came to clear the glens. The young men were away, engaged in a foreign war, seduced by their ancient devotion to their Chief, now played on by the Government to lead them away from the ancient ways. The women are left with helpless old men and children. It is not without reason that the book is focused on the tragic figure of Dark Mairi. She personifies the ancient ways; and the novel opens with her represented as almost a figure graven from stone, timeless and enduring. It closes with her symbolic death. Gunn sees History as the legendary continuity of 'innumerable women whose suffering and endurance were like little black knots holding the web of history together'. Her death points the conflict between a mythic and a historic view of life. The figure of Mairi, symbol of eternal wisdom, is crushed down by History and Progress. In the coming new order there is not room for such a person. Her spirit only can be remembered as the vital and earthbound spirit of

> the human mother carrying on her ancient solitary business with the earth talking good and familiar sense with boulder and flower and rock and now and then following a root below the surface; in easy accord, the communion sensible and so full of understanding that silence might extend into eternal silence for wind and sun to play upon.

In *Sun Circle* Aniel and Breeta are not overtaken by

Progress and History. They achieve mastery of these forces because they are both urged by the fire of youth. In fact these two books point out how the ancient self survives through legend, transcending and translating its commonness into something 'eternally right like the movement of a figure through the mesh of fate in one of Old Hector's stories or like a swan in the Irish Sea in the legend of Finn, son of Angus'. This quotation from *The Silver Darlings* shows how central the theme is for Gunn.

Nevertheless in few of his novels does one find the enchantingly optimistic atmosphere and the high symbolism present in *Sun Circle*. While *Butcher's Broom* represents with superb elegy the passing of an archetypal world, it lacks the density of event, image and symbol of *Sun Circle*. Yet separately and together they must surely be held among Neil Gunn's most ambitious and stirring work.

The Source of Joy : Highland River

DOUGLAS GIFFORD

The dedication of *Highland River* signalises that Gunn's fiction has taken a new turn; that he is moving on to explore the inner, as well as the outer, landscape. Indeed, the very act of writing the novel seems to have surprised himself.

> Certainly it is not the description I anticipated . . . some ancestral instinct, at first glimpse of the river, must have taken control and set me off on a queerer hunt than we have yet tackled.

And after acknowledging the connection, nevertheless, with the earlier fiction by spotting stray characters from *Morning Tide* present here, he then sums up the essential difference. The hunts, the forays after rabbits and salmon are concrete and actual—but they are also part of the mature novelist's other hunt—' a poaching expedition to the source of delight '.

Looking at Gunn's work as a whole, it is difficult not to see *Highland River* and the final work, the spiritual autobiography *The Atom of Delight*, published as far apart as 1937 and 1954, as first and last great explicit statements of the same theme—the theme of the significance of the moment of delight, round which the other novels revolve. Nowhere else does he enunciate so clearly his central ideas—although one must immediately qualify this by adding that one or two other novels like *The Silver Darlings* are more complete and satisfying works of art. Yet *Highland River* must mark the deepening and intensifying point in Gunn's own flow of development—and deserves inclusion amongst his greatest novels for several reasons: because it sings his major theme of delight; because it introduces motifs and symbols like those of serpent and circle which will recur throughout his work; because, in its complex but extremely satisfying structure and time sequence, it shows Gunn the deliberate artist experimenting in a manner reminiscent of Proust or Virginia Woolf with the entire methodology of the novel form; and finally because as a result of all these he produces a magnificent, if not unflawed, 'Prelude'-like account, somewhere between the novel and the long poem, of the growth of a sensitive mind to the point where it finds itself. It is Gunn's portrait of the artist as a young man. Yet it is typical of his humility that he should portray Kenn—so close to himself—first as one of the folk, and second as a scientist, devoid of Stephen Daedulus's egotism about the special nature of the artist.

Possibly the best way into this apparently simple but actually very rich and complex work is to follow the image and the idea of the river itself. It obviously has to do with the theme of delight, since Gunn talks of finding delight's source. In fact, exploration of this river will reveal just what Gunn's theme is; the river is to this novel what the image and idea of the circle and the ring of stones known as the 'house of peace' is to *The Silver Darlings*. It runs through the novel from first chapter to last. All through the novel we move from the sea it joins, to the populated places round its mouth, to the crofting country higher up its banks, to the lonelier Pict and pagan haunted places close to the moors, and finally on to the bare, eternally desolate moors in which the river has its source. Whatever flashes forward in time to war or maturity occur, careful reading will show how the growing Kenn has several important points of development which are measured by the progress he makes in adventuring farther up the river.

But it must be stressed that this is a very real river in a very real strath. It produces real salmon—as Gunn reminds us, Kenn ' was hunting nothing abstract. The " salmon of knowledge " for him had real silver scales and a desirable shape; the eyes he feared were the telescope eyes of game-keepers '. And on this real level one must simply acknow-ledge that Gunn has no superiors at evoking seasonal change in a country landscape. While regarding this descriptive and evocative ability as one of Gunn's major claims to greatness as a writer, one feels that at this level he speaks for himself so clearly that little comment is needed. Read Chapter VI alone, if this is still doubted, with its description of the stormy winter; of the sea thundering on the beach ' with reverberations that would be heard far inland '; of the dim afternoon light where drizzle thickens into rain, where the drop at the end of an old woman's nose is ' distilled from misery's final self '. The river in this chapter takes on its own cruel power, has ' a submerged sound of grinding boulders ' as it boils and seethes.

It is a real river. But we should also appreciate how richly Gunn develops its meaning beyond this. As Kurt Wittig said in *The Scottish Tradition in Literature* :

in *Highland River*, even in hunting the salmon as it pursues its pilgrimage between light and darkness back to the source of its life, Kenn himself is making a similar journey back to the source of his own life.

That is to say that Kenn also follows a river which winds deep back into the recesses of his own mind.

Yet even then one must enlarge the river's scope, for the river's connection with the sea and its salmon is an idea that Gunn develops in relation to Kenn. Indeed one must broaden the river's scope to include the entire strath and its creatures, since they are so interconnected. The subtlety of Gunn's art could be overlooked in this respect, as it is so apparently simple. What he does is to make the boy Kenn a creature, a part of the changing seasons and the natural skirmishes and hunts taking place throughout the strath. He describes—including the humans—an animal landscape which merges with the physical; without trace of false sentiment or extra respect for any part of the whole. The way this is done is by describing Kenn in animal metaphors. As a boy, in winter as the river rushes past at night, Kenn curls up in the hollow of his bed.

> It was great fun to be so safe in this warm hole, while the dark cold river rolled on its way to the distant thunder of the sea . . . animals, furry and warm, were curled up in their dens . . . curled up, like himself, and heard, waking or in sleep, the rushing of the river. . . . The picture made him snuggle in his own den, and smell the thick warmth out of his own pelt.

This is the technique throughout. Kenn and Beel and Art are creatures in a landscape; they sniff ' with the action of a stag '; their cheeks are ' petals of the dogrose '; their eyes are ' quicker than tits or finches '. Chapter XV has at its centre a ' stream of consciousness ' passage where the attempt is to represent purely animal states of mind, immediately savouring the smells, tastes and glimpses of summer. Later the same chapter has the boys naked in a

pool. Beel is a water-rat, Kenn a seal; they are as persistent
as otters; they dam the pool like beavers.

This is no casual method—for Gunn uses the converse.
Usually human terms are applied to natural phenomena.
When Kenn listens to the river he hears a heart beating—
' contract and expand, systole and diastole; the river flows '.
And throughout the novel there is the evocation in lonely
and deserted places of a presence—of something which
animates the landscape—not merely the threat of the keepers,
but something which can be glimpsed in the inhuman but
more than animal eye of a gull, or

> that inexplicable sensation of there being an eye about
> somewhere, a non-human eye, a peat-hag eye under
> heather tufts. . . .

Gunn emphasises the animal in the human, and the more
than animal or merely physical in the landscape behind the
human. And thus, to return to the river, one can now see
little incongruous in the fact that the salmon which comes
from the dark continental shelf of the Atlantic at the
stirrings of some long-sleeping instinct to enter the freshwater currents of the river and to explore, almost despite
himself, the remote reaches from which he once came, in
time dimly remembered—that this salmon is a parallel, an
echo to Kenn. There is a deliberate play made on the
instinctive quest of both for the source. This is first developed in Chapter II; where the continental ledge, that
deep and comfortable water within which the adult salmon
passes his unthinking existence, is used as a metaphor for
Kenn's mind, when in a state of abstraction, ' where story
and meaning run into a silver glimmer '. Both Kenn and the
salmon are in the middle stages of their development

here. (In Chapter XVII Gunn says there are three divisions of the river.) They have as yet no thought of exploring for the source, but are content to move unthinking at a level of sensual enjoyment. And it is worthwhile remembering that this view of the salmon is Kenn's, as he muses in the classroom in Chapter II. The two are explicitly paralleled at this point.

> And here the grown-up Kenn pauses because it was this very point of what the salmon may feel at such a moment [the moment when the salmon begins his search for the source] that first launched him on this search into lost times.

Kenn the adult will search for his source in a way that is utterly natural, just as earlier the boys, going upriver

> came to the base of an overhanging rock with a slanting passageway to either hand, as salmon might come to a pool where two rivers meet. Which way now? They had no memory of ever having chosen before. Yet they hardly hesitated, all three going to the left. And if one had gone to the right, he would very soon have sniffed and returned, just as an old salmon has been known to go a short distance up one stream, then inexplicably to return and follow the other, that, unknown to him, had been chosen of his brethren for thousands of years.

Thus Kenn shares the instincts of animal creation; and later, when as a soldier he is beset by horror and death and life seems unbearable, he is sustained by this same kinship with the animal.

> . . . this blinding by gas followed at a considerable interval an incident on the Somme that still makes him smile, because in its cool river cunning, it shows so clearly the effect of his early environment.

There is nothing slovenly in the action of a salmon. By the time Kenn was seventeen, he had almost an instinct for precision. . . .

And time and again the movement of Kenn's mind, as it flashes with delight or takes refuge deep within itself, is expressed in this salmon metaphor, this movement within the ' river of life ' which Kenn's home river has become so sustainingly to him. We remember, too, Gunn's play on the old Celtic symbolism that the salmon is the salmon of wisdom, eating the hazelnuts of knowledge which drop into the pools of the river of life. In this early novel Gunn does not develop this symbolism to the level at which it operates in, say, *The Green Isle of the Great Deep*; but the fact that the book presents Kenn's development towards self-awareness as often in terms of salmon-catching as anything else surely carries a symbolic overtone: that Kenn is gathering and becoming one with the salmon of wisdom.

There is another light in which the salmon should be seen, and that is in the same way as other beautiful, surprising elusive creatures are seen too. These animals are of a different order from the pig, cow, goat; they are still linked with the river, but they are somehow marvellous; ' magical ' is a word which Gunn associates with this kind of animal or creature—in the sense that nature rarely vouchsafes their appearance, let alone their entire presence, as a gift.

We come close here to the importance of the ' delightful moment '—not to be used or taken casually in the Gunn world. At this point let it merely be argued that this salmon category of creature or event—for a sunset, a flower like the primrose or a smell of birches after rain can have the same effect of epiphany—is one which precipitates the moment of delight. The book is presented totally in terms of such moments, whether they be the sighting of a *black* rabbit, the discovery of the sudden grace of hinds at the source of the river or the catching of the salmon itself. And after a while the reader becomes aware of a great skill in the weaving together of these animal glimpses or events which occur as Kenn moves upriver through his boyhood. The technique is not dissimilar to Joyce's in *Portrait of the Artist;* it is the arrangement of *motifs,* of certain central images, ideas, phrases even, which, as they are reused and reoccur, take on a deeper significance. Kenn's response to the same stimulus, the same motif, changes as he develops— and by recognising the motif we are not only able to measure the extent of his development, but our minds are cast backwards in time, time is momentarily cancelled out, and we are simultaneously aware of every other occasion on which Kenn hunted salmon, tried to trap linnets, or felt the presence of desolate places.

It is worth considering this method a bit more fully, since it is probably the main way in which Gunn binds the apparently random events spread over twenty-eight years of Kenn's life. It takes a little while to realise the method, since Gunn has obviously to state his motifs, the images and ideas which will later be echoed or varied, for a first time. The most obvious example is in the simple recurrence of the *pool*; the well pool at the beginning gives way to the higher Achglas pool, which gives way to the Lodge pool even higher, till the final small loch at the end. Each has its separate character, yet they are linked. We recognise Kenn's spiritual progress at each new pool—and we remember with a sense of timelessness, the smaller and younger Kenns. And this kind of juxtaposition of separate times

forms the very texture of the novel. When Kenn very
early has to learn that Leicester is famous for boots, we read
this as a part of a sensitive condemnation by Gunn of the
teaching of inert, unrelated facts. The children do not get
taught local, vivid folk-history, or anything of the culture
which relates to their lives; they learn the lives of long-
dead English kings. The passage is self-sufficient—but
Gunn weaves it into a bigger pattern by having it echoed
years later in the hospital where Kenn, blinded by gas, finds
a moment of ironic delight when he realises he *is* in Leicester.
The memory, as he murmurs the old school lesson to himself, takes him back to the strath. Time is cancelled by
delight, his deafness from shell noise clears, and he hears
the rumble of hospital noise as ' the far cry of brown water
in the hollow of a strath'. Even then the motif is not
finished, as the nurse who tends him there recurs at the
end; he is still in touch with her, and we are still in touch
with several moments of Kenn's life simultaneously.

This method is used with so many events and images
that only the most important need be indicated. One of
the often-used ideas is that of the presence, the strange and
sometimes threatening life within the inanimate world.
The boy is conscious of it in an empty house—the very
furniture seems to be aware of him. He will see this later
in a gull's eye, where the eye seems to be that of more than
gull, the very spirit of wilderness, ' wild and cold and
watchful'; and he will find on his poaching expeditions
that more than the keepers have eyes. The motif runs all
through—and thus it is the climax to this that he finds,
in maturity, he fears neither the darkness nor the watching
eyes. The use of the motif enables us to realise his coming
to maturity, to complete self-awareness, in much the same

way as Finn, in the last chapter of *The Silver Darlings*—significantly called ' Finn at the Heart of the Circle '—has arrived at *his* moment of completion. They are at one with whatever spirit may (or may not) be there. They can accept.

People are used in the same way. They are at once themselves—mother, father, brother—and motifs. The father's " Bless me, boy " occurs at beginning and end as a phrase the same in its warmth, kindliness, but subtly different in the way it relates to Kenn's development. The father himself has shrunk through the course of time from bearded giant and benevolent patriarch to something just as dignified but somehow more vulnerable, more human. The mother, too, is real, yet part of a recurrent pattern of archetypal womanhood; the nurse, the old woman who is considered by Kenn the fittest human being to represent the race to God, even the young girl Annie—all are linked, deliberately, by recurrence of descriptive phrase and image, to a central figure who is simply Woman. None of Kenn's family or friends is presented in the usual narrative fashion, whereby we follow them chronologically in the secondary roles. They are not secondary, since they are a part of the whole Kenn is part of too. But they emerge before us in flashes, in moments which, while exceptionally graphic in the amount they tell us about them as individuals, are nevertheless primarily important in that they develop previous moments and combine with these earlier and related episodes to form a thematic thread which leads to the central theme of delight.

And again we come back to the main characteristic of these motifs, these groups of linked episodes. They are carefully chosen *moments*. The word is not trivial for

Gunn—indeed it is probably the most used word in all his work, and certainly so in this novel. What Gunn is doing in *Highland River* is picking *moments* of delight and wonder from Kenn's childhood and adolescence, moments which will contribute towards his central revelation. Is it then at all surprising that they sould be in clusters, similar, manifesting Kenn's growing insight? Indeed, sometimes one feels that the repeated image becomes so strongly indicative of the theme that it has become more than motif, but symbol in itself. The salmon obviously takes on this extra dimension of meaning; and at the end the hinds are symbolic of the same meaning. But the best example of motif growing into symbol is found in the way Gunn develops the bird motif into the specific symbol of delight, the green linnet—so reminiscent of Joyce's green rose in *Portrait of the Artist*. Curlews, peewits, gulls haunt the book —they are ever present at the back of Kenn's consciousness as he wanders through the strath. The green linnet *is* the elusive moment of delight; it is the one bird than Kenn has never caught, only glimpsed. Even more than salmon or hind, there is something particularly apt in the use of this bird to symbolise the fleeting, unpredictable point in time when sheer surprise and pleasure are glimpsed.

We are, it must be realised, still within the central river theme of the work. But now the river has taken on even wider scope. It is now quite deliberately meant by Gunn to be a river of time and of space. And by using the motif method, Gunn can place us as he wishes at any and several of the branches and pools which are the significant developing points in Kenn's life. Gunn quite explicitly refers throughout to ' straths of the past ', and develops the notion that Kenn the adult, in deliberately remembering his past, is moving up a river of time.

Gunn has been criticised for his use of several different time-sequences in the novel, for not telling his story in a straightforward manner. I do not think this is valid. His intention justifies the method; and the intention is to show how the child is father of the man. Mature Kenn is actively remembering the moments which he thinks made him; thus Gunn must have at least a dual time-sequence since we must know two Kenns to know the relation between them. The method confuses for a little while, but the sensitive reader soon grasps the principle behind each chapter, whereby childhood moment of delight, intense moulding experience, is followed by an adult or adolescent experience which has somehow been conditioned by the earlier episode. The Leicester-linked passages may be seen as example; the scenes with Angus in childhood and then Angus in war as another. (Notice the typical attention to detail in the motif which links these two, the use of the same image of pellets of earth being displaced as though by a serpent.) In most cases the childhood experience provides the sustaining, strath-rooted memory which enables Kenn to face city squalor, war horrors, cynicism of colleagues—and himself. And the effect of juxtaposing time past with time present is usually forceful and effective. Time is momentarily cancelled, and the river of the past rolls into Kenn's spirit, filling him with the sense of wonder and delight he needs to sustain him. And likewise, this river of time which knows no temporal barrier is a river in space too—for Kenn finds in France that the Somme can become his Highland river.

Indeed the river defies label as symbol, motif, structural

device—simply because it is so much. It is a river of memory, it is a river which, like that of *Heart of Darkness*, as it moves from coast to interior, represents the movement from the conscious to the unconscious. Yet it is also itself and the *sine qua non* of the strath. And then we change perspective yet again, and it becomes a river of humanity, the river of Highland folk and all their ways, stories and songs which surround Kenn. And here one must consider Gunn's fundamental belief that for most Western people the river took a wrong turning. Kenn muses:

> It's a far cry to the golden age, to the blue smoke of the heath fire and the scent of the primrose! Our river took a wrong turning somewhere! But we haven't forgotten the source.

Like Lewis Grassic Gibbon in *Sunset Song*, Gunn believes that primitive pre-Christian and pre-institutionalised man possessed an innocence and a communion with his organic surroundings—albeit his life was filled with the facts of hardship and suffering. It is not necessary to prove or disprove the validity of this diffusionist theory here; but for a true appreciation of Gunn's *art* one must recognise this informing vision. Other essays in this collection, like that on *Sun Circle*, discuss Gunn's presentation of these ' elder people ', these ancient and innocent folk, more fully than this essay can—so let it suffice to point at the bare bones of Gunn's anthropological beliefs, and at the use he makes of them aesthetically. The point is that the river, in all its aspects as a central image, is the link with the past. Kenn, in seeking the source of the real river, is also doing several other related things, exploring several other sources. Not only is he in search of himself as a *separate* person—the destiny of all Gunn's heroes—but, although at first this may seem a contradiction, he is also in search of his community, present and past. It is not a contradiction; one is, in Gunn's view, first a clearly defined and essentially alone person—but this does not destroy the further need of the individual for family and friends and community identity. There is nothing solipsistic in Gunn's concept of the essential loneliness of man.

And in searching for himself in this fuller social sense, Kenn finds that the river takes on wider implications as symbol and image. It becomes the river of men, with Spartacus, Copernicus, Galileo, Leonardo da Vinci, as well as the river of fishermen and peasants. But for all its illustrious salmon, Kenn, as he considers who of humanity should talk with God at the source of this river, finds that the essence of the river is that it is of the folk, and that he himself is of the folk. For it is the old woman, wasted almost to pure spirit, shy and withdrawn in her cottage by the river, whom Kenn chooses.

This realisation does not come at once to Kenn. He is given insight bit by bit, in these moments of surprise or delight—as in the first chapter of the novel, when, hunting the huge salmon in the Well pool,

> Out of that noiseless world in the grey of the morning, all his ancestors came at him. They tapped his breast until the bird inside it fluttered madly; they drew a hand along his hair until the scalp crinkled; they made the blood within him tingle to a dance that had him leaping from boulder to boulder. . . . Not only did his hunting ancestors of the Caledonian forest come at him, but his grown up brothers and his brothers' friends, with their wild forays and epic stories. . . .

Here is Jung's 'collective unconscious' in operation; and it is this inner instinct which impels Kenn upriver, giving him glimpse after glimpse of the next stage, the higher value or beauty of the river of life; it is the same instinct as moves the salmon. Legends, song and story carry this ancient knowledge—which is why Gunn in all his work sets such high value on the act of story-telling or singing. The knowledge of the bones is developed by seeing and hearing the traces of the elder people in ruins of brochs or fragments of lore, in story or song. And once the instincts have been awakened, they remain—witness Kenn's coolness, the instinct of the hunter for survival, in France.

In all this discovery by Kenn of his complete, detached self as a nevertheless organic part of the community of past and present there is a dark counter current, broadly summed up in the use of the motif of 'the keepers'. For many—indeed, for most—of society, the river has taken a wrong turning. Gunn begins this theme by stressing that within Kenn's mind, as he hunts the salmon in the Well pool,

> the fear ... of the fish itself ... was also infinitely complicated by fear of gamekeepers, of the horror and violence of lawcourts, of our modern social fear.

And throughout 'fear of the keepers' is used as a covering motif for all oppression; a kind of shorthand which originates naturally in the strath, where so obviously there is something sick in the fact that the people who have fished and hunted the strath for a millenium are now legally forbidden to do so; the fish and game being the 'property' of, in all probability, an absentee landlord. There is much of Grassic Gibbon's feeling that the 'elder' people have been cheated—in terms of political and religious oppression as well as simple economic exploitation. But there is nothing of Gibbon's hysteria, which makes the climax of the theme of ' the keepers ' all the more deadly in effect, just as the method of understating the press-gang's brutal treatment of the simple fishermen in *The Silver Darlings* is more effective than any amount of lavish brutal detail. Compare Gibbon's treatment of the demoralisation and degradation of Ewan in *Sunset Song* with Gunn's expression of the same theme in showing how Kenn's brother Angus has been drained of the strength of the strath by the horror he has seen. There is no viciousness in Angus, as in Ewan; no demonstration of his debased state through acts of sadism, aided by physical description which, in Gibbon's case, is emotive, since it associates Ewan's close-cropped hair, his scars (putrescent) with his inner fall. Instead, we juxtapose the Angus we have met at odd intervals poaching with Kenn, humouring his younger brother, clowning goodnaturedly, with the shifty-eyed new Angus, advising Kenn to take no unnecessary chances—Angus, the childhood chancer, the daredevil tree-swinger, who found in chances his delight! Gunn puts in an odd, effective touch here; Angus of the strath is dead before he dies, but *another* Angus, from Canada, carries on his attitudes, lives in the tradition. Just as in *The Silver Darlings* Gunn has young Finn born as Kirstie's father dies—the implication being that the spirit passes from one to the other—so there seems to be the hint that the spirit of Angus is not lost here either, despite all that sick society can do. The war is the worst it can manage; and even that cannot cancel the fact that Angus had his moments of delight. Notice how Kenn tries, by recalling these to him in the trenches, to recreate him, to relocate him in the river that matters, and not the

river which has taken a wrong turning and which is guarded
by keepers at every point. But Angus has become a ghost;
and Gunn's skill is nowhere better seen than in the way he
makes the trenches scene a natural development of the
earlier episode when Angus and Kenn were almost caught
by the keepers. For all Angus's basic decency, he seems
to lack Kenn's deeper wellsprings of strength; he is like
Ronnie of *The Silver Darlings*, with an inner weakness that
gives in to the pressures of the sick society. As they lay
hiding from the keepers

> Kenn looked at Angus's face. It had whitened, and play-
> ing on it was a weak surface smile.
> All the dark proud life was gone.
> Doom was in the nervous lips, in the shallow glitter
> of the eyes. The spirit, netted in the white smile,
> haunted Kenn through all the rest of his years. . . .

This ghost-face becomes another motif of the novel; in it is
prefigured Angus's spiritual defeat. He will be too weak
to hold the river in his mind—Kenn is appalled by his
attitude of

> take care, do no more than you must. . . . And all the
> time the river as pure memory, receding . . . receding . . .
> until their talk became forced. . . .

The ghost face of Angus joins the other hidden fears of
the younger Kenn; only in maturity will he fully conquer
them, and in so doing he conquers all threats to the river
of his own development, be they the obvious assaults of
Calvinism, the horrors of slums or war, or the more
insidious cynicism of the scientist Radzyn. Destroying
Angus is as near as these forces come to him; but they

cannot overthrow the validity of Kenn's memories of his river.

And thus we come to the last meaning which the river takes on. For a river—or rivers—which is simply a river of memory, or of humanity, or even of time, would not provide the source Kenn is looking for. Something of value must be found, or at least glimpsed, however moment-arily, to give meaning to all these rivers of life. We remember Gunn's dedication, his statement that he, as well as Kenn, is looking for the source of the river of delight.

For Gunn and for Kenn this notion of the river as a continual pouring from somewhere of moments of delight is the one which illuminates and unites all the other aspects of the river and all the other motifs. They all depend on this central concept—because only here does Gunn provide a reason for the river of humanity or the internal river of consciousness to flow at all. It is the moment of delight which blesses the human condition. And, although to say so oversimplifies the novel, it is basically true to say that the entire form of the novel derives from such moments—in so far as every chapter presents one or two such moments which, when recollected in stress or tranquillity in later life, provide a timeless refuge. They are Wordsworthian glimp-ses of another landscape; and from *Highland River* onwards nearly all Gunn's novels carry a title which symbolises this place or condition of timeless harmony with all creation and with oneself—usually with the added implication that this state comes as water in a parched land, as a much-needed sanctuary. *The Well at the World's End, The Drinking Well; The Lost Chart; The Other Landscape; Wild Geese Overhead*—all are images drawing on this basic idea of transition through the moment of delight to a condition in which all fragmentation of experience is lost and there is unity of self and surroundings.

Such moments are magical for Gunn—it is significant that, next to ' moment ', ' magic ' should be the most used word of the novel. Again one must stress that whether one agrees or has shared this kind of experience or not is irrelevant as a basis for criticism—Gunn has felt them, and has based his aesthetic organisation on them, just as Wordsworth did in ' The Prelude '. Let us look briefly at one such moment, and see how it forms the heart of his inspiration.

Young Kenn's capture of the salmon bigger than himself at the beginning of the novel is one of the finest descriptions of its kind in English. It is also a classic example of the setting and context of Gunn's ' moment of delight '. To begin with, it comes as a surprise, as unexpected—there is a sense of wonder about the sly unpredictability of nature, and already we see that Gunn has cajoled us into seeing the natural world as animate, as possessing even a sense of humour: all through, it will play such tricks on Kenn with black rabbits and green linnets and false sources for his river that mock his seriousness. He is sleepy—and unexpectedly, ' as at a signal in a weird fairy tale ', the world suddenly changes. The fabulous mood has been arranged by that beginning; and the sense of comic myth is increased by the emphasis that this huge salmon which ploughs at his feet is the ' allfather of fish; it will be a ' saga ' of a fight.

But the moment does more than surprise; it *develops* Kenn, since for the first time his instincts, all the memories of his race, are awakened in him. And notice that in the fight that ensues, there is utterly nothing that is at all sentimental or idealised—there is nothing about Gunn's conception of such episodes of delight that forbids healthy violence or takes a soft view of animal creation. The salmon is hunted remorselessly—and Kenn will accept this in wartime as his lot. Unnecessary cruelty is one thing— the facts of life another.

The fight with the salmon awakens Kenn to his racial past; to his ' collective inconscious '. It draws out instincts for ferocity and animal cunning he did not know he possessed. But it also, afterwards, redefines his relationship with his family—as the mother realises, she cannot take the attitudes she used to towards a boy changed like this—

> . . . there was a flame, an intolerant fighting spirit, that knit him together, and separated him from her in a way that suddenly pulled at her heart.

And this separation is more than just from family; he is being individualised, and he folds his achievement and the glorious memory of it to himself—thereby getting into trouble from the schoolmaster who cannot understand this kind of privacy. And, completing the way in which an episode like this gathers into itself all the themes of the book, notice how in musing about the salmon Kenn *becomes* the salmon, moving from the salt depths to the freshwater river in his mind. The episode has integrated himself, defined him as a separate person and helped to define his relationship with his background.

This is an exceptionally intense episode of delight—so much so that the moments of delight resulting from this are many, welling up inside Kenn whenever his mind turns to what he has done. Gunn also says that it is difficult to know how much Kenn consciously appreciated at this very young age. But after this the moments become simpler. Kenn does not look for them—indeed, he is often only half-conscious of the natural setting to his adventures. But increasingly he is able to distil more and more personal meaning from them—as with his moment of short-circuiting time, when he and Beel creep into the broch and find that time telescopes, and ' from two thousand years back time's fingers could touch them in less than an instant '. He now gathers more than simple wonder from such experiences— going on in maturity to feel that he has occasionally ' had an impression of very nearly visualising the fourth dimension '.

And this idea of moving into realms uncharted by scientific method leads to the final significance of the moment of delight. It must finally be realised that Gunn is moving into areas normally discussed in religious terms. He has obviously been affected by ideas from Zen Buddhist and Taoist philosophies. He leaves the conclusion of *Highland River* open, but there is no doubt the implications point to a God who vouchsafes us these moments when all leaps into significance. Indeed God figures in this novel and at the end of *The Green Isle of the Great Deep*. Always, however, such a figure is presented with a certain dry humour which seems to mock the notion as it is presented— and it does seem to me that herein lies an area of weakness in these more metaphysical novels. Gunn seems to hover between two interpretations of the world. One asserts the validity of scientific research—this being one of the most refreshing qualities of his fiction, a lack of any ' backlash ' against the material and technological world. In this interpretation Gunn seems, reasonably enough, to be

E

arguing that since man is an organic creature, his full development, spiritual and physical, will be realised in harmony with an organic and natural background. The ending of the novel stresses that Kenn sees his strath in the setting of Northern Scotland and thence set on ' a ball turning slowly in the immense chasm of space '. The anthropological attitudes are part of a science, albeit one which values intuition and instinct highly.

But occasionally beyond this it seems that Gunn implies more—that the animism which moves in trees and hills and makes Kenn aware of a *presence* is not merely attributable to projection on Kenn's part. This way, Gunn seems to hint, lies God—no Christian God, indeed a God of no creed whatever, but the source, the conscious source, of the river of delight. We never see him (unless in a Gunn fantasy). Kenn's final vision at the source is, one notices, undivulged— we are told he is in a state which is ripe for vision, for time- less harmony—and we next join him an hour later.

Perhaps this is as it should be—that we should be taken, enthralled, to the final mystery, and left wondering. And certainly, if Gunn has not shown us the real source of delight, but merely peeled several layers of the onion, he has achieved some wonderful things. His river of delight does banish time, since for ourselves as well as Kenn, the memory of fish, of bird, of boy in pool, is immediate and lasting. If meaning is to be found at all, we agree that it will be found in the pools of Kenn's Highland river.

Folk Epic : The Silver Darlings

ALEXANDER SCOTT

The roots of *The Silver Darlings* go deep into the history of the Highlands, and equally deep into the author's own personal history, into his childhood and boyhood in just such another Highland fishing village as those which provide the scene and background for many of his finest novels. Like those of his heroes who are presented most intimately, Gunn was born into a family of fisher-folk, as he tells us in ' The Sea ', Chapter 13 of his highly individual and indeed idiosyncratic collection of autobiographical and speculative essays, *The Atom of Delight* (1956), where he writes of himself in the third person, as ' the boy ', expressing his own youth in the same terms as those used for his fictional characters.

> As his existence had two parents, so it had the earth and the sea. In fact he could hardly think of his father without thinking of the sea. Out of the sea came the livelihood of the household. They depended on the sea, and of all the elements it was the least dependable. When a storm blew up . . . at sea you had to fight it out, with only an inch of planking between you and what lay beneath. . . . Snatches of such fights the boy heard now and then when on a winter's night a half-circle of men hemmed in the kitchen fire . . . telling stories.

In a profound sense, it is those same stories that Gunn is retelling in much of his fiction, including *The Silver Darlings*. Since his own father, the skipper of a boat, was closely concerned in many of those tales, either as a daring hero or as a lucky escaper from disaster at sea, their fascination for Gunn was intimate, deep and abiding. It is not without significance that his first widely acclaimed critical success was with *Morning Tide* (1931), a novel whose relationship to the sea is declared by its very title and whose origin in the author's early experience is indicated by Professor George Gordon's description, ' a fine piece of work, this picture of a Scotch fisher family, choicely designed and close to the gravity of Nature '.[1] A novelist of a generation older than Gunn's, John Buchan, found *Morning Tide* ' remarkable '[2]—an adjective remarkable enough in itself, when applied as here to the presentation of the way of life of a family of fisher-folk in a remote village in Caithness, for Scottish fiction has been hag-ridden by stories of provincial life, by sketches of the *mores* of small local communities, from Galt to the Kailyarders and beyond. The clue to the quality of remarkableness in Gunn's novels of provincial life lies in Professor Gordon's praise of his control of form and his attitude to existence—' choicely designed and close to the gravity of Nature '. Unlike so much provincial Scottish fiction, Gunn's best novels are functional both in design and in emotional variation.

Morning Tide is the first, and *The Silver Darlings* is not the last, of a series of Gunn novels presenting a kind of initiation ceremony, by means of which an adolescent hero is shaken awake out of the dream of childhood into a realisation of the complex responsibilities of adult life. (Other works of this kind include *Highland River*, *Young Art and Old Hector* and *The Drinking Well*.) In all of these novels the principal protagonist is at once individual and archetypal, at once a particular boy called ' Hugh ' or ' Finn ' or ' Kenn ' or ' Art ' or ' Iain ' and a representative of all boys. For while Gunn writes prose fiction, his attitude to life has much in common with that of such poets as Edwin Muir and George Mackay Brown—as Kurt Wittig remarks, ' He is not interested in chance happenings; he is looking for the pattern of life, the underlying ritual, the myth.' [3] The incidents in *The Silver Darlings*, and the other successful Gunn novels of this type, are presented in order to illustrate and exemplify universal truths of experience rather than to provide examples of unusual adventure; and the leading characters, while they have their own personalities, are drawn not as oddities or eccentrics but as the living embodi- ments of essential human qualities.

Sometimes this mythical, archetypal, symbolical quality of Gunn's characters is expressed quite explicitly, as in a striking sentence from *Butcher's Broom* (1934) which he singled out, with a brief introduction, as a passage in his volume of selected prose, *Storm and Precipice* (1942) [4]—' In the centre of this gloom was the fire, and sitting round it, their knees drawn together, were the old woman, like fate, the young woman, like love, and the small boy with the swallow of life in his hand.' This is the boy who is at the centre of all the ' initiation-ceremony ' novels, every one of which might be given the title of Conrad's study of growth from adolescence into manhood, *Youth*. All of them are fables expressing the sense of the opening sentence of *Morning Tide*, ' The boy's eyes opened in wonder ', and if (as I believe) *The Silver Darlings* is a greater work than any of the others, it is because of the successful combination of this fable of personal development with the story of the historical experience of a whole community in a particular place and period.

For while Gunn's characters in these novels are to some extent archetypes, representatives of world-wide humanity, the setting in which they live, move and have their being and their breakfast—on those occasions when there is any breakfast to be had—is far from universal, being localised in a scene which is quite narrowly circumscribed, the action seldom straying far from the coast and the sea and the islands between the Dornoch Firth in the extreme north-east of Scotland to the Outer Hebrides in the far west. (*The Drinking Well*, with its Edinburgh chapters, is an exception here.)   Yet his work has avoided the reproach of 'parish-pump parochialism' so frequently levelled at writers of the Kailyard school.   For this there would appear to be a number of reasons, all operating together.   The scene is painted so evocatively, it is so evidently *present* to the senses, that the reader scarcely recollects that it is in fact somewhere far far away on the other side of the Great Glen.   The behaviour of the characters is so normal, in the sense of always being in contact with the central concerns of men and women everywhere, that it is impossible to regard them as picturesque provincials, as queer fish in a local backwater.   The picture of the small communities is so rounded, the author shows us so much of all the vital aspects of their way of life, at work as well as at play, their religion, their art, their domestic customs, their general social activities, that the impression made upon the reader is one of wholeness rather than of the fractional or the fragmentary.   And the local scene is not hermetically sealed off from the rest of the world, but is inevitably influenced by external as well as internal pressures. This is particularly the case in *The Silver Darlings*, where external pressures are on occasion so overwhelming as to come dangerously close to destroying not only the personal relationships of the characters but also the social organisation of the community as a whole.

Indeed, the novel begins from destruction, after the Highland Clearances (themselves the subject of another Gunn novel, *Butcher's Broom*), when the landlords drove the clansmen from the fertile inland glens to the barren coasts in order that the crofting lands might be given over to the more profitable grazing of sheep—a catastrophic uprooting of a whole people from a centuries-old tradition. In some respects, and for some of the people, the disaster is total, as Gunn reveals in 'The Derelict Boat', the opening chapter—'The landlord had . . . set them here against the sea-shore to live if they could and, if not, to die. . . . Many had died.' Here the horror of the situation is increased by the careful understatement of the style, and the appalling callousness behind the landlord's action is rendered all the more reprehensible by the nonchalance of the phrase, 'to live if they could and, if not, to die'—as though the choice were the people's and not the proprietor's.

'Many had died' because their new environment, utterly unfamiliar, seemed also to be utterly hostile, with 'little or nothing to live on but shell-fish and sea-weed. Often they ate the wrong thing and colic and dysentery were everywhere'. But if the products of the sea were dangerous when not properly understood, the sea itself was the greater enemy, murderously implacable, destroying even the best of the people, as when the young heroine Catrine's uncle, 'one of the most heartening men in their little colony . . . with the gaiety in him', a 'nimble' and 'daring' scavenger of the beach, was snatched by the water and drowned in one unwary moment—'following the suction of the receding wave, he slipped . . . and the next wave had him and sucked him over a shallow ledge '.

Yet the people, friendless, have been compelled to make a friend of their enemy the sea. Forced to turn their backs on the land that once nurtured them, they have had no option but to become fishermen, involved in ' the beginning of the herring fisheries ' after the Napoleonic Wars, a new craft through which ' the people would yet live, the people themselves, for no landlord owned the sea '. *The Silver Darlings*, then, is to be concerned with ordinary folk, with the lives of working men and women who wrest from the sea not only prosperity of a modest kind, but also freedom; and in the creation of a little wealth and a wider liberty they will also create their own legend—' it was the beginning of a busy, fabulous time among the common people of that weathered northern land '. Occurring as early as Chapter I, that adjective ' fabulous ' indicates the quality of myth which is to underlie the whole narrative.

The opening chapter also stresses the love-hate relationship between the people and the sea, between the men and women of the shore and the sea which is at once their preserver and their destroyer, and this is another thread which is to run through the book from the first page to the last. The nineteen-year-old heroine, Catrine, pregnant with her first child, feared and hated the sea because the fishing took away her young husband, Tormad, an apprentice to the new craft, and she struggled fiercely to prevent him going out in the boat which he had bought by ' selling his second beast ' from the croft; but this new way of living, and of making a living, had ' so stirred the imagination of the people that it seemed to them uncanny '—that last word indicating that the fascination of the sea was dangerous as well as delicious. Tormad, unable to resist its lure, rowed out to the fishing grounds.

In the event, Catrine's premonition of disaster was all too disastrously justified, for Tormad and his crew, a set of novices—once again Gunn emphasises the novelty of the fishing as a way of life—were seized by the press-gang of a warship while alone and far out at sea, and in the struggle Tormad received a fatal blow. It is to be many long years before Catrine receives confirmation of his death, from the only member of the crew to return alive from naval service; yet, without any ' factual ' evidence, she has been convinced of that death from the moment of its occurrence, and Gunn's success in persuading the reader of the truth of her conviction is the result of a very high degree of stylistic skill, imaginative insight, and emotional verisimilitude.

Like that earlier twentieth-century Scottish novelist who was born and bred north of the Highland Line, J. MacDougall Hay, author of *Gillespie* (1914), Gunn is able to employ in his work elements of Celtic superstition, the background of half-believed magic which had survived from the remote past in relatively isolated and primitive communities, the acceptance of certain old women as witches, the fear of old prophecies of disaster, the belief in the premonitory qualities of dreams. Just such a dream of Catrine's—in which a black horse carried Tormad into a deep pool and vanished with him beneath the surface— was responsible for her apparently irrational efforts to prevent her husband from going to sea; and another, five days after his capture, when ' he appeared before her . . . but stood there mute, asking her forgiveness ', made her utterly certain of his death in her own mind. The reader, if he cares, can interpret both of those dreams as hysterical by-products of Catrine's pregnancy; but they are presented with such vividness, and yet with such restraint, as to create the maximum inducement towards a willing suspension of disbelief. And where, after the researches of Jung, should disbelief end and belief begin with regard to this question? However the reader interprets those dreams of Catrine's, as self-induced fantasies or as flashes of some kind of supernatural revelation beyond our rational understanding, there is never the least doubt of their influence over the heroine herself, and never the least hesitation over acceptance of that influence as emotionally overwhelming.

From Tormad's death flowed another new beginning, when Catrine—emotionally unprepared to face the prospect of living on alone in the house in Helmsdale which she had shared for so short a time as a newly married wife—determined to go north to the village of Dunster and stay with her mother's old friend Kirsty Mackay. In Chapter III, 'Catrine Goes into a Strange Country', this journey towards a new life for the heroine is most splendidly described, almost as if it were an epic march in Xenophon, and her arrival, when she met the youngest skipper in the place, Roddie Sinclair, leads on, in Chapter IV, 'The First Hunt for the Silver Darlings', to the description of yet another new beginning, the story of how the herring-fishing had begun in Dunster, and the related tale of the emergence of Roddie as the most daring and skilful of all the fishermen there.

Chapter V presents still another new departure, the first appearance—as a hunter of butterflies—of Catrine's son, Finn, then five years old. From an expedition which introduced him to both death and terror, and which led him far astray, the young hunter was brought home by

Roddie Sinclair, and through this encounter Gunn establishes the link between the boy who is to be the central character of the rest of the book, the boy whose initiation into the ways of society and the ways of the sea is to provide the principal development of the action, and the man who is to be the hero, his mentor, his exemplar, his rival—for the love of Catrine, mother of one and sweetheart of the other—and eventually his friend and fellow-skipper.

For the next eight chapters, VI to XIII, which span a decade of Finn's young life, the action is land-bound, although the sea is always on the horizon, and frequently much closer—as is evident from such chapter-headings as ' The Land and the Sea ' and ' The Seashore '. Those chapters demonstrate the growing fascination which the maritime way of life exercised over the boy, and the ever-deepening struggle on this account between himself and his mother, who hated the sea for the death it had brought to her husband and feared that her son too might perish by it. In particular, Chapter IX, ' The Seashore ', exemplifies this developing situation. Finn had deceived Kirsty Mackay and dodged his mother in order to go fishing from the rocks in the bay, where he became so intent on trying to catch a monster eel—far too big for his equipment to tackle successfully—that he found that the tide had risen and surrounded the rocks. Although he showed his coolness in a tight fix, and the self-reliance which the necessities of a fishing community had made a prime virtue, by the way in which he extricated himself from that tricky situation, Finn nevertheless fell foul of his mother's terrified anger when he succeeded in reaching shore safely.

Eventually, words of warning from Kirsty Mackay, speaking on her death-bed, brought Catrine to realise that if she persisted in opposing the boy's desire to go to sea she might warp his nature, and she acquiesced in his ambition to become one of Roddie's crew. Chapter XIV begins—another new beginning—the story of Finn's apprenticeship to the fishing; and, more particularly, it starts a sequence of five chapters which constitute the most sustained passage of narrative adventure in the whole novel—or in any of Gunn's novels—with the tale of ' the first time a Dunster boat was to venture beyond the Moray Firth . . . bound for Stornoway '.

In the course of the events contained in those chapters, the still adolescent Finn began to learn how to come to terms with the world of men—and also, to some extent, with the world of women, for he was also initiated, if to a lesser degree, into some of the relationships between the sexes as well as into a realisation of the attitudes and customs and responsibilities of those who go down to the sea in fishing-boats. Danger, endurance, courage, achievement and failure, the comedy of verbal sparring-matches between the members of the crew (each nicely differentiated) and the strength of their co-operative endeavour, the savage flare-up of wild individualism, the power of song and story, the passion (and the denial of passion) created by the fervour of evangelical revivalism—these chapters have them all, and the sea surges through every page in always-changing waves, at times delectable, at others deadly. For the present writer, Chapter XV, ' Storm and Precipice ', represents the peak of Gunn's achievement in narrative prose, and it would seem that the novelist himself once held this opinion too, since he gave the same title to the volume of excerpts from his writings published in 1942, the year after *The Silver Darlings* first appeared in print. This tale

of Finn's climb of an almost unscalable cliff-face in search
of water for the crew, parched after days and nights of
fighting for survival in the wild Atlantic, is superb not
only in the incisive evocation of the cool daring of the feat
but also in the subtle penetration of the interplay of character
among everyone involved and the sensuous force of the
physical presence of wind and water, the vertical towering
of rock and the wheeling width of empty air.

From that saga of high adventure in the Western Isles,
Finn returned to face a more complex situation than any
that could be created by external circumstances, a psychological problem—which only he could resolve—raised by
the all-too-belated factual evidence of his father's death,
brought to his mother by an eye-witness of the event.
Although the way was now open for marriage between
Catrine and Roddie, Finn found himself unable to accept
that relationship, a refusal to face reality which is succinctly
defined in the title of Chapter XXII, 'Finn Denies His
Mother'.

Necessary recognition of the inevitably weaving
patterns of destiny was achieved by Finn only as a result of
a second voyage to the Outer Hebrides, when a storm
compelled the crew to seek refuge ashore with a remote
community on the island of North Uist. The influence
upon Finn of that community, which in its isolation had
preserved unspoiled the ancient arts of oral story-telling and
song, was both profound and permanent, 'never to be
forgotten', and it was a charm exercised, significantly,
upon his imagination rather than his rationalising intelligence—'Finn was now deeply interested in the customs
and ways of the people, for the more he knew of them the
more he seemed to discover what had long lain hidden in

himself; and that not seriously, but with a humour prompting his eyes to glisten or his mouth to laugh.' As he listened to the singing of a lullaby, all his bitterness against his mother dissolved, and he in turn was able to sing a moving song of acceptance in love, ' As the rose grows merry in time ', the refrain from which this Chapter XXIV derives its title.

That voyage over, Finn returned to Dunster with gifts for his new half-brother, and returned also to the courting of his own sweetheart, Una, the building of his own boat, and marriage. The last sentence of the novel is, ' Life had come for him.' The long initiation ceremony is over, and the responsibilities of manhood have begun. ' Growing pains! A man had to live long enough to learn many a thing! '

What Finn has learned, as a result of his apprenticeship, is mastery of a craft, and emotional self-control. Throughout most of the novel, he has been at the mercy of his emotions, even in those incidents and episodes which show him to possess innate qualities which are themselves highly admirable. In Chapters X and XII, on ' The Coming of the Plague ' of cholera to Dunster, when Kirsty Mackay fell victim to it and Catrine, nursing her, was inevitably exposed to the deadly infection, Finn was alone among the children of the community in having the intelligence and initiative to act on the information that a new doctor who specialised in the treatment of the disease had arrived in the nearest town, to travel the many miles there and back on foot across the moors, and to procure the medicines necessary to avert the otherwise unavoidable end. Yet an irrational fear of meeting strangers on the road—' when at last he came, while it was yet early, within sight of what might be the haunted bridge, and saw furtive human heads bobbing out of sight'—sent him the long way round, at a time when every minute was precious; and on his return to Dunster, in ' Ordeal by Plague ' (Chapter XIII), Roddie had to use force as well as persuasion to obstruct Finn's unreasoning impulse to join his mother in the house where she had gone into quarantine—' Roddie bore him away in his arms, writhing and fighting. " Listen, Finn. If you went in, what would your mother say? Damn it, boy, listen to me. Have sense. Do you want to go in and break her heart? " '

Even in the ' Storm and Precipice ' incident, where Finn's courage, resource and skill combined in heroic action, he expressed uncontrollable adolescent rebellion in his resentment against Roddie's exercise of a skipper's authority; and in his self-glorying delight over his own achievement in climbing the apparently unclimbable cliff he forgot about the dire straits of his companions, desperate for water in the boat below, and amused himself by playing tricks on the animals grazing on top of the island—' The next time they saw him appear he was astride a sheep, holding it by the horns. It was a joke on Finn's part, for he knew they could do nothing with a sheep.' When the crew were much less than amused by his behaviour— " You were hours. We thought you were gone "—he reacted with ' anger like a red worm of hate ' and ' bitter self-pity '.

Nevertheless, through all the experiences shared with the rest of the crew on that memorable first voyage, Finn began to learn mastery over the thrust of his adolescent emotions, a process completed by the greater self-discovery resulting from his stay on North Uist. Nor is Finn the only character in the novel to achieve self-control. Catrine also, through force of circumstances, has been compelled to conquer her fear of the sea and to come to terms with her resistance to Roddie, whom she had held at arm's length for so long during the years when she was neither wife nor widow that she found herself in terror at the implications of being her own woman at last, free to give herself to him. Again, with Finn's sweetheart, Una, the power of her maturing love for him enabled her to defy her superstitious panic over his sudden appearance in circumstances which generations of folk-lore had represented as being supernatural. In all three, self-knowledge has been accompanied by self-mastery.

But if *The Silver Darlings* is immensely impressive as a psychological study of individual development, it is at least equally so as a study of communal relationships, as a picture of men and women of all kinds of character engaged in the endeavour to establish a new way of life. A whole folk-group are involved in the action, not only the fishermen but everyone in the district, from the inn-keeper (called ' Special ' after his best whisky) who first finances the boats to the coopers who build the barrels for the fish and the women and the girls who work on the shore to gut them. They are all involved in one another, too, in communal celebrations like the annual fair as well as in the general rallying-round for rescue attempts when a sudden unexpected storm threatens to drive the boats on the rocks.

This novel provides a view of a particular people during a specific historical period, the twenty years after the fall of Napoleon opened the markets of Europe to the fishing fleets fostered by the Government of these islands, and it has a definite ' documentary ' interest as a picture of the growth of a great industry. But, beyond and above this, it also succeeds as epic. The characters are drawn as archetypes as well as individuals, and the whole narrative has the amplitude and the altitude of myth, a universal significance.

The characters appear as archetypes because they see one another as such, because each is aware, at particularly revealing moments in the action, of qualities in the others which have value always and everywhere, qualities not limited to any one time and place. In Chapter V, ' Finn and the Butterfly ', Roddie glances through the window of Kirsty Mackay's house and sees Catrine, ' her features against the red glow, warm and soft, not only with her own beauty, but with all women's beauty. It was a picture a man might glimpse once in a lifetime, and have a picture of woman in his mind that time or chance, good or evil, would never change'. Again, in Chapter XVII, ' Drink and Religion ', Finn watches Roddie go berserk in a Stornoway pub and sees him as ' beyond the littleness of men to-day, looming like the far solitary figure of another place and time. Not evil, not good; imminent and terrible'. Or again, in the greatest episode of all, Chapter XV, ' Storm and Precipice ', the rest of the crew look up from the boat and see Finn on the summit of the rock, ' laughing, like an immortal youth '.

It is highly significant that the hero of *The Silver Darlings* has been given the same forename as Finn MacCoul, the great legendary hero of Celtic mythology. Gunn expects the reader to see his fictitious Finn as a kind of nineteenth-century equivalent, or even reincarnation, of the legendary Finn, a point which is made three times, explicitly and quite unmistakably. In Chapter XX,

' Finn Goes to Helmsdale ', where the young hero tells the story of the first Stornoway voyage to a gathering at a *ceilidh*, one listener praises him in the loaded sentence, " You gave me a vision—of the youth of Finn MacCoul himself." This sentiment is echoed in Chapter XXII, ' Finn Denies His Mother ', when the same listener, after hearing another episode in the Stornoway saga, asks, " Are the days of Finn MacCoul coming back upon us? "—a question to which the author expects the reader to respond with at least a qualified affirmation. Most pointedly of all, in the North Uist chapter, ' As the Rose Grows Merry in Time ', the following passage makes the identification as complete as it could be without being spelled out in so many words.

> Much knowledge Finn received from this old man, who was one of the three story-tellers of the district. He could have listened to him for hours on end, because as he listened something in himself that had hitherto been dry, like dry soil, was moistened as by summer rain, and became charged with an understanding of life and with an upper movement of wonder like fragrant air. There was perhaps some special concentration of the self in it, too, for the old man's first name was the same as Finn's, which was likewise Finn MacCoul's, the great hero of the noble Fians, whose marvellous exploits were this story-teller's province in learning and art.

The epic quality of the novel's narrative action scarcely requires to be remarked upon. The characters, as well as being themselves, are also representatives of a whole people, and many of their experiences are the fundamental experiences of all mankind—child-birth, development from childhood through adolescence to maturity, apprenticeship to a craft, the growth of love, the experience of death.

Death from old age, death from disease, death as the result of natural catastrophe, from the treacherous violence of the sea—it is out of the ceaseless battle against the many forms of death that the community wrests its hard-won triumph, the creation of a new way of living.

Not only men and women are involved in the story, but also (as in all great epic) the gods—or if the forces evoked are not exactly the gods, whose forms and faces are lost in the hard dazzle of our age of reason (!), they are still spiritual and supernatural. Gunn's talent is at its most tactful in the way that he uses the age-old superstitions in which the minds of early nineteenth-century Highlanders were saturated in order to suggest a world behind this world and to imply an immortal immunity to change interpenetrating the continuous changes of history. The scene which is principally associated with those forces—however their nature may be interpreted—is the ruins of an ancient monastery, called the House of Peace, which Catrine first sees and hears named on her earliest arrival in Dunster, when ' the name had been like a benediction sounded softly in her mind ' (Chapter III). The House of Peace plays the same part in *The Silver Darlings*, the paradoxical part of being at one and the same time a refuge to the individual from communal activities and a reminder of the age-long history which lies behind the community, as the ruined broch in Gunn's earlier novel, *Morning Tide* (1931), or the Standing Stones in Lewis Grassic Gibbon's *Sunset Song* (1932)—a conception which Gibbon may well have derived from Gunn. It is among those ruins that Finn, having heard the story of a monk who was slaughtered by a viking in the House of Peace (Chapter IX), sees a vision of that same monk as he lies day-dreaming (Chapter X). But

Finn also experiences the feeling that ' he was not alone' in a ruined chapel on the rocky island of Chapter XV, ' Storm and Precipice', and such hints of supernatural associations are none the less powerful for being most delicately understressed.

The Silver Darlings has been described as ' the longest . . . and the richest '[5] of Gunn's novels. In the present writer's view, it is also the greatest, a folk epic on the major theme of human indomitability, a triumph-song of the Gael.

NOTES ON REFERENCES

1   Quoted on the dust-jacket of the eighth impression (1944).
2   Ibid.
3   *The Scottish Tradition in Literature* (Oliver & Boyd, Edinburgh and London, 1958), pp. 335-6.
4   This title is also that of Chapter XV of *The Silver Darlings* (1941).
5   *The Times Literary Supplement*, quoted on the dust-jacket of the fifth impression (1945).

True Imagination : The Silver Darlings

DONALD CAMPBELL

Truth is the strangest and most elusive of virtues. A fact may be a fact—and a hard one at that—but the degree of truth it generates is nevertheless governed by the manner in which it is regarded. This, I think, is what Edwin Muir meant when he wrote (in his *Autobiography*) that ' It is as easy for the false imagination to hate a whole class as it is difficult for the true imagination to hate a single human being '. In the consideration of much of Scottish social history (by which I mean those events in our past that have most affected the present) the false imagination has been employed to an astonishing if all too understandable degree.

One area of which this is certainly true is that period known as the Highland Clearances. From roughly the end of the eighteenth century to the middle of the nine-teenth, crofters all over the Highlands were evicted from the land they had cultivated and defended for centuries in order to make room for the more profitable sheep walks. The first (and most infamous) of these evictions took place in the county of Sutherland, where the Duchess of Suther-land's factor Patrick Sellar carried out the evictions (or ' improvements ' as they were called at the time) with such barbarism that the name of Patrick Sellar can hardly be mentioned in Gaelic company even today without the blood rising. In an interview in May 1970, the Gaelic poet Sorley Maclean tells of how, at the mere mention of

Disraeli, one of his uncles cried, " The bloody Tories, who did the Clearances! " And in the same interview, Maclean himself says that " Franco and his landowners and the big capitalists and the Catholic Church looked to me awful like the landlords of the Clearances and the Church of Scotland at that time ".

The trouble with such responses (understandable though they are) is that they dodge the issue. If we accept the story that the victims of the Clearances were a happy, peace-loving people living in an idyllic, prosperous *Ghaidealteachd* where the storehouses were always full and the cattle were fat, we can draw only one conclusion about the landlords. They were nothing more nor less than racialists (I have often heard the word ' genocide ' used in connection with the Clearances), and all the problems of the Highlands—the depopulation, the death of the Gaelic way of life, the dying position of the Gaelic language itself—can be laid at their door. There are no more questions to be asked—the blame has been apportioned and the hating can begin. This is the false imagination at work.

Unfortunately, life is not that easy. The plain truth is that, to begin with, the Highlanders were not in such a happy state. Contented with their struggle they may have been (most poor people are), but they were barely scraping a living from the land, and happiness is impossible when you are continually wondering where the rent is going to come from. Secondly, the Clearances were barbaric only in their execution. The ruling motive of the landlords was at all times genuine improvement, and where the sheep walks were introduced with some sort of humanity (in Caithness, for instance—although such instances were admittedly rare), the results proved beneficial to both landlord and tenant alike. (It is of course true that people like the Duchess of Sutherland and her husband regarded the tenants as inferior beings, but men must be judged within the context of their times, and any contrary belief would have been held to be revolutionary in the extreme. Certainly, to draw comparisons with twentieth-century Fascism seems grossly unfair.) Lastly, it must be borne in mind that, heavy though the emigration was, it was not total. Some of the people remained.

Taking all of this into account, we find that, far from having received all the answers, we are left with a further number of questions. If the Clearances were instituted as an attempt to bring economic health to a depressed area, to what extent were they successful? And what did the people get out of it—not just in material terms, but in social and cultural and moral terms too? I believe that these questions were very much in the mind of Neil Gunn when he wrote his most successful and most vitally readable book, *The Silver Darlings.*

This novel is not concerned directly with the Clearances, but the characters are people who have suffered from them. They have come through a terrible time and are beginning to make a fresh start in a new life. As Gunn says in the first chapter:

> That first winter had been a terror. For one long spell, they had had little or nothing to live on but shellfish and seaweed. Often they ate the wrong thing and colic and dysentery were everywhere. . . .
> Yet it was out of that very sea that hope was now coming to them. . . . The people would yet live, the people themselves, for no landlord owned the sea, and what the people caught there would be their own. . . .

No landlord owned the sea. Over and over again throughout the novel, Gunn impresses this on us. The people may have been victims of a barbarous eviction but they are victims no longer. They may (and do) suffer again—but not at the hands of any landlord. When the herring boom came to the north-east coast, it had the effect of a minor revolution in that it gave the fishermen both the means of production *and* the product itself. As mere crofters, they had not been much more than agricultural labourers. As herring-fishers, they not only caught the fish, they owned (or held part-shares in) their boats and took the proceeds from the sale of their catch. Thus they had more than financial security, they had independence and could take pride in their way of life.

This, however, was not achieved without many problems and much hardship. They had to learn to live with the sea, to learn new skills. To begin with, at least, they continued to live in crofts (poor land, near the coast) and they had to develop a new relationship with the land. Then again, the influx of a great deal of money on a community that is used to poverty must inevitably bring social evils in its wake. There had to be a transitional period, and it is with this period that Gunn is dealing in *The Silver Darlings*.

The novel is essentially an allegory, the main characters being representative of the community and the social tensions that were set up during this period. The central character, Finn, is a hero-figure (as his name suggests) and the story of his growing-up is the story of the development of the herring industry. The land is represented by Catrine, Finn's mother, and the sea by Roddie Sinclair, the giant Caithness skipper whom she eventually marries. Lastly, there is Tormad, Finn's father who, although he appears only in the first chapter, haunts almost the entire narrative and is not only representative of the lost manhood of the community but (since, as we shall see, Finn and Tormad are really one and the same) is symbolic of the immortal spirit of the people and, by definition, humanity itself.

The story begins with Tormad and his friends putting to sea in their first attempt to catch fish. After some clumsy attempts with the line, they try the net and are lucky enough to get into herring. Their luck stops there, however, and they are taken by a press-gang. Tormad, it seems, is swept out of the novel as suddenly as if a heavy sea had taken him overboard. (Neil Gunn once remarked of Lewis Grassic Gibbon's work that ' you could smell the earth '. It may be as well to mention in passing that the sea, if not evidenced by smell, is ever-present in Gunn's narrative, and there are a number of such moments in the course of the book.) Catrine, deprived of her husband and heavy with his child, is faced with the prospect of either remaining on their meagre croft or returning to her family. Then, five nights after Tormad's capture, she dreams of him and knows for certain that he is dead. She decides to go to Caithness and it is there that Finn is born.

This remove to Caithness is logical when we consider that the effects of the Clearances were a great deal less severe in that county. Its significance is heightened by the fact that she enters the new land with the fear of a *shepherd* in her heart. This man, a Scots-speaking Lowlander whom she meets on the road, is friendly enough but he terrifies Catrine. It is as if, in entering Caithness, she is leaving sheep and the inevitable eviction behind her. Something else, too, is hinted at later on in the novel when Finn accompanies his young cousin Barbara back to her home in Helmsdale:

At the Grey Hen's Well, Barbara drank twice.
" Once for Aunt Catrine and once for myself," she
murmured, wiping the water from her nose.
   " Why that? " he asked, astonished.
   " This is where your mother rested," she said,
" long, long ago, when for the first time she crossed the
Ord and entered into a strange land."
   He smiled at her legendary tone, but he saw, too,
that there was something behind it and, whatever it
was, all in a moment it touched his heart. So he got
down and drank—hesitated—and drank for a second
time.

One of the first people Catrine meets on her arrival is
Roddie Sinclair, at this time nineteen years of age and
already becoming a legend on the coast. Roddie is representative not just of the sea but of the knowledge of the sea.
There is never any suggestion that Roddie has ever been
anything else but a fisherman and he is completely dedicated
to what he would regard as his calling. In the earlier part
of the book it is as if the life of the community depends on
Roddie's skill. One old greybeard even goes as far as to
suggest that Roddie had " come himself up out of the sea
like—like one sent to deliver us ". Special Hendry, the
curer, regards Roddie as a talisman, and Roddie himself
makes the strange and sober declaration (in the midst of a
wedding celebration) that he is " married to the sea ".
   Roddie and Catrine are attracted to each other almost
instantly—yet they hold back and make no real contact for
years. Roddie's dedication to the sea and his regard for
Catrine's good name (he does not know, of course, that
Tormad is dead) prevent his approaching her, while
Catrine, for her part, is afraid of him—afraid of what she is
unable to understand.

He stood quite still. She could hardly see him, but in his stillness there could always be something strong and ominous. Had it been Ronnie she would have known exactly what he felt. She was never sure of Roddie.

" Good night," he said in the same clear voice, and walked away.

" Good night," she called and, going inside, quickly found her hands fumbling with the bar, and her heart beating as if something tremendous had happened from which she had narrowly escaped.

There is a parallel with Catrine's fear of Roddie in the initial fear that the men had for the sea. Going back to the first chapter, we find that

> Their hearts went across them. The beat rose on the heave of the sea. Now that they were clear of the land, a gentle wind darkened the surface of the waters. A small ripple suddenly slapped the clinched planking like a hand slapping a face. The sound startled them.

When I first read *The Silver Darlings* I felt rather disappointed with what I considered to be a lack of development not only in the relationship between Catrine and Roddie but in the character studies of some of the minor figures (Special Hendry, for instance, that quintessential Caithnesian. I still wish that there was more of him in the book). Of course, at that time I was reading the book as a mere adventure story (as so many people unfortunately do), and it took a closer reading for me to realise that, far from being understated, these characters and situations are set in exactly the correct perspective. The love affair of Catrine and Roddie, the career of Special Hendry, the hopes and fears of the fishermen—all of these are important only in so far as they affect and influence the character of Finn. Finn symbolises the community, and the influences which shape his character as he grows to manhood are the influences which bring the community back to prosperity—so that, in considering the characters of Catrine and Roddie (and the impasse that lies between them), we must of necessity consider them in their relationship to Finn.

The first thing that must be said about Finn is that he is more of a hero in the legendary or mythical sense than in the popular one. I have mentioned earlier that Finn and Tormad are one and the same and there is ample evidence of this in the narrative—in fact, at one point Finn even admits it to himself:

> He got up and as they walked back to the house a deep feeling came over him of being himself and his own father, responsible for this woman walking by his side, who was his mother; deeper even it was than the resentment against the odds which had murdered his father, and within it, too, sustaining it, was a strange new element, quiet as this dim half-light, of peace that was like happiness.

This peace that Finn feels within himself, this ' strange new element ', is perhaps more important than the feeling of being ' himself and his own father '. The awareness that he is both Finn and Tormad constitutes a recognition of the continuity of life—but the peace and happiness that lie within this feeling are an intimation of the changing nature of life and a coming-to-terms with the hard fact of the situation. When the herring fishing began, the men who put to sea were basically crofters. It must have taken many years before they were to think of themselves as being primarily fishermen and during this time there would be much nostalgia for the old way of life. It would have taken more than the mere acquisition of skills to turn them from landsmen to seamen. They would have to realise first of all that the past was dead and buried and, having made that admission, make the further admission that no matter how things had changed they were still men and could take as much pride in their new ways as they had in the old. The sharp contrast between the old and the new is emphasised still further in the passage that follows immediately after the one I have just quoted. I have italicised what appears to me to be the important sentence.

> Not even a visit by the ground officer depressed his spirit unduly. " You have a good place here," said that reserved and ominous man. " We're trying to improve it," replied Finn quietly, leaning on his spade. " It's as well," said the man and walked down through the croft, aloof and noting all things. Finn tore into the ground to ease his apprehension.
>
> " I wonder what he's after? " Catrine came and asked Finn when the man had gone. *She still had the feeling that they were strangers here and might be driven out.* " You needn't worry," said Finn. " It's money he's after."

Money! That is no problem to Finn who is a fisherman and can make more in one night at sea than any crofter could hope to gain from a year's work on the land. He might well be apprehensive at the sight of the ground officer (his rent, after all, could well be increased) but he has none of Catrine's fear of eviction.

It is of course true that Finn has never known the Clearance and has no reason to feel a stranger in Caithness where he was born and bred—yet it is important that Finn's attitude is not seen to be that of a generation which

is unafraid of something it has not experienced. If we turn
to that part of the narrative that is set in Lewis, and specifically to Finn's attraction for the Lewis girl Catrine, we find
an incident which underlines the correspondence between
Finn and Tormad (and therefore the eternal). In addition,
there is a reaction which is almost the exact counterpart of
Catrine's (*i.e.* Finn's mother's) acceptance of Tormad's
death.

> The sadness of the song came over him in a mood
> that had something strange and bitter in it. He could
> have held her in his arms and kissed her; that would
> have suddenly swamped her nervousness. But at the
> very sign of the half-scared spirit moving in her, at
> the sound of his own voice calling her by the name
> Catrine, he found that he could not force himself upon
> her, and somehow did not greatly mind. . . .
> My sorrow! My sorrow! said the song.
> What sorrow? Sorrow for death, said the words.
> But, for the first time, Finn saw it went beyond
> death.

Finn is eighteen years old, far from home and the Lewis
girl has the same name as his mother. So it is quite natural
that he should be both attracted and disturbed by her.
Yet there is a suggestion—evidenced by Finn's feeling that
' he somehow did not greatly mind '—of the presence of
much deeper forces. Finn senses a mutual attraction
between the girl and himself, yet recognises that its further
development is impossible—and turns away from it without
regret. Moreover, it is a *shared* experience, affecting Catrine
as well as himself. What they have received is an intimation
of the past—but an intimation of a past that is *theirs*. They
have caught a glimpse of a relationship that exists between

them, a relationship that is timeless and ' goes beyond death .' To what extent Catrine understands this we can never be sure—but what is plain is that she recognises her association with Finn and is afraid of it. Finn understands it fully and, while realising that the past cannot die, knows that it cannot be repeated and that regretfully he must inevitably turn his back on it.

But if Finn has managed to come to terms with the past his position regarding the present is less secure. For Finn there is only one reality, one certainty, one present and one future and that is the element by which he lives—the sea. Finn's relationship with the sea is exactly reflected in his relationship with Roddie. Roddie has been many things to Finn—he has been both father and brother, he has been hero and teacher, he has been friend and enemy. Finn has worshipped him, has loved him, has hated him at times and often enough has challenged him. Yet, although he has never ceased to respect him, he has never been afraid of him.

The real conflict between Finn and Roddie gets under way only when Finn goes to sea. Until that time, Finn's feeling for Roddie is much the same as any boy will have for a father or elder brother—a vague mixture of hero-worship and familiarity. He takes him for granted, yet remains in awe of him. He knows that his future is connected with Roddie as surely as it is with the sea—yet he does not have the slightest intimation of the nature of that future.

Finn's first brush with Roddie coincides exactly with the first real challenge of his life—his ascent of Eilean Mor. Having become lost on their way to Lewis, the crew of the *Seafoam* are hove to in the lee of the Seven Hunters, desperately short of water and unsure of what to do next. Finn volunteers to climb the cliff and Roddie forbids him to attempt it. They clash and Finn taunts Roddie, asking him what he's frightened of. Roddie snaps back at him and even the other men notice the significance of the moment.

> In their exhausted, thirst-tormented, overwrought condition, a bout of irritation or short temper was understandable enough, but the others felt that what had flared so swiftly between Roddie and Finn was deeper than irritation. They were like two with a blood-secret between them. . . .
> Finn said nothing, his face to the rock. It was between Roddie and himself and he was aware that Roddie did not care for cliffs. It was quite possible that he hadn't the head. But, far beyond that, he knew what was troubling him. Roddie would not like to be the bearer of the tidings of Finn's death to Finn's mother! Something deep inside Finn exulted over Roddie, over his bitter predicament, with a sustained feeling of ruthless triumph. Death itself was neither here nor there, because it never entered Finn's head except as an imaginary counter in his triumph of enmity.

This, of course, is the zealous arrogance of youth which is always to come through its first trials well ahead—and always full of exultation when it does so. Finn gets as big a kick from Roddie's discomfiture as he does from scaling the cliff. But he is soon to get a bigger one—and of an altogether different kind!

When they eventually arrive in Lewis (they had in fact missed it all together, having gone out round the Butt) the Caithness men are dogged by ill-luck of one kind and another. Roddie takes it all as a slur on his ability and is seen by the others to be boiling up to an outburst. On the first Saturday night of their stay in Lewis, they are drinking at the Sloop Inn and Big Angus, a local giant who is said to

' rule the world ' on a Saturday night, taunts Roddie for missing the Butt. That is all the excuse Roddie needs and Finn is unwise enough to try to intervene.

> Roddie had broken loose. Swaying on the outer edges of his feet, fists clenched, he let out a challenging roar. But no-one was interfering with him now. " I'll sail you round your bloody Butt! " yelled Roddie. " Come on! "
>
> . . . And at that moment, with the whole company paralysed, it came upon Finn to approach Roddie.
>
> The actuating motive may have been a desire to help Roddie, to get him away in time. Standing before him, he said, " Come on, Roddie. Let's get away now." Roddie's left arm was still outstretched, the back of the open hand towards Finn's face. Through the foot that separated it from that face, Roddie brought it with such an explosive force that the resounding slap almost lifted Finn off his feet.

This is youthful arrogance stepping in where angels fear to tread. If we understand that Finn represents the community and Roddie the sea, these two instances can be seen as growing points in the one's attempt to come to terms with the other. Towards the end of the novel, in one of the most moving episodes of sea life that Neil Gunn has ever written, we see the final consummation of this relationship.

Coming in from the fishing, the Dunster fleet is caught in a storm and one of the boats founders on the rocks at the foot of a tall cliff. Finn volunteers to go down for the crew.

> " I'll go down on the rope," said Finn, " if you hold on."
>
> Roddie's face paled in a drawn concentration.
>
> Finn sat down and began to take off his boots. He

liked to feel the rock with his bare toes. In trousers and jersey, he stood up lightly.

Roddie turned on those pressing about them. " Get back! " His voice cracked like a whiplash, and even old men took a backward step as if the primal force in the man had struck them.

" Are you ready? " asked Finn, and he met Roddie's eyes.

" Will you try it, boy? " asked Roddie, and his voice was gentle.

It was a moment of communion so profound that Finn felt a light-heartedness and exaltation come upon him. This was where Roddie and himself met, in the region of comradeship that lies beyond all the trials of the world.

The Silver Darlings begins with a man, impoverished and humiliated by an inhuman eviction, putting out to sea in an attempt to earn his livelihood from hunting fish. In the final chapter, a man goes to sea on a similar errand—the same man, but he has changed. Compare the two:

They changed places in the boat so warily that she scarcely rocked. Tormad wiped the sweat from his eyes and Ian leaned forward, drawing his shoulders from his sticky vest. Not until that moment did they fully realize that they were by themselves, cut off, on the breast of the ocean.

And:

The great happiness that came upon the crew was kept in control by their eager labour, drawn taut as the back-rope upon which Finn and Tomas hauled, hauled until their necks swelled and the blood congested in their faces.

Now Finn felt like a great hunter, like the leader of hunting men. Assurance of his strength and power was

in him like a song. But when he spoke, he spoke
quietly, as if deep in his throat there was a gentle laugh.

It is the same man—he has conquered his inexperience
and the inbred instincts of centuries of life on the land.
He has defeated hardship and danger and has triumphed
over death itself. He feels himself to be free and independent and is at peace with himself.

I have often heard *The Silver Darlings* described as a
mere adventure yarn, not to be compared with deeper,
more intellectually satisfying later books like *The Well at the
World's End* and *The Key of the Chest*. Quite apart from the
fact that this attitude obviously irritates me, I often wonder
why. I think the answer must lie in the book's uniqueness
when seen in the context of twentieth-century Scottish
fiction. It has none of the macabre mysticism of *Gillespie*,
the morbid satire of *The House with the Green Shutters*, the
sentimental pessimism of *A Scots Quair*, or the haunted
bitterness of *And the Cock Crew*. In saying this, I mean no
disrespect. All of these books (and one or two of them have
suffered as much neglect, in a critical sense, as has *The
Silver Darlings*) are, in their separate ways, fine novels,
among the best that this century has had to offer in the
waste-land that is Scottish novel-writing. Yet they all
have one thing in common—they are all basically negative
in approach, while *The Silver Darlings* (and the whole
corpus of Neil Gunn's fiction) is exactly the opposite.
Where others see misery and point accusing fingers, Gunn
sees hope and applauds the human spirit. *The Silver
Darlings* was written in the 'thirties, a time of high un-
employment and poverty (*industrial* clearances, if you like),
social unrest and even greater tension in the world than that

which confronts us today. Perhaps Neil Gunn, like Sorley Maclean, saw a similarity between the Clearances and the Spanish Civil War. If he did, he was not depressed by it. Instead, he chose to utter a hymn of joy to mankind, in the sure belief, no doubt, that just as the community of the North of Scotland had risen like a phoenix from the flames of the Clearances, so too could humanity endure and survive whatever trials time and circumstance might bring.

The Silver Darlings is the work of a writer of great compassion, a man who not only cares deeply about his fellow human beings but who knows them intimately and who has derived great wisdom from that knowledge. Let me end with one final quotation from the end of the novel, the last paragraph in fact. On the night before his wedding, Finn is hiding from his friends (who wish to put him through ' certain heathenish practices ') on a wooded knoll close to his home. He is thinking of the future and all its possibilities when suddenly he realises that he is about to be discovered.

> . . . Finn's thought suddenly quickened and for an intense moment the knoll took on its immemorial calm. Time became a stilled heart-beat. Stealthy, climbing sounds. Finn's body drew taut, heaved up on to supporting palms. Whisperings, the movement of the top of a small birch-tree here and there whose trunk invisible hands gripped. The hunters in their primordial humour were closing in. Life had come for him.

The Way to Wisdom :
Young Art and Old Hector

GILLIAN SHEPHERD

" There was a time before now," began Old Hector
in the storyteller's voice, " when there lived an old man
who had the Druid's knowledge. In truth he was a
Druid himself, but though he had the knowledge, he
hadn't the great wisdom, which is the wisdom of all the
ages. The only thing in the wide world at that time
which had the great wisdom was a salmon which lived
in a pool in a river. There were some hazel-trees that
grew over this pool, and on the hazel-trees grew nuts,
and these nuts were the Nuts of Knowledge. As the
seasons came and the seasons went, time out of mind,
the nuts would be falling quietly into the pool where
the salmon lay. Well did the Druid know this, and he
knew, moreover, that if only he could catch the salmon
and eat him, then he would have himself the great
wisdom of the salmon. But try as he would, he could
not catch the salmon. Well, on a day of days, who
should come along to the Druid to get lessons from him
but young Finn MacCoul. . . ." (Chapter I)

So begins the first of Old Hector's parables, in which he
shows Art how 'to get wisdom without having a whisker'.
In *Young Art and Old Hector* (1942) Gunn, in his own unique
storyteller's voice, presents his variation on the theme: his
Druid, Old Hector, has both knowledge and the wisdom,
if not of the ages, then certainly of age, and his Finn,
Young Art, will in time reach the River, the Hazel Pool
and the Salmon. It is with Young Art's journey, actual
and spiritual, that Gunn is primarily concerned.

The richness of the relationship between Young Art and Old Hector is first indicated in their designation. The significance of 'Young' and 'Old' will be discussed later; the significance of 'Art' and 'Hector' emerges by analogy and implication, and receives no explicit statement until *The Green Isle of the Great Deep*, the sequel to *Young Art and Old Hector*. In *The Green Isle*, the legend of Art is accorded two possible interpretations:

> The first school said that Art was merely a name used to connote the activities of certain individuals in an earthly existence. These individuals had always been a source of trouble to those who had desired permanence in established thought and institution. . . .

> The second school had quite a different approach to the story. They advanced the theory that Art was an obvious—and even a known—contraction of Arthur. Now Arthur was the original Chief of the Round Table. He was of Celtic Stock. As the Celts had always been pushed back by predatory savage tribes into the bens and glens, into the west coast of every country, it was quite natural that some reflection of the Arthurian legend should appear in the Thirteenth Region. For thirteen was an unlucky number and, true to type, the Celts of the bens and glens had naturally landed on the Thirteenth Region (as Art and Old Hector had done). Further, the conditions of life in the bens and glens and on the adjacent sea-coasts had always been of such an austere nature as not to permit of riotous living.
> Accordingly when the predatory tribes who had driven them into their fastnesses returned at a later date to take from them what little they had in order to give it to flocks of grey sheep, the folk found that there was practically nothing left to live on but their own legends.

They thus continued to die out quickly in a legendary atmosphere. So what was more natural than that such a story as was now under discussion should be ferried across? The one remarkable feature in it was that Arthur or Art should now assume not the appearance of a knight in armour but of a bare-legged boy, for this showed clearly that in the core of the legend there had always existed a youthful hope. In short, the story was no more than the personification of a legendary hope. (Chapter XVII)

The first of these theories has no apparent relevance to *Young Art and Old Hector;* the second is central to it.[1] The Celtic myth of a lost leader who will return in time of his people's need is given, if not substance, a well-defined shadow. Hector, Art's spiritual guardian—who bears the name of the guardian and foster-father of Malory's Arthur [2]—nourishes in Art, by precept and parable, the consciousness of his identity as part of a pattern of existence. Past, present and future are seen in relation to each other; the heroes of legend are archetypal figures which may appear in different form at any time. It is clear that Art has already accepted this concept in terms of himself:

> " Cuchulain was the greatest, easy," declared Art with quiet triumph.
> " That is as may be," replied Old Hector doubtfully. " Perhaps you're only thinking so because Cuchulain was a small dark man, and you yourself are small and dark."
> Even as Art repudiated the suggestion his eyes opened wide. " Was he like that? " he asked.
> " He was," said Old Hector.
> Art looked far away and smiled secretly. " Everyone knows," he declared, " that Cuchulain was a greater fighter than Finn MacCoul."

"Perhaps so. I'm not denying it, though I have my own opinion. A man is entitled to his own opinion."

"You are not," said Art. "He was the greatest! He was!"

"Very well so. All right. All right. He was a great fighter certainly."

"He could have—he could have—" Art paused to look over his shoulder. "He could have cut the head off the Ground Officer easily. Could he?"

Old Hector laughed. "Ha! ha! ha! Ho! ho! ho!" His head waggled. "Yes and twenty Ground Officers. And he wouldn't have cut them off, either. He would have put his finger against his thumb like that and— flick! off they were."

"It's a pity we hadn't him now," said Art.

"Never you mind," said Old Hector. "There's no saying who may grow up to be a Cuchulain some day."

Art's forefinger came of itself against the ball of his thumb and made a little flick so that no-one could see it. (Chapter I) [3]

The resentment of the men of Clachdrum against the Ground Officer and the gaugers, the representatives of 'the predatory tribes' who took the Clash for sheep, manifests itself largely in wary but good-humoured attempts to outwit them; their consciousness of injustice derives in the main from a sense of economic deprivation. Old Hector acknowledges this deprivation, but he is unshakeable in his conviction that 'human dealings are founded—*founded*—not on money but on what is fair and just all round'. His concern is with 'rights' and with the judgement of 'a court higher than the Sheriff's'. Hector is 'the last living of the Clash folk', the present embodiment of past ways and values which will survive him only if they

are transferred to Young Art as the link between present
and future. This process of transmission is in many respects
conscious; Old Hector is aware of his own place in the
pattern of existence and is aware too that the elements of
the pattern are mutually sustaining.

> " You see, I know every corner of this land, every
> little burn and stream, and even the boulders in the
> stream. And I know the moors and every lochan on
> them. And I know the hills, and the passes, and the
> ruins, and I know of things that happened here on our
> land long long ago, and men who are long dead I
> knew, and women. I knew them all. They are part
> of me. And more than that I can never know now. . . .
> ". . . There are many places, many many places,
> with names that no-one knows but myself, and they
> will pass away with me."
> "Will you tell them to me? " asked Art eagerly.
> " I will indeed, and gladly, for I would not like the
> little places to die."
> " Will they die if they lose their names? "
> " Something in them will die. They will be like
> the clan that lost its name. They will be nameless."
> . . . Art took a small dance to himself by Old Hector's
> side. " And when I have all the names of the places
> that no-one else knows, then, when you're gone, I'll
> be the only one who'll have their names, the only one
> in the world? "
> " The only one," agreed Old Hector pleasantly.
> " I'll like that," said Art. " And some day, some
> day in a long time, I'll tell someone too. Won't I? "
> (Chapter VI)

This vision of life as a continuum informs the whole of
Young Art and Old Hector. Gunn represents it most frequently in terms of a circle, the Celtic symbol of completeness and

eternity. The central relationship of the book, that between Young Art and Old Hector, circumscribes every other relationship, and every experience; within it Art finds stability which enables him to trace without restriction and without harm the paths of other concentric or intersecting circles.

The youth of Young Art and the age of Old Hector are seen not as opposite ends of a spectrum but as different points on the circumference of one circle:

> . . . The greatest difference between first and second childhood was not a matter of experience, of knowledge; not a mental difference so much as a difference of sheer time. . . .
> Yet the wonderful thing was the resemblance between the two states. When a young boy was alone with you, talking quietly and asking questions, he rarely grew obstreperous, as he so often did before an audience. And then suddenly, all in a bright moment, you would see the open wonder of his mind. It was there before you, as a bird or a rabbit might be. . . . That early rapt wonder, which had been lost for so many years, opened its own eyes in you once more and beheld the world. But now it was not the same world, not quite, for it had grown selfless and was altogether clear vision. It asked for nothing. This vision of the circle completing itself was all the mind desired, so marvellous it was, and supporting that vision came a feeling of such well-being that panic or time could no more intrude. (Chapter V)

The resemblance between the two states is, indeed, so strong as to overcome the difference of sheer time and permit unspoken communication. Old Hector has the ability not so much to read Art's mind as to share the

images which people it, an ability which is involuntary and
often inexplicable to him, although he recognises its existence. During Young Art's temporary dislocation from the
circle of his family, immediately after Henry James's
enlargement of it, Old Hector experiences this phenomenon
and gains some understanding of it. He is impelled to go
to the Clash to look for the missing boy, ' and this was
curious even to himself, because the farther he went, the
more time he had to think, and the more he thought the
more foolish seemed his vision of Art's body lying curled
up in sleep under the old gooseberry bush that stood in
front of the ruins of his grandfather's house '. It seems
' beyond sense ' to Old Hector until he reaches the Clash,
where the conjunction of time—the quality of youth which
is transmitted from Art—and space—the setting of his own
youth—works on his memory and enables him to go
beyond the confines of time and space.

> Perhaps it was because he had been driven out of
> here with his folk, at about Art's age, that the mind of
> Art in its fears and quick imaginings could touch him
> so naturally now. He remembered—ah, how he
> remembered! He remembered so vividly that it seemed
> to him that his young body flashed by in a half light
> round the walls and corners of a legendary place.
> (Chapter V)

In effect, there has been a fusion of consciousness:
Art's present consciousness of the present, Hector's present
consciousness of the past and Hector's past consciousness
of the past. The fusion results in what may be termed the
' collective conscious ', in contrast to the Jungian concept
of the ' collective unconscious ', which also has a place in
Gunn's world. The collective unconscious is not confined

to old age, nor does it derive only from the unconscious fruits of felt experience. Art draws upon its source, with little or no understanding of its nature:

> It was too cold to sit long in any one place, and, besides, the body was restless in this keen air with its ancient tingling fragrance. Art was disturbed by the notion that something striking and wonderful could be done on such a morning if only it would ' come to him ', come into his mind. It seemed on the verge of coming, out of years long ago, that were not really long ago, but in the present, bright mornings in a present that was very near him but not just at him, so that he was baffled and restless. . . .

Attempting to explain this in terms of his own experience, Art equates expectancy of the unknown with expectancy of the known—a letter from Donul in the outside world or the acquisition of a knife: ' everything was a short distance beyond him, but he knew he would suddenly be in that place, if only he could get a real knife '. The knife assumes for Art a greater significance than its intrinsic value would suggest; it becomes a symbol both of stability and of independence, giving him the confidence to accept each new experience as it presents itself. By hanging on to the knife he can hang on to the familiar world whenever he enters the unfamiliar, or when the unfamiliar enters his familiar world. During the first stages of Art's journey towards wisdom it is the latter of these types of experience which guides his feet; the coming and going of his father and his brother Duncan, the friendships outside the family circle of Duncan and Morag, the arrival of Henry James and the departure of Donul create paths to and from his own world and the other, paths along which Art can send

his imagination in preparation for his own actual progression.
Again Gunn sees life in the round:

> There were two worlds for Art: his own and the
> one beyond. He lived in his own world, as inside a
> circle, and here things happened but never changed.
> The crops moved about on the fields as he did himself,
> but the fields remained where they were. So did the
> braes and the hollows and the outlines of the land
> against the sky, whether in snow or summer sunshine,
> in dryness or in flood. From Shivering Eye to Loch of
> the Rushes, from the lonely grey ruins of the Clash to
> the smuggling cave in the Little Glen, he knew the feel
> of the earth under his bare feet. Sometimes his legs
> tucked themselves beneath him while he made things
> with his knife or created fables with his mind, and
> sometimes his legs rushed in panic from that which
> seemed more real than the knife itself. But whatever
> happened, the earth remained in its abiding outlines,
> the houses in the same place, and men and women tall
> and secure and moving about. Here was the permanent,
> changeless as Old Hector's whiskers.
>   So much for his own world. Beyond its known
> rim there was, however, the other world, the world
> outside. Folk talked sometimes in solemn voices of
> great changes taking place in it, and now and then they
> would shake their heads in wonder. . . .
>   Now between these two worlds the boundary line
> was a circle vague as what lay beyond the horizon—
> except in one place, and that place was the River.
> Many times Art had tried to reach this River, but he had
> never succeeded, yet so much had he thought about it
> that it ran clearly through his own mind.

So often is Art diverted in his course towards the River
that it becomes ' the fabled River and the Hazel Pool—
the River that he sometimes thought he would never be

allowed to reach in this life '. Indeed, he is not allowed to reach it within the pages of *Young Art and Old Hector*; the last chapter sees him on his way there with Hector, but the first chapter of *The Green Isle of the Great Deep* makes it clear that once again Art has had to turn back— this time because the little red cow carelessly allows a turnip to stick in her throat. In the context of this first record of Young Art and Old Hector, therefore, the River exists only in ' the other landscape '. It represents the ultimate experience, the transition from the world of childhood and innocence to the world of maturity and wisdom.

Art's growth is reflected in his changing response to situations in which the River figures. We first meet him in Chapter I in a fury at being prevented from following Donul and Hamish to the River; Old Hector succeeds in distracting his attention from his grievances comparatively easily by feeding Young Art's appetite for conundrums. Art's first experience of the paradox of existence is second-hand, verbal; his understanding of the abstract quality of wisdom, distinct from knowledge, is necessarily limited by his youthfulness and is best satisfied by the terms of Old Hector's parable of Finn and the Salmon. The fabled River is more real to him than the actual for the time being.

In Chapter VII, his second attempt to reach the River is frustrated in the same circumstances: Donul again leaves him behind in tears of rage, from which he is diverted, this time by Morag. Her technique is similar to Hector's, for she catches Art's attention with a conundrum on the nature of Nowhere and Somewhere. Nowhere and Somewhere represent a real world for Art, a world peopled by No-one and Some-one. They are outside his own experience, within which ' where ' has always an identity. Art is almost sure that Somewhere is at the River, but he has been deceived before, and for the moment he is content to leave the idea, still paradoxical, in the nebulous world of partial but unlocated reality.

The third attempt, in the next chapter, takes place under circumstances entirely new to Art. The River becomes now the symbol of male superiority, for Mary Ann requires to be impressed and Art's claim to have done things that would frighten her must be substantiated. For the first time in his life Art is the leader instead of the disciple. For the first time he is, in a sense, forming experience instead of accepting it already formed, and it is the novelty of this which prevents their reaching the River. Art manufactures ' a little house ' for them at Mary Ann's request, and their energy is diverted towards the enjoyment of the world of imagination, away from the world of the River and the Pool.

In Chapter X, Art is on his way to the River when hard physical reality intervenes in the shape of a thorn in Art's foot. Once again Old Hector attempts to distract him with a conundrum, but this time Art's response is different. He has begun to realise that it represents only a verbal, and therefore insubstantial reality, but he has learned at the same time that, used in the right way, it has its own value. ' They both knew it was a trick, but it was a trick, they also knew, for withdrawing them into the male region of stoical courage.' Even so, Art gains some measure of comfort from translating his recent experience with the thorn into a conundrum, as if in some way he can lessen the reality of its effect on him, an effect of which he is in retrospect slightly ashamed.

Art's next hope of an expedition to the River is removed

by a change in the inner world of home, a change which affects Donul's reactions and, by extension, Art's.

> This was not the Donul who had first given Art the courage to put his hand in a calf's mouth or hunt peewit's eggs on a Sunday morning. Keenly had Art been looking forward to the time when Father would be away, and Duncan too, because then it was certain life would be much more free and full of fun. Donul and himself would have the greatest times and, in particular, Donul would be able to take him to the fabled River and the Hazel Pool—the River that sometimes he thought he would never be allowed to reach in this life.
>
> . . . The thought of work was dull. A brightness went out of the landscape, and he saw his home and the coloured fields around it go still and lonely as if they were aware that Father and Duncan had been withdrawn from them. Where there should have been an overflowing there was, instead, a draining away. (Chapter XI)

By the withdrawing of Father and Duncan from the inner world a path has been opened to the outer world and along this path has come the concept of duty and responsibility. These are abstract ideas, as was that of wisdom in the first chapter, but Art has now sufficient understanding to accept the abstract and to translate it to the physical: he gives up again the notion of the River and replaces it with a concrete contribution to his real world.

Chapter XIII presents Art, displaced and disconcerted by wedding preparations, in a strangely altered world in which, for the moment, he has no part. He is, consequently, easily drawn out of it by the distant River. The world he enters, however, is as strangely altered as the one he has just left:

> In the little Glen he was all alone, going away off to find the fabled River and the Hazel Pool, and because this fatal mood was upon him and there was no help for it, he wanted to cry. It was hard on him, having to do all this alone. When the cry mounted he took a little run to himself and the tears that came out bounced off.
>
> Presently he noticed that the glen was quieter and more watchful than when he had gone down it before, perhaps because Mary Ann had been with him then.
>
> But the glen itself seemed to have changed, too. There were curious little places which he had not noticed before, and one or two bends which he could have sworn were not in it the last time. And then he observed, on the other side, the small ravine of a burn which issued a noisy trickle of water. He certainly had never seen *that* before, so he stood and stared at it until it began to stare back. Whereupon he went on, but with the corner of his left eye on the ravine to prevent a surprise, and while he was thus politely not really looking at the ravine, the earth itself bobbed clean from under his foot and he went face first into a ditch. It was the one he had told Mary Ann how to jump.
>
> So he was on the right road, and even if things could be enchanted, as he had heard Donul say before now, they clearly had not been enchanted entirely.

As Art goes deeper into the glen, its aspect becomes more sinister. Fear of the unpleasant natural world, personified in the three gaugers, the Great Ones, is mixed with fear of the unnatural, the little folk. His progress from now on has the quality of nightmare.

> No sooner were [the three men] out of sight, than Art got to his feet and ran on as fast as he could, indeed a

little faster, but when he fell he let no yelp out of him now. The next time he fell was from fright at a big black bird that flapped up from below him. As he gazed down the short steep slope, he saw the body of a dead sheep. Where the wool was off its side, the skin was black, and white maggots were crawling over it. A rotten smell attacked his nostrils, and, pushing back his head, he saw, far across from him on the other side of the small glen, the ravine of the foxgloves and the wild beast's den. He would have run then, but for one infernal circumstance—the roots of the heather above the den breathed out a faint but unmistakable blue smoke.

Art's mind became a whirling place of wild beasts' dens and little houses of fairy folk and legend and dread that set the world itself going up and down and round like the machinery in the meal mill. Then out of the little door, which Art had discovered on the day Mary Ann and himself had set off to find the fabled River, out of the little door that gave entry to the dark den, came the shaggy head of a great beast, and all at once, O torrents of the mountain, it was not a beast's head, but the hairy *oorishk* itself, the fabulous beast-human. There were legends of this human monster that could chill the heart's blood of grown folk. On all fours it came forth, and slowly it reared itself, and looked around, and Art saw, as in a strange and powerful dream, that the *oorishk* was Old Hector.

This world is subjective to the point of animism; it is a world of the unnatural and the supernatural, peopled with bogles and monsters from Art's imagination, which is full of the old fables and legends. Each of these malevolent phenomena has, of course, a perfectly natural cause, but because Art observes only the effect and not the cause, he is forced to provide an explanation for himself. Such an explanation can only be in terms of his own experience, which has been moulded and directed by stories of the little folk, of bird-beasts, and beast-humans.

On the very day that Donul has solemnly promised to take Art to the River, the world outside stretches out its 'long, dark, menacing arm' and takes Donul away. This is to be one of the most significant of the events of Art's life, for it introduces him gradually, if with some sadness, to the world beyond. It gathers 'a certain brightness' for Art, although he prefers the little places himself. More than this, it alters his concept of the River. In this chapter (XV), the River ceases for the first time to be 'the fabled River' and becomes simply 'the River'. He has shed in a natural fashion some of the magic scales which had clothed the legend of the salmon and the hazel nuts, for in the company of Donul and Hamish rational theories are more fitting than mystical. In the aftermath of Donul's departure, indeed, the River loses for a time all of its magical influence:

> [Art] did not want to see or speak to anybody. The River flowed on in its darkling waters, remote and sad. He had never been able to reach that River, and its flow held no urgency for him now.

This pathetic fallacy indicates the shift which has taken place in the nature of Art's subjectivism. His concept of the River is still totally subjective—unseen, it has only a hypothetical existence for him—but because of his experiences the River has assumed dimensions within the control of his conscious and rational imaginings.

Each stage in his journey has contributed to his concept of reality, has given it breadth and depth and has balanced in correct proportion its relation to physical, mental and spiritual development. The seven situations which have been examined have combined to create in Art a rounded view of existence. They have presented to him in turn the intangible reality of the world of legend, the indefinite reality of Nowhere and Somewhere, the subjective reality of childish imagination, the physical reality of pain and release, the abstract reality of responsibility manifested in physical labour, the animistic reality of physical phenomena explained in psychic terms, and finally, the fusion of the inner world and the outer, with its consequent necessity to accept the whole of experience.

The ability to distinguish the real from the fabled is a necessary part of his spiritual development, and his spiritual development in turn is a necessary part of his relation to the pattern of creation. Such ability cannot be manufactured; it can be nourished and directed—and is, by Old Hector—but its source is instinctive. Jung's theory of the collective unconscious is again relevant:

> Although our inheritance consists in physiological paths, it was nevertheless mental processes in our ancestors that traced these paths. If they came to consciousness again in the individual, they can do so only in the form of other mental processes; and although these processes can become conscious only through individual experience and consequently appear as individual acquisitions, they are nevertheless pre-existent traces which are merely 'filled out' by the individual experience. Probably every 'impressive' experience is just such a break-through into an old, previously unconscious river-bed.[4]

Art's failure yet to reach the River, seen in these terms, is not only irrelevant, but also, in a sense, inevitable. The river-bed of his consciousness cannot be filled until he has amassed sufficient experience to establish his unique identity and until he has the wisdom to understand the forces which motivate him. In exploring the territory between his own world and its boundary, the River, he is exploring his own nature. It is the journey that has mattered, for in its course he has learned lessons which will enable him to retain his integrity on the Green Isle of the Great Deep.

In the closing chapter, 'To the River', Young Art and Old Hector set out on the last stage of their journey. For Old Hector the circle is about to be completed, his final trip to the River fusing with and taking new life from Art's first. For Young Art the fabled has become the real; soon he will reach the boundary between his own world and the world beyond. He accepts Old Hector's inheritance of the knowledge of the little places, and shares his vision of the continuity of existence.

> " Do you think," he asked, trying to control his voice, " we'll see a salmon in the Hazel Pool? "
> " There's no saying," replied Old Hector. " But I know a flagstone I can poke with a stick, and if I don't put a fellow out from under it, it will be a wonder."
> " Where will you get the stick? "
> " You can help me to cut one with a knife from a hazel tree. And the nuts will be ripe. We forgot that! They'll be falling out of their clusters."
> " Will they? " said Art on a breath.
> " They will," said Old Hector.

The storyteller has returned to his beginning and the circle is closed.

NOTES ON REFERENCES

1 See Nigel Macneill's *The Literature of the Highlanders* (Eneas Mackay, Stirling, 1892) for a discussion of the theory that ' the existence of the Feinne is only a myth—part and parcel of an old world system, not unconnected with the classical and oriental—a system of which we have the same with variations in the Militia of Ireland, and in the Knights of the Round Table of the ancient British. It is held that Fingal and King Arthur are the same personages . . .' (Intro. p. 33).

2 Malory, *Le Morte d'Arthur* (Everyman ed., 1906): " Well, said Merlin, I know a lord of yours in this land, that is a passing true man, and a faithful, and he shall have the nourishing of your child, and his name is Sir Ector " [Volume I, Chapter III]

3 There is another example of this prophetic style of address in *The Silver Darlings* (Chapter XXIV): ' Before Finn went to sleep that night on his heather bed, old Finn-son-of-Angus said to him: " You told the story well. . . . It was done, too, with the humour that is the play of drift on the wave. And you were modest. Yet—all that is only a little—you had something more, my hero, something you will not know—until you look at it through your eyes, when they are as old as mine." " What do you mean by that? " asked Finn. But the old man shook his head and turned away. " Go to your sleep, my boy. Many a one may come in the guise of a stranger.'

4 ' On Psychic Energy ' in *The Structure and Dynamics of the Psyche* (Volume VIII, Collected Works, pub. 1960 by Routledge & Kegan Paul).

Fable of Freedom :
The Green Isle of the Great Deep

ANDREW NOBLE

> The Bible says That Cultivated Life Existed First. Un-
> cultivated Life comes afterwards from Satan's Hirelings. Necessaries,
> Accommodations & Ornaments are the whole of Life. Satan took
> away Ornament First. Next he took away Accommodations,
> Then he became Lord & Master of Necessaries.
>
> Blake: *Annotations to Reynolds*

In this essay I wish to discuss Neil M. Gunn's peculiarly
complex and relevant novel *The Green Isle of the Great Deep*.
While most of this paper will be devoted to the work's
complexity I would also like to stress the book's specific
relevance for our age. There is, I believe, an all too common
assumption that Gunn is a novelist of limited geographical
and dubious psychical talent. The basic premise underlying
what I have written here is that Gunn is, by any standards,
a major writer and that what he has to say about the modern
world and the contemporary mind is totally pertinent to
the condition we find ourselves in. For me he is one
of the few modern writers, in an age of despair, who can
still speak honestly and profoundly about the possibility
of human possibility.

It is this sense of possibility, of freedom, that lies at the
core of what I want to say. There seems to me no theme
more central to Gunn than that of freedom. If, as Hugh
MacDiarmid tells us, ' freedom—the free development of
human consciousness '[1] is of the essence of the Scottish

genius, then Gunn is indeed a worthy member of such a tradition. With the help of that remarkable piece of autobiographical writing, *The Atom of Delight*, which takes as its basic theme the relationship between childhood and freedom, I hope that my study of the novel will make this obvious. Obvious, too, I trust, will be the fact that Gunn is a writer of major stature and, in the course of this essay, I have deliberately sought to create realistic and credible parallels between him and those writers with whom I consider him comparable. One of the benefits of such a procedure is that the writers I have chosen, principally Fyodor Dostoevsky and William Faulkner, have achieved a recognised critical awareness, and that our advanced understanding of them might enable us to see Gunn in a more appropriate perspective.

William Faulkner, a novelist who was also at one time considered as a rather limited and regional talent, offers a peculiarly fruitful parallel. There are, of course, obvious differences between the two men. The fecund Deep South gives rise to a more torrid rhetoric than anything coming from Gunn's vision of the Highlands. Both novelists, however, have a similar capacity to subserve the aesthetic innovations of modern fiction to their own more traditional visions of spiritual worth. Consider, for example, Faulkner's use of time and consciousness in *The Sound and the Fury* and Gunn's use of Proustian techniques in *Highland River*. Both, too, have a predilection for plots of a near melo-dramatic intensity. In terms of their social vision each writer presents a rural community poised between decay and possible rebirth and brought to this pass by historical tragedy. In Faulkner this tragedy is the Civil War, in Gunn Culloden and the Clearances. It is tragedy of a kind that has left a near overwhelming burden of guilt and despair.

The final belief of each writer is, however, that man will not be overwhelmed. Man, for Faulkner in his Nobel speech, is that creature who will not only endure but prevail. Both men share a sense of the elemental worth and nobility of the figures in their landscape: a belief in the depth of the best man to outlive the depthlessness of the present age. Isaac Rosenfeld says that the principle of life in Faulkner's characters is that ' their goodness is their profound submissiveness ',[2] and while we will have reason in *The Green Isle of the Great Deep* to return to the relationship between submission and endurance, it is sufficient to say that the latter value is the final ground for optimism in both men.

The nature of depth in the human being is also something to which we will return. Faulkner and Gunn both feel that this quality of depth in the individual is being eroded because the individuality itself is being stifled in modern society. Thus Faulkner says:

A belief that there is no place any more where individual man of such simple things as honesty with oneself and responsibility toward others and protection for the weak and compassion and pity for all, because such individual things as honesty and pity and responsibility and compassion no longer exist and man himself can hope to continue only by relinquishing and denying his individuality into a regimented group of his arbitrary factional kind, arrayed against an opposite opposed arbitrary factional regimented group, both filling the same air at the same time with the same double-barrelled abstractions of ' people's democracy ' and ' minority rights ' and ' equal justice ' and ' social welfare '—all the synonyms which take all the shame out of irresponsibility by not merely inviting but compelling everyone to participate in it.[3]

Here we have a perfect introduction to that strange land of Gunn's, the Green Isle, that runs between life and death and where the very air itself seems to be part of the pressure on the individual to conform for the alleged good of all; where the old virtues have of necessity to be surrendered so that the new materialism can succeed. Bearing this in mind we can allow our Faulkner parallel to run even closer to Gunn. In this same lecture, ' A Word to Young Writers ', he goes on to adumbrate the difficulty for the contemporary writer in creating character because so much of our present experience is experience of a social vacuum:

> Let me repeat: I have not read all the work of this present generation of writing; I have not had time yet. So I must speak only of the ones I do know. I am thinking now of what I rate the best one: Salinger's *Catcher in the Rye*, perhaps because this one expresses so completely what I have tried to say: a youth, father to what will, must someday be a man, more intelligent than some and more sensitive than most, who (he would not even have called it by instinct because he did not know he possessed it) because God perhaps had put it there, loved man and wished to be a part of mankind, humanity, who tried to join the human race and failed. To me, his tragedy was not that he was, as he perhaps thought, not tough enough or brave enough or deserving enough to be accepted into humanity. His tragedy was that when he attempted to enter the human race, there was no human race there. There was nothing for him to do save buzz, frantic

and inviolate, inside the glass walls of his tumbler until
he either gave up or was himself by himself, by his own
frantic buzzing, destroyed.   One thinks of course
immediately of Huck Finn, another youth already
father to what will some day soon now be a man.
But in Huck's case all he had to combat was his small
size, which time would cure for him; in time he would
be as big as any man he had to cope with; and even
as it was, all the adult world could do to harm him was
to skin his nose a little: humanity, the human race,
would and was accepting him already; all he needed
to do was just to grow up in it.

    That is the young writer's dilemma as I see it.   Not
just his, but all our problems, is to save mankind from
being desouled as the stallion or boar or bull is gelded;
to save the individual from anonymity before it is too
late and humanity has vanished from the animal called
man.   And who better to save man's humanity than
the writer, the poet, the artist, since who should fear
the loss of it more since the humanity of man is the
artist's life's blood.[4]

Here again Faulkner's relevance cannot be overstressed,
for there is no more important theme to Gunn in life and
fiction than the growth of the child through the crisis of
adolescence to his final mature involvement in communal
life.[5]   Thus for both Gunn and Faulkner, the latter nourished
by Twain, there is no greater horror than the destruction
of children within a social vacuum.   The supreme virtue
of communal life for both men is that it nourishes the child
both in a physical and spiritual sense.   They see the child's
free growth as a necessary prelude to his mature participation.   A society which does not allow this is bent on
destruction, or at least castration.   For both men part of
the potential of modern man is to be the castrated animal.

In fact, in *The Green Isle of the Great Deep*, Robert tells Old Hector that " they castrate the mind ".[6]

To my mind the best way of getting further into the heart of Gunn's thinking on childhood and freedom is to begin with that radical and radically underestimated autobiographical study of his own childhood called *The Atom of Delight*. The book is not only an unsurpassed source for events in and insights into Gunn's own fiction but is also, in its own right, a work of wisdom and provides ground for creating deep speculative excitement in the reader. In a way quite unique in my knowledge, Gunn takes his own childhood activities and from his comprehension of their deepest meanings is able to use them as a springboard for the most profound kind of thinking about the nature of the self, the condition of freedom and the forces opposing freedom in modern society.

The fundamental argument in the book is about the ultimate reality of childhood's physical *and* psychical experience. Gunn recognises no division between the physical and the psychical. He approvingly quotes Freud's dictum that adults have greatly undervalued ' the psychic life of the child [in] its richness and fineness of feeling ',[7] but the path he takes from this point is the very reverse of that taken by reductive psychoanalysis. Gunn is interested throughout the book in that area of the self that lies beyond analysis and he believes that such an area is innate to the child and provides him with a kind of inner core, a *second self*, a kind of centre of vitality and spirit. This is the very ' atom of delight ', which is *not* indestructible in the cyclotron of modern society and modern cynical analysis but which, once destroyed, leaves merely an adult shell, a disintegrated personality. This inner essence although autonomous is not finally self-centred, since it is the area which generates our freedom and, therefore, our ability to assume responsibility for others, and is also the centre and source of our ability both to receive and communicate animal and aesthetic pleasure.

Now before going further, and lest these ideas about the relation of childhood memory, psychic health, freedom and artistic creativity seem rather *passé* in a world of psycho-analysis and behavioural psychology, it might be well to call to Gunn's defence some other novelists who share his belief in the essential fountainhead of childhood and its relation to adult life and art. Patrick White, for example, talks about his persistent ' longing to return to the scenes of childhood, which is, after all, the purest well from which the creative artist draws '.[8]   Saul Bellow, too, discussing his style says that:

> I wouldn't really know how to describe it. I don't care to trouble my mind to find an exact description for it, but it has something to do with a kind of readiness to record impressions arising from a source of which we know little. I suppose that all of us have a primitive commentator within who from earliest years has been advising us, telling us what the real world is. . . .   There is that observing instrument in us—in childhood at any rate. At the sight of a man's face, his shoes, the color of light, a woman's mouth or perhaps her ear, one receives a word, a phrase, at times nothing but a non-sense-syllable from the primitive commentator.[9]

Thus Bellow agrees with Gunn's belief that the primitive and the child are peculiarly rich in their awareness of immediate sensory experience and the necessary relation of this power to the creativity of the ' mature ' artist.

Dostoevsky, too, provides much of interest on the subject of the child and the man. In this characteristic passage from his *Diary of a Writer* he recounts his visit to the village, the 'dear scenes' of his childhood, and this leads him to speculate on how the present generation of Russian children will remember their own childhood:

> That our contemporary children will also have such sacred memories there can be no doubt, since otherwise 'live life' would cease. Man cannot live without something sacred and precious carried away into life from the memories of childhood. Some people, apparently, do not think about this; nevertheless, unconsciously, they do preserve such recollections. They may even be painful and bitter; however, even suffering endured in one's life may subsequently transform itself into a sanctuary of the soul. Generally speaking, man has been so created that he loves his past suffering. Besides, man, of necessity, is inclined to mark points, as it were, in his past in order to be subsequently guided by them and to deduce from them something whole—as a matter of routine and for his own edification.
>
> The strongest and most influential recollections are those produced in childhood. Therefore, unquestionably, those memories and impressions—possibly the strongest and most sacred ones—will be carried into life also by present-day children.[10]

This passage, with its precise location of the 'sacred' in the life of the child and the potential for this spiritual quality to organically develop into and through the life of the man, is very close to Gunn's own thinking. Close, too, is Dostoevsky's idea that if the sacred is broken and lost 'live life' is also lost; the adult life becomes a shell without a core as vitality and inner meaning leak from it.

Finally we can note in the thought of both men the concept that the gravest cultural peril is implicit in the treatment of our children.   In *The Brothers Karamazov* it is desperately difficult, and Dostoevsky meant it so to be, not to admit the truth of Ivan's case against God: that God permits the death and suffering of children.   It would be well to remember that equally in Dostoevsky's fiction is his case against his contemporaries: that they cause physically and spiritually the death of children with their egotism, ideological blindness, sheer cruelty and atheism.   Time and again he presents characters, Raskolnikov, Stavrogin, Ivan himself, who are the warped and twisted victims of parental megalomania and a community which projects its darkest desires into the education of its children.

While Gunn understands the consequences of such darkness, it is both his personal and fictional strength that his own creative roots lie, in a time transcending way, in a blessed childhood within the circle of a family and a community marked by common sense and genuine charity. Thus he describes this society:

> The old feeling of equality among themselves remained, of that independence which being dependence on one-self was not directed against any other but, on the contrary, respected a similar independence in all others.[11]

It is Gunn's formative years spent in such a genuine spiritual democracy that has created in him a sense of the elemental goodness in man that appears everywhere in his fiction.   It is this rural community, too, that allowed the boy the physical freedom of running, hunting, fishing and exploring that become archetypal emblems for more complex adult states.   For Gunn the physical realities of childhood, however, have a value which is utterly primary and without which there is nothing. They are the basic ground on which the adult builds.

> From such high-flying over the terrain, let me get down to *living* passages, in boyhood, the body, the senses, where delights are first come upon and mental complexity is a burden. Get rid of the burden, drop the shackles and run.
>
> How often as a boy I did just that! To run until you forgot what you were running from, until the running itself became an exhilaration that flew until the wind of your speed brought water to your eyes and your toes touched the ground so lightly that with the very smallest of extra aids they could have skimmed it. When the Greeks carved their figure of Hermes, the swift messenger of the gods, they put a small wing on each sandal.
>
> The slowing-up, the gasping, the return of the body's weight, the glance over each shoulder, and " I'm off! " has become " I'm away! " [12]

This cry of freedom echoes through *The Atom of Delight*. If the Highland community is a model democracy, then, for Gunn, the boy in his assertion of freedom over all restriction is the essential and primary democrat. The essence of childhood is for Gunn the desire for freedom which is attained by the body's acceleration into open country. It is a freedom the boy attains by all sorts of ruses against the restrictions of parents, adults and teachers, but the child is correct in so acting because he is nourishing in himself a *pre-moral* essence which is the basis of his subsequent adult moral sense of freedom, responsibility, creativity and powers of aesthetic response.

This area of childhood reached through, and always

part of, the body Gunn calls the second self. It is this second self that is absolutely fundamental and even the child's peculiar powers of spiritual awareness, especially his innate ability to sense evil, and his sense of justice are consequent upon the thing itself.

> But when we come to the second self even the sense of justice is left behind. I have tried hard to think of ways of describing it but cannot get beyond the mere assertion that it simply *is*. If I remember my school Euclid correctly the four or five basic axioms *were* in much the same way, yet with the difference that in being taken for granted they are assumed to exist, they remain assumptions, even though they 'work' with unvarying success. The second self is not an assumption. It is the fount from which assumptions proceed. In the beginning it is. I am myself, trying to describe it.[13]

Before cries of 'empirical' disbelief rend the air at this assertion, it would be well to show how Gunn came upon this awareness of an inner and deeper self. We are presented with this beautiful incident when, as a child, he is squatting on a rock in mid-stream attempting to break open hazel nuts with a stone and bathed in sunlight.

> Then the next thing happened, and happened, so far as I can remember, for the first time. I have tried hard but can find no simpler way of expressing what happened than by saying: *I came upon myself sitting there.*
>
> Within the mood of content, as I have tried to recreate it, was this self and this self was me.
>
> The state of content deepened wonderfully and everything around was embraced in it.
>
> There was no 'losing' of the self in the sense that

G

there was a blank from which I awoke or came to. The self may have thinned away—it did—but so delightfully that it also remained at the centre in a continuous and perfectly natural way. And then within this amplitude the self as it were became aware of seeing itself, not as ' I ' or an ' ego ' but rather as a stranger it had come upon and was even a little shy of.

Transitory, evanescent—no doubt, but the scene comes back across half a century, vivid to the crack in the boulder that held the nut.[14]

Here, I believe, we see the strength of Gunn's position because it is so rooted in experience. Not a definition of experience that would please the logical positivist, constricted by his definition of the senses, a definition which makes man a captive of a tyrannical nervous system rather than allowing him the freedom of the body; nor a definition that would please the behavioural psychologist or the analyst. It is, however, the triumph of *The Atom of Delight* that it has a kind of unpretentious wisdom that understands these systems and their imprisoning limitations. By returning the child to his body Gunn is able also to allow mind and soul a truer definition. Throughout the book, and indeed throughout all his writing, Gunn is deeply aware of the modern sensibility that wants to reject childhood and joy. Thus he says in talking of such intuitive conditions of the psyche:

How easy is this deflating, this debunking of the extravagant, the lyrical moment! With what hidden malice, too, it so often achieves the stale and unprofitable end! Until at last one can do it oneself by a sort of introverted trick; until one is hypnotized into the grey belief that life itself, the world, is going out with a wail, when in fact the scientific realities point to it going out with a very extravagant bang.[15]

Gunn, therefore, is acutely aware of this desire to dominate and destroy certain types of experience; of the terrible confusion in the modern mind that knowledge is not an infinite, free and open-ended pursuit but rather a power of limitation. He understands, too, that limitation demands systems and that systems are of their very nature deterministic and potentially totalitarian. If *The Atom of Delight* is about the light and joy of boyhood the dark side of it is its deep awareness of how fiercely such qualities are under attack. Modern thought Gunn describes as ' the infiltrating authoritarian '[16] ready to attack man at his very root, his innate freedom. Thus he describes the process of choice:

> After the choice is made it may be contended that the choice was inevitable, that it was predetermined. But determinism is always wise after the psychic event. And being wise after the event is tantamount to saying that it happened because it happened. If determinism were really omniscient it would be wise before the event. But determinism, as a rational process, cannot be wise before the event if the event embraced the exercise of non-rational factors, including those incalculable upsurges from the Unconscious, or from the intromissions of archetypes in the Collective Unconscious, not to mention ongoings in weird realms where perceptions are extra-sensory in a way that would have shaken Hume to his Edinburgh roots and may yet produce another kind of smile on the face of a physicist. To provide for all this (and the still unknown more) determinism would have to be omniscient, and omniscience of this order is as unknowable as God, of whom it is accordingly postulated as an attribute.

> The materialism which makes use of determinism finds itself, if taken far enough along its own way, in ideal country.[17]

The irony of the last sentence will be returned to, but for the moment one cannot emphasise too strongly how deep is the critique of determinism and closed systems in the autobiography. In MacDiarmid there is a thematic struggle between the divine artist and the demonic bureaucrat and in Gunn there is a parallel line of development in his concept of the inner, second self, the innate self of the child and the adult's centre of artistic vitality and creativity, being under constant onslaught by the pressures of our age for conformity.

> Critics, ideologists, philosophers, theologians are forever trying to do this essential work of cleaning up and arranging, confining and stabilising, and when in the first flush of success they make a good job of it, the second self finds freedom for a time to pursue its search in a wonderfully creative fashion; but always the system hardens as the theologians or ideologists take over its active control and justify their rule by use of a practical force toward a reasoned end, and as the second self now begins to feel the curb of a system which has the first self in control—for that is roughly what it amounts to—it begins to wriggle and want to break through for it knows that rigid confinement will ultimately stifle it. It has got to be off and away. It has got to be about its implicit business. But because of the potency of the business, and because it is at least latent in every one, the rulers of the system fear its disruptive force and so have it crucified, or poisoned or otherwise liquidated according to the manners of the time.[18]

Thus for Gunn the anxiety, enormity and possible apocalypse of our time is centred in our capacity for destruction of our own inner religious and artistic dimension. His relation of Christ and the artist is, in some ways, close to Blake. 'In our most modern moment,' says Gunn, 'we are back in the Garden where the Devil entered in the serpent and broke the circle.'[19]   Fundamentally this ultimate dilemma lies not so much in the fact that the genuinely religious person or artist will inevitably be assailed by authority and demagoguery but that our condition in modern society is really that of suicide rather than ritual sacrifice. If we recall *Crime and Punishment* we can better understand this point. Spiritual self-destruction is the necessary prelude to the destruction of others; indeed in the Dostoevskyian world (our world) murder is the consequence not the cause of the sin.

Paradoxically, too, we murder in the name of our supposed best interests. From the depths of a profound personal and communal unease—indeed disease—we strive for false security believing that control of our environment, of other men, the creation of systems and vacuums, the determination of possibilities, the extension of our rational capacity will be our salvation. The profound and tragic ironies of such behaviour lie all round us; achieving their ultimate expression in the notion that our technological control of nuclear weapons is our salvation. We have reached the Kafkaesque point of deifying our institutions and bureaucracies and being agonised by the fact that they do not respond with the 'goods' that we need. The humming in our telephone wires is most decidedly not that of angels singing.

It would be wrong, however, to leave *The Atom of*

Delight on such a black note. While it does full justice to the terror of this time, it is no more a pessimistic book than Gunn is a pessimistic writer. Perhaps this is so because it does not fall victim to the literary plague of our time that is caused by the fusion of creativity and notions of historical determinism. Literature for Gunn, as for MacDiarmid, is always a creative opposition to the excesses and authority of the age, and part of his opposition lies in the belief that the child, the creative imagination and, therefore, mankind itself are innately free. While we may destroy ourselves we are not mere victims. More hopefully Gunn looks towards an evolution beyond the apparent present impasse.

> Freedom may be an ambiguous word, but its nature is at least indicated, as has been suggested, in the spontaneity of the whole child in achieving its delight. Without consciously thinking or striving, 'It' is achieved, spontaneity comes into its own, the arrow lands in the bull. Musical composers, scientists, painters, writers, know how in the midst of their striving 'It' takes charge, strife ceases, and the 'marked passage' is born. In that moment of delight freedom is known...
>
> The future remains open to this kind of freedom. Through freedom the adventure continues. The way goes into the future, and the end of it cannot be known. One can know it only as far as one has gone. Freedom has its growth like the second self, and along with the the growth of the second self.[20]

Having established the basis of our discussion we may now turn to that peculiarly complex fable, *The Green Isle of the Great Deep*. Simone Weil, the French religious philosopher, gives one of the best definitions of complexity in art that I know of. 'Simultaneous composition on several planes at once,' she says, ' is the law of artistic creation, and wherein, in fact, lies its difficulty.' [21]   True to her premise, *The Green Isle* has a multilevelled and simultaneous existence and the critic can only hope that his process of simplifying and abstracting the work will, in Coleridge's sense, better allow the reader to return with greater understanding to the whole.   I shall begin, then, by summarising the plot and then develop, or tease out, the different levels of meaning.

As a word of preliminary personal and general caution it should also be noted that Gunn is very sceptical about the general level of critical awareness.   His belief, like mine, is that art communicates only if the reader shares its ground of experience and insight.   Too often, I believe, modern criticism believes that it is art that has to prove itself, to meet the tests of the analytical weaponry we have evolved—close analysis, study of symbolism, depth psychology, sociology etc.—rather than that it is we the critics and readers who are being tested.   We are in danger of creating a critical ideology to imprison the freedom and power of art.   Rather than recognising the spirit of things we are obsessed with reducing them to the level of our own awareness.   Blake, in his celebrated letter to Dr Trussler, puts this rather more cogently:

> You say that I want somebody to Elucidate my Ideas.   But you ought to know that What is Grand is necessarily obscure to Weak men.   That which can be made Explicit to the Idiot is not worth my care.   The wisest of the Ancients consider'd what is not too Explicit as the fittest for Instruction, because it rouzes the faculties to act.
> . . . to the Eyes of the Man of Imagination, Nature is Imagination itself.   As man is, So he Sees.   As the

Eye is formed, such are its powers. You certainly
Mistake, when you say that the Visions of Fancy are
not to be found in This World. To Me This World is
all One continued Vision of Fancy or Imagination, &
I feel Flatter'd when I am told so.[22]

Now few, if any of us, have either Blake's powers of
vision or confidence, but I think it would well become us
to meet such qualities with humility rather than rage.
Certainly if we are to gain even partial entry to Gunn's
world we must accept, as he does, that the elemental things
are mysterious and sacred and that they are communicated
by the artist in his art. They are not, however, made
available as a commodity. Vision for Gunn is elusive,
fleeting, ' the fawn in the glen ', but it *is* there. However,
for

the inadequate critic—the critic who has not had the
glimpse—what he has to say can manifestly have no
relevance in this region of experience. When the
glimpse is the touchstone anything less is nothing.[23]

The Green Isle of the Great Deep begins, naturalistically
enough, in a typical small Highland community during
the Second World War. There is, too, Gunn's customary
ability to catch the warmth, intimacy and banter of such a
community. The people, however, are not untouched by
the greater shadows beyond. Like scraps of sodden grey
newsprint blown across the land, word has come to them
of the concentration camps and of what Red Dougal
describes as man's new power to ' break the mind '. To
this Old Hector Macdonald, who with young Art Macrae
is to be one of the book's two main characters, replies:

" I do not know what to make of it. The mind is all

we have finally.   If they take that from us—if they change that—then we will not be ourselves, and all meaning goes from us, here—and hereafter." [24]

"Here—and hereafter": this should serve sufficient notice to us that the territory we are about to enter will transcend the merely social; though, of course, the social will have its part.

Art and Hector leave the house and embark on a poaching trip, Art's first, to the river, which he has never seen. The river is a strange place, 'a place that might at any moment be some other place'.[25]   Art picks some wondrously large and ripe nuts from the topmost boughs of a hazel tree.   They then move down to the salmon pool and in the process of trying to land a huge salmon Hector loses his balance and falls, taking Art with him, into the depths of the pool.   Gunn in his autobiography refers to his being so near the point of death by drowning that he experienced the dream that lies between life and death.   It is into a similar dream that the man and boy plunge.   We enter an area that transcends the temporal, and the book's naturalism gives way to a more mythical and legendary awareness without surrendering its factual precision of person, event and object.   Like Kafka, Gunn has the ability to make the most solid also the most deceptive.

They come to themselves in a bright yet strangely brittle countryside.   It is a land that seems fertile, even idyllic, and in both its terrain and inhabitants has a superficial resemblance to their own countryside.   This apparent likeness, however, serves only to give the whole thing a terrifying, nightmarish quality.   The atmosphere is taut with fear: 'as if terror might come with wing and talon out of the invisible air'.[26]   The people, too, laugh, but their

G 2

laughter has an undercurrent of cruelty and, in a peculiar way the two cannot understand, they seem to be people without depth. In so far as they live they seem to exist purely on the surface of their faces so that they appear like ' clean empty shells on a strange seashore '.[27]

Art and Hector meet the Coastwatcher, the first in an ascending power sequence of Civil Servants and administrators, and they are ordered to proceed to the capital, the Seat on the Rock, and to travel only by day and to stay at one of the Inns overnight. This, prompted by Art's intuition, they do not do, but travel towards the Seat and stay in the fields at night, living off the abundance of fruit that hangs from the trees. In its bounty the land is a literal paradise.

It is at this point that Art and Hector have their first *human* contact. They are taken in and given food by a married couple, Mary and Tom. The woman is sympathetic, but the man seems uneasy and evasive. He is peculiarly disturbed that they have been eating fruit and avoiding the Inns. Continuing on their way they come to the Seat and have their first meeting with the bureaucratic powers. Art is instinctively terrified of them and attempts to fight and break free. Old Hector, however, is tired in mind and body and almost willingly succumbs to their order to enter the rest room. The course of much that follows in the book is controlled by this initial pattern. Art unremittingly struggles against his oppressors and their plans for him to the point of making three successful escapes from them, while Old Hector is increasingly undermined by the persistence of his questioners' probing analysis into his nature and motives. The dramatic structure of the book is, therefore, created by Art's escapes and development in his freedom, Mary and Tom's involvement in his rebellion, and the assaults made on Old Hector to betray Art to them so that the general good will be restored.

The general good of this administration is, of course, that their society has evolved beyond its savage beginnings into a safe, static condition where all individuals engender the common good and consciousness by responding to an absolutely controlled and determined industrial environment. In practical terms this is done by their creation of a closed, mechanised food cycle and by making everyone allergic to any food, especially fruit, other than the gruel-like porridge spewed out from the underground factories. One fashion, therefore, in which Art threatens to undermine this whole structure is his refusal to be caught and his magical ability, to the eyes of the programmed inhabitants, to eat fresh fruit.

Art, helped by Mary until her arrest, does precisely this. He evades all attempts at capture and develops a fantastic fleetness of foot. The people soon begin to see in him a legendary quality. Old Hector, too, driven by constant questioning, indeed brainwashing, finally turns against his captors and demands that he should be allowed to talk to that power above their power, God himself.

The culmination of the book, consequently, is God's reappearance in the land, summoned from his meditation by hearing of Art's legend and Hector's request for an audience. Being Gunn's vision of God he is a very human and endearing one; a person of wit and charity and power of insight that terrifies the senior administrators who are called forward to account for the 'rational' society they have created. The book ends in their failure to do so, the freeing of the population from their mechanical and

spiritual torpor and the end of the ' dream '. Art and Hector
return to consciousness on the river-bank with the water
being pumped out of them by Art's sister and her boyfriend.
Then, as a final touch, they find lying on the bank the huge
salmon whose attempted capture had caused them to plunge
into the pool.

> He had a girth which makes length deceptive, so that
> his proportions had the perfection which becomes
> legendary. Then there was his colour. It was not,
> below the blue back, pure silver. It was silver
> invaded by gold, as knowledge might be invaded
> by wisdom. And finally beyond the mouth, which was
> closed, lay also on the grass two hazel nuts which had
> fallen out of a ripe cluster from the bough overhead.[28]

These symbols, archetypal in Gunn's work, of the hazel
nuts of knowledge and the salmon of wisdom, bring the
book full circle. The journey began with them provoking
physical pursuit and ends on the other side with Art and
Hector's understanding of what they represent at the
deepest level. Wisdom, knowledge, magic, love, these are
the elements that exist within man but that have been so
repressed. In *The Green Isle* they have been almost entirely
usurped by man's will-to-power and his unloosing of his
rational and administrative faculties. Thus when Old
Hector had his audience with God he is led to understand
of what the good society should consist:

> Old Hector nodded. As the conception of the Council
> of the wise men grew clear, he was greatly heartened.
> And particularly was he pleased when he saw that the
> Council was to have no power. For well he knew that
> a wise man will give the best he can distil with the
> finest grace when he gives freely and without reward.

Where administrators seek the counsel of the wise, blessed will be that land.

Most of the present Administrators, then, would be removed, and in their place would come those who had the urge to serve in an administrative capacity and who from time to time would have to consult with the Council of the wise men.

Old Hector could not help nodding. For behind the wise men was this Wisdom that saw. And this Widsom haunted man. That was its awful potency, its strange and elusive delight. Man might get power in the head and destroy without measure, but the Wisdom would haunt and draw him. The mathematician knew the direction; the saint knew the way. Too long had the head-hunters ruled them without mercy, turning their mathematics in the direction of death and their saintliness to the way of disintegration in the atomic psychology chamber. Too long, O Wisdom!

Knowledge and wisdom—

" And magic," murmured Old Hector, " which is the scent of the flower, the young feet of the runner, and the deep smile in the face."

And these three are all?

" All," nodded Old Hector.

Have you forgotten the Creator?

From staring into the distance, Old Hector turned his head and looked at the face of his Host. And so it came upon him that here indeed was the last place and the final occasion.

The Creator? That which creates?

" Love," breathed Old Hector.

The eyes of his Host were deep as the salmon pool that stirs gently on its surface when the fish moves below.[29]

At a primary level, then, what Gunn's fable represents

is an image of the gross confusion in the modern mind attained by *deifying* the practical, ordering, administering faculties and suppressing those ' inner ' primary qualities which form the sole basis of genuinely charitable adminis- tration *in so far as* it is administration that is necessary among us. If we make order and administration, man as controlled response, absolute values we also make power an absolute value and we reach the ultimate confusion of power and truth as being the same thing. We consequently canonise those who wield this power; we may even—Hitler, Stalin *et al,*—go the lengths of making Gods of them. We can now, perhaps, better understand Gunn's remark that beginning with an exclusively materialist philosophy we end in ideal country. Hell, it should be remarked, is ideal country of a kind. I would also like to note, though I am not competent to do more, that Gunn, from the evidence of *The Atom of Delight*, is obviously aware of and influenced by the work of C. G. Jung, and the model of mind he presents us with is very similar to Jung's, who also sees modern man detached from his soul, his psyche, and chained to ' a habitual misuse of reason and intellect for an egotistical power purpose '.[30]

In part, too, this explains Gunn's belief in the elemental power for good of the truly feminine woman—Mary and Morag in this book—with her capacity for instinctive action and response to the actual rather than theoretical needs of life. Thus Morag is described when Art is dragged half-dead from the river:

> Morag, in fact, was little beside herself. She sat and stood at the same time. . . . She was more than a wild rose; she was a fire. And she was to it that silence had no more chance than the snowflake on the river. After

all, she was the only woman among them and life was her concern.[31]

Gunn's capacity to understand what is wrong with us and with our society also gives the book for me a deeply prophetic quality. Like Bartok's music this novel emerges from an intense awareness of Fascism. Gunn, however, is too honest a writer to descend to a propagandist account of what the concentration camps represent for us. What he is saying, I think, is that a deification of power, irrationalism in the name of rationalism, a society controlled by terror, is within the capacity of all modern society. The devil is within the circle of our society; indeed he is within the self. If we consider the books of sociology which have appeared within the last decade we can see, too, how much Gunn understood of what was happening in his earlier creative work. Here, for example, is part of Herbert Marcuse's vision of the fate of man in the closed industrial state where, controlled by the stimulus and response of productivity, man becomes a ' happy ' slave of his society, in such a condition of alienation that he cannot consider any other possibility:

> The Happy Consciousness—the belief that the real is rational and that the system delivers the goods— reflects the new conformism which is a facet of technological rationality translated into social behaviour. It is new because it is rational to an unprecedented degree. It sustains a society which has reduced—and in its most advanced areas eliminated—the more primitive irrationality of the preceding stages, which prolongs and improves life more regularly than before. The war of annihilation has not yet occurred; the Nazi extermination camps have been abolished. The Happy

Consciousness repels the connection. Torture has been re-introduced as a normal affair, but in a colonial war which takes place at the margin of the civilized world. And there it is practised with good conscience for war is war. And this war, too, is at the margin—it ravages only the ' underdeveloped ' countries. Otherwise peace reigns.

The power over man which this society has acquired is daily absolved by its efficacy and productiveness. If it assimilates everything it touches, if it absorbs the opposition, if it plays with the contradiction, it demonstrates its cultural superiority. And in the same way the destruction of resources and the proliferation of waste demonstrated its opulence and the ' high levels of well-being '; ' the Community is too well off to care! ' [32]

If we look, too, at *The Informed Heart*, Bruno Bettelheim's book of his experiences in Dachau and Buchenwald, we again find an area very similar to the Green Isle where men are reduced to ants because their freedom has been withdrawn and they behave purely in terms of a murderous insane closed system. ' The very essence of the total mass state,' says Bettelheim, ' is that it sets out to destroy individual *autonomy*.' [33]   Bettelheim relates much of the behaviour in the camps to a regressive, sadistic infantile parent/child relationship, and this again returns us to Gunn's central insight that the nature and quality of life depend fundamentally on the damage we do *not* do to our children. Perhaps nothing can now be more important to our survival than a renewed understanding of what Christ really meant in his teaching on the loving care that must be extended to the child.

Thus it is that the boy, Art, is the focus of value and rebellion in the book. He is the one person who will not allow his autonomy, his second self, to be broken. In this child Gunn creates a sense of superior integrity and, in spite of innocence, a superior wisdom. Thus Art is described at the moment of Old Hector's attempt to betray him by asking for Art, for the general good, to give himself up:

> As his clear child's eyes passed from one face to the other, in that remarkable interval of holding his rage, they were judged and condemned more surely than if the eyes were conscious of what they were doing. And, as if taken from them. there came into his eyes, too, a shadowy incredible simulacrum of age and cunning.[34]

We have already seen in *The Atom of Delight* Gunn's belief in the child's peculiar, innate ability to sense evil, and throughout the story Art is the only person who understands the pragmatism of what is happening for what it actually is, evil. He, therefore, is the exception that breaks the rule. ' In the end,' says Gunn, ' the diversion becomes the deviation that wrecks the system.' [35] And if the child diverts itself in the delight of running, it is a diversion that has deeper meaning. Gunn puts it thus in the autobiography:

> It was as if he had two selves and found the second self after going through the speed barrier. . . . That the boy raced away from the social complex that normally had him in its toils, from the breeding ground of emotional ambivalence, into a freedom where with his second self he got his second wind and a powerful feeling of delight there is no doubt.[36]

Thus in the fabulous and increasing quality of Art's running there is metaphysical as well as physical rebellion against a system of total restraint. It is this ability to run that creates in the population at first amazement, then a kind of legendary wonder and, finally, a kind of total and cleansing laughter as Art, assisted by God, makes his final escape from the Hunt.

Part of Art's legend is, of course, obviously derived from Celtic mythology. The book is developed from *Young Art and Old Hector*, and Art is both Cuchulain with his great hounds and Arthur, the king who will return when the land is most in need of him. He is both the mythical redeemer and art as well. Since Gunn believes that the child's powers are in any case innate to the creative artist, this is no mere name play. Thus, at the initial stage of Art's rebellion, the administration's analysis of his conduct is as follows:

> The first school said that Art was merely a name used to connote the activities of certain individuals in an earthly existence. These individuals had always been a source of trouble to those who had desired permanence in established thought and institution. These Art folk had a certain stinging or poisonous power.
> ... They found quite a subtle way of extracting his poison from the Art man or artist, for they discovered he was susceptible to flattery and loved to be paid enormous prices for his work. Why not therefore use him—to decorate their institutions.
> ... The technical term for this value was propaganda, and thus it became logically clear that all art not only partook of, but was in itself propaganda.[37]

Here, again, I consider Gunn to be socially prophetic. What I believe is extensively happening to art's powers of critique and protest in our time is that they are being metamorphosed by technology into the language of

consumer desire, the voice of advertising, and by bureau-
cracy into academic literary criticism. The wonderful
world of Marshall McLuhan provides the, as yet, culmination of both systems so that high finance, the academe, the
misuse of aesthetic form, the new technological media,
melodrama as the power to shape behaviour, are promoted
by a ranting demagogue in the name of a communal and,
inevitably, benevolent consciousness. It can only bleakly
be remarked that Gunn's belief in art as communal therapy
is of a very different level, and that which exists in the
Jungian Collective Unconscious is a different kind of beast
from the factory farm animals of the global village. Blake
believed that '. . . There is a vast Majority on the side of
Imagination or Spiritual Sensation '.[38] Gunn also believes
that the capacity for vision and imagination is latent in the
least of us and it is this potential that Art's rebellion taps.
We can only hope that he is correct.

If Art is the positive side of freedom in *The Green Isle
of the Great Deep* then it is surely man's analytic powers
that provide the negative. In *The Atom of Delight* Gunn
denotes the relationship between freedom and analysis
thus:

> In the same way, freedom is a fact while it is being
> experienced. Afterwards analysis in its familiar fashion
> will attempt to rationalise it, to find its determinants,
> but if the determinants are non-rational the attempt
> must fail, and accordingly any ' explanation ' will
> *appear* to explain away. One might say that as analysis
> destroys life in the amoeba so it destroys spontaneity
> in freedom. And if all this may look like an exercise
> in reason—I hope it does—at least it is directed towards
> indicating reason's sphere of action. For reason by its
> very nature will make an effort to work in all spheres,

and though this is one of its most valuable urges it has
got to be watched or presently it begins to develop
the familiar arrogance of the dictator and pooh-poohs
what is beyond its power to grasp, then inhibits or
suppresses it. . . . [39]

It is this kind of analytic power that is of the essence of
administrative practice in the novel. Gunn's presentation
of the blindness, shortcomings and power seeking of the
purely analytic mind is masterly. Analysis is brought to
bear by those rising *apparatchiks* Merk and Axle, and their
master—for it is a very hierarchic world—the Questioner,
on the virtues of Art, art, Old Hector, the 'peasant'
psychology and freedom itself. In these activities we
begin to understand the true nature of this kind of conduct.
The manner of analysis is neither neutral nor objective, as
one might innocently suppose, but rather in its stress on the
neutral and the objective, the logical and the positive,
wildly prejudiced. It is also arrogant in the sense that,
like technology itself, it has an implicit belief in the obso-
letion of the traditional values it assaults. Rather than a
scientific spirit, indeed, it is more a kind of superstitious
credo that the ability to classify things either renders them
impotent or explains them away. Its instinctive bias is
towards a cynical nominalism and a belief that the reduction
of virtue and value to its own terminology is somehow
an explanation or expression of these things.

What Gunn shows us in the autobiography and the
novel is that this kind of analysis is a dominant characteristic
of the modern mind and that its source lies in malice and in a
frightened, fundamental ignorance. That is to say that
analysis has misunderstood, perhaps deliberately, the way
in which 'non-rational determinants' are available to it

and, like the totalitarian mind itself, its real aim is to control without understanding and to reduce the higher functions of mind to a level with which it can feel comfortable. Implicit in the whole process is a deep-rooted fear of virtue, a subconscious terror of the mysterious religious dimension, and a consequent need to have power over it, by means of its pseudo-scientific black magic. Its final error, and final evil, is that its only perspective on things is one which sees everything—men, their relationships, their social systems, as aspects of power: a world of masters or victims.

It is Old Hector's fate in the novel to be the subject of the administration's full analytic drive. They attempt to peel him like an onion, believing in the void they are sure to find at the centre. Gunn finally describes the modern process of brainwashing which holds the promise of ' freedom ' if the victim will only surrender.

> There is a pitch beyond which no burden, no pressure can be borne. Once the dam is burst, confession comes in a stream, complete and absolute, destroying every barrier, washing away every obstruction. It is freedom, freedom, and the body and the mind wallow in it.
> . . . The Questioner's eyes, watching the old man narrowed. It was truly remarkable—the fight left in that aged body. Clearly, here was the case of the primitive mind with its parallel in the lower forms of animal life. Break it into bits, and each bit wriggles.
> For the first time, the lust of his quest got into the Questioner's eyes. His breathing became a trifle more rapid. For interest now lay in some new suggestion of an indefinable region where the old man might have achieved a primitive integration, a certain living wisdom. The old man's weakness, his only personal

lust, was a manifest hatred of cruelty. But that again was unfortunately balanced by an equal capacity to take punishment.

. . . Until at last the old man could bear no more, and crashing round, like some old stag of his native forest, raised his stricken head and stood at bay.

The Questioner felt a small shiver from that challenge. The whole primordial world stood still, this world, and all the universe of men and time.

And upon this silence, holding the Questioner by the eyes, Old Hector spoke deep out of his throat:

" I want to see God." [40]

In dramatic form this presents us with Gunn's belief that analysis finally comes to that which its paranoidal self-awareness has perhaps always feared. It breaks through not into a void but a final core of irreducible freedom and plenitude: that area in which neither the child nor the old man will surrender. We will turn in a moment to our final discussion of the book as a religious statement, but it can be noted that Gunn suggests that if we have the courage and integrity God can be summoned.

Thus Old Hector's testing of his courage and wisdom takes place in the full fury of the modern mind. Nor is it any easy victory for him—some forgone symbolic conclusion. The book's considerable triumph is that it is able to present, at one and the same time, character realistically as well as metaphysically. The physical, psychological and spiritual elements are perfectly blended so that the dialogue is consistently ambivalent though rarely ambiguous. Gunn has an innate talent for fusing different dimensions of experience within his characters so that, while having a symbolic function, they are never merely that alone.

Old Hector is, therefore, a man of strengths and weaknesses. If his ancestral wisdom grants him enormous virtue there is also within his heritage potential sources for disaster. There is in him, perhaps as a consequence of Calvinism, a debilitating sense of his own unworthiness, a peculiar mixture of admirable natural modesty and masochistic inferiority, to which the Highland personality seems particularly prone. Calvinism as a religion can also have terrifying consequences either in the fatalism or the megalomania it induces in the social sphere. Thus, when he asks Robert if they ever rebelled against the encroaching power of the administration, Robert replies:

> " Did you rise against the lairds and the factors and the clergy when they told you that you had to be cleared off your own ancient lands and your homes burnt down? "
> " No," said Old Hector sadly.[41]

Thus Old Hector's physical exhaustion in the face of constant questionings is also indicative of a deeper spiritual weariness, a sense of unworthiness and a sense of cultural defeat engendering quietism, even defeatism, in the face of the challenge. Gunn's sense of tradition, then, is not that it exists as an unmixed force for good. It may also entail a loss of nerve. Indeed Iain Crichton Smith, a younger Highland writer, takes an even more pessimistic view of his inheritance.

> In fact, the thing I find most terrifying about the Highlands is the passiveness of the Highlander. My book about the Highland Clearances [*Consider the Lilies*] is not historically great, but I certainly did read certain things about the Clearances, and the thing that struck me and everybody at the time was the way

in which the Highlanders seemed to accept what happened to them at the Highland Clearances without doing anything about it.[42]

Old Hector's ability, however, is, to repeat Faulkner's terms, not only to endure but prevail. His innate strength overcomes his weakness and his final request to have an audience with God causes the book to enter in overt, dramatic terms the dimension of religious myth that has from the beginning been embodied in its symbolism and meaning. To understand this remarkable novel deeply we must see it in terms of religious legend similar to that which Dostoevsky created in *The Brothers Karamazov*. Gunn, indeed, has Dostoevsky capacity to see through the texture of society and psychology into the underlying movement of the spirit.

Thus it is that we find religious legend and parable running like sinews through the flesh of the story. We are reminded of the consequences of selling our birthright for a mess of pottage and, more important, of the archetypal Genesis story of the fall. If, Gunn says, the fall brought us into a tragic, terrifying awareness of good and evil, how much more terrible would it be to go beyond this to a state where we did *not* know good from evil. In such a condition we would not be free but in a condition of spiritual entropy. We would be beyond good and evil not in Nietzsche's self-aggrandising way, the triumphant dance of the *Ubermensch*, but in the treadmill of the herd animal. This, of course, is why the administration prevents the people from eating the fruit of the trees. Old Hector asks Robert:

" Was the fruit on the trees forbidden? "

" If I offered you such fruit now, would you take
it? " asked Robert with a mocking glance.

" But why did they bother with the fruit? "

" Because the fruit is the fruit of life," answered
Robert.

" *The tree of life also in the midst of the garden,*" issued
Old Hector's voice softly from the Book of Genesis.[43]

Thus for Gunn the tree of knowledge is also the tree of
life, because without knowledge of good and evil man is
not free. The consequence of this knowledge can be
tragic, are never less than painful, frequently agonising,
but the knowledge is necessary to the divine within us.
This is precisely the ground of Dostoevsky's Grand Inquisitor's complaint against Christ.

Thou didst know, Thou couldst not but have known,
this fundamental secret of human nature, but Thou
didst reject the one infallible banner which was offered
Thee to make all men bow down to Thee alone—the
banner of earthly bread; and Thou hast rejected it for
the sake of freedom and the bread of Heaven. . . . But
what happened? Instead of taking men's freedom
from them, Thou didst make it greater than ever!
Didst Thou forget that man prefers peace and even
death, to freedom of choice in the knowledge of good
and evil? Nothing is more seductive for man than his
freedom of conscience, but nothing is a greater cause
of suffering. And behold, instead of giving a firm
foundation for setting the conscience of man at rest for
ever, Thou didst choose all that is exceptional, vague and
enigmatic; Thou didst choose what was utterly beyond
the strength of men, acting as though Thou didst not
love them at all—Thou who didst come to give Thy
life for them! Instead of taking possession of men's
freedom, Thou didst increase it, and burdened the

spiritual kingdom of mankind with its sufferings for
ever. Thou didst desire man's free love, that he should
follow Thee freely, enticed and taken captive by Thee.
In place of the rigid ancient law, man must hereafter
with free heart decide for himself what is good and what
is evil, having only Thy image before him as his guide.[44]

It is the Grand Inquisitor's atheistic contention, as it is
the Devil's struggling with Christ in the wilderness, that
men will refuse to accept the suffering that freedom entails.
It is, consequently, the basis of *The Green Isle of the Great
Deep* as it is *The Brothers Karamazov* to provide creative
and credible answers to the voice of the devil in his latest
manifestation of power politics and humanitarian benevolence. Both books are in the form of a dialectic between
the forces of oppression and individuals struggling to find
freedom and faith.

Thus it is that there is in them no division between the
political and the spiritual spheres of action since one entails
the other. Dostoevsky, prophetically, and Gunn through
undoubtedly bitter personal experience, perceive the
development of the political forces in our age as being in
response to our desire for, and yet terror of, freedom.
For the political mind of our time the answer is an easy
one: the practical demands of the situation are such that
modern technology and social structure require mass
obedience. Obedience that is imposed from above. As
Robert tells Hector:

> "One day there and all your doubts will vanish.
> You will understand with a new freshness the sin of
> disobedience. You will realise that obedience is the
> highest of all virtues, for in it is order, and seemliness,

and an end to the burden of thought and decision. Man's curse has been the curse of disobedience." [45]

Later in the book the Newcomer elaborates the consequences of such order:

> " For the truth was so obvious—that every nation was seeking order, an order in which their only possible salvation as social communities lay. And we had almost perfected the means of achieving it! Earth folk, being what they are, order can be achieved only by the few at the top. Earth folk instinctively realise that. They have always made, and still make, gods of their leaders. In war that is essential. In peace time, should they no longer do it, they crumble. You cannot have obedience without belief, and without obedience you perish. That's the historic law—everywhere. We were merely advanced enough to give it body and form—and to create the machinery that would ensure its permanence." [46]

Thus what Gunn so clearly portrays in *The Green Isle* is the capacity of modern politics and technology to do evil in the name of good. They have created a mechanised food system in factories cut into the mountains, a literal turning of stones into bread. The population is impotent before such ' miracles ' of ingenuity. They are apostles of the belief in closed systems, in the redundance of individual conscience, and they place their faith in the historically determining force of materialism and their ability to administrate the necessary conformity to this force.

Thus Gunn's administrators dwell in a world of statistics and benevolence. But what is the final nature of this benevolence? As Gunn has the voice of God say in his final interview with the Head:

Meantime you might think over the contention that at the core of a theory or a plan, *in addition to the highest intention there can abide self-delusion and the last refinement of cruelty.*[47]

Like Dostoevsky's legend, this novel also understands the temptation of the administrative mind to move from the candied hand to the iron fist. Starting with expressions of pragmatic goodwill, we enter the iron kingdom of necessity and find that the deepest desire of the functionary is to have his way at whatever cost, and that the need to control other men is related to self-deification. Thus again we move from social and political comment to those more mysterious regions of the spirit where man in the name of good does evil. The tragedy of this sort of mind, as well as the terror it must inevitably cause, is its lack of self-consciousness. It usurps human rights, especially freedom, because it is cynical of man's nature and yet it fails to understand that the very things it despises in the human—cruelty, aggression, power-seeking—must exist in even more concentrated form in the allegedly divine structures it creates to control these forces. As Mark Schorer says of Blake:

The conception of man as a selfish creature, and the resulting necessity of authority, which passes into the hands of the most selfish, ends in every tragic social paradox Blake pursues.[48]

The Green Isle of the Great Deep, although profoundly serious, does not end in tragedy but comedy. In opposition to authoritarian terror Gunn presents us with characters and forces which he believes are the fundamental and finally triumphant human ones.

What marks these characters is their depth, their sense of commitment and belonging, and their capacity to endure suffering. For Art it is the capacity to endure the loneliness of the woods cut off from all men, unable to trust even Old Hector. Old Hector himself suffers, indeed he almost gives way not because of his own suffering but his terror of causing suffering in others—an act of genuine benevolence which, even so, still endangers freedom. Mary, too, because she has not lost the capacity to suffer for the child she lost on earth, suffers for Art and, in her wisdom, will not be broken and betray him.

All this, for me, makes Gunn a profoundly religious writer because he understands creatively the relationship between suffering and truth. He sees, like Dostoevsky and Faulkner, that without a final sense of truth that transcends all relative and pragmatic actions we are lost and that freedom and truth are related. He also understands that if we chain ourselves to the necessity of a purely materialist philosophy we again destroy our freedom and our capacity for charity—our capacity to give freely. When Art and Hector first appear Tom tells Mary that it is not their business to feed the stranger. The book's final meaning is that this is precisely our business and in this it is like all Gunn's work: an appeal for grace and charity, spontaneity of the body and freedom of the mind. In a nation like ours, so given over to legalised moralising, there can be no more meaningful appeal.

NOTES ON REFERENCES

1   While it is far beyond the scope of the present paper to discuss the validity of MacDiarmid's assertion about the

place of freedom in the Scottish tradition, it can certainly
be advanced that in their thinking about freedom Gunn
and MacDiarmid are very similar. Both writers believe
that freedom and imagination are essential to one another
and that such freedom must be sought outwith systems.
Thus in *The Drunk Man Looks at the Thistle* MacDiarmid
says:

> I ha'e nae doot some foreign philosopher
> Has wrocht a system oot to justify
> A' this: but I'm a Scot wha' blin'ly follows
> Auld Scottish instincts, and I winna try.
>
> For I've nae faith in ocht I can explain,
> And stert whaur the philosophers leave aff,
> Content to glimpse its loops I dinna ettle
> To land the sea serpent's sel' wi' ony gaff.

Thus, too, in both men creativity is constantly at war
with what is felt to be a kind of spiritual deadness: a
calcifying of spirit into mere organisation. As MacDiarmid ironically puts it in his ' Lament for the Great Music ',
a superb poem written round this theme:

> The great music has had a real if imponderable influence
> On subsequent piping after all—like Christ on the Kirk!

Indeed one could say that MacDiarmid's major
preoccupation is a war he wages for the divine artist
against the demonic bureaucrat: life against death, spirit
against matter, genuine individuality against mass coercion.
  Finally both men are attracted to Dostoevsky's thought
on the nature of freedom, especially the Legend of the
Grand Inquisitor, for, as MacDiarmid says, this shows how
' all human organizations become conspiracies to short-
circuit the development of human consciousness. . . .'

2 Isaac Rosenfeld, ' Faulkner's Two Styles ', *An Age of
   Enormity* (New York: World Publishing Co., 1962), 269.
3 William Faulkner, ' A Word to Young Writers ', *Faulkner
   in the University* (Charlottesville: The University of
   Virginia Press, 1959), 242.
4 Ibid., 244-5.
5 Finn in *The Silver Darlings* is probably the best-known
   example.

6   Gunn, *The Green Isle of the Great Deep* (London: Faber, 1944), 114.
7   Gunn, *The Atom of Delight* (Faber, 1956), 69.
8   Patrick White, 'The Prodigal Son', *Australian Letters* (April 1958), 38.
9   Saul Bellow, 'The Art of Fiction XXXVII', *Paris Review*, 36 (Winter 1966), 57. This passage can be interestingly compared with Gunn's statement in *The Atom of Delight* (294) that in the creative act 'possibly an underlying prompter has been concerned to give even an autobiographic fragment some sort of design as though, haunted by the old feeling " this is not what matters ", the prompter had to find from experience what did matter. But as the prompter is no longer the boy, though he includes the boy, what did matter will also tend to be what does matter. What mattered and what matters will be on the same way. The selective process, forever active in whatever man does or makes, will see to that, even thought it be as non-rational as a coral polyp'.
10 F. M. Dostoevsky, 'A Conversation with a Moscow Acquaintance of Mine', *Diary of a Writer* (New York: George Braziller, 1954), 752-3.
11 Gunn, *The Atom of Delight*, 119.
12 Ibid., 24.
13 Ibid., 87.
14 Ibid., 29-30.
15 Ibid., 145.
16 Ibid., 133.
17 Ibid., 289.
18 Ibid., 162.
19 Ibid., 222.
20 Ibid., 284-5.
21 Simone Weil, *The Need for Roots* (London: Routledge & Kegan Paul, 1952), 207. Mme Weil's notion of a modern industrial and rural Christian society—post Capitalist *and* post Marxist—seems to me to offer many fruitful parallels with Gunn's social thought.
22 William Blake, 'Letter 5. To Dr Trussler, 23 August 1799', *Complete Writings* (London: Oxford University Press, 1966), 793-4.
23 Gunn, *The Atom of Delight*, 22.

24   *The Green Isle of the Great Deep*, 13.
25   Ibid., 22.
26   Ibid., 68.
27   Ibid., 41.
28   Ibid., 255.
29   Ibid., 245-6.
30   C. G. Jung, *Psychology and Religion* (New Haven: Yale University Press, 1964), 18. A wealth of fruitful material would almost certainly emerge from a deeper study of Gunn in relation to Jung's psychological and religious thought.
31   *The Green Isle of the Great Deep*, 254.
32   Herbert Marcuse, *One Dimensional Man* (London: Sphere Books, 1970), 77.
33   Bruno Bettelheim, *The Informed Heart* (London: Paladin, 1970), 267.
34   *The Green Isle of the Great Deep*, 117.
35   *The Atom of Delight*, 10.
36   Ibid., 83/90.
37   *The Green Isle of the Great Deep*, 131-2.
38   Blake, 'Letter to Dr Trussler', 794.
39   *The Atom of Delight*, 289-90.
40   *The Green Isle of the Great Deep*, 154-5.
41   Ibid., 98.
42   'Poet in Bourgeois Land', Interview with Iain Crichton Smith, *Scottish International* (September 1971), 27.
43   *The Green Isle of the Great Deep*, 98.
44   F. M. Dostoevsky, *The Brothers Karamazov* (London: Four Square, 1958), 266-77.
45   *The Green Isle of the Great Deep*, 92.
46   Ibid., 46.
47   Ibid., 218.
48   Mark Schorer, *William Blake—The Politics of Vision* (New York: Vintage Books, 1959), 242.

NEIL M. GUNN

Three portraits

Handling the Unbearable :
The Serpent *and* The Drinking Well

GEORGE BRUCE

The bird flies in the mind and more than bird—

Norman MacCaig

'They forget,' wrote William Carlos Williams of literary critics, 'that literature, like all other effects by genius, transcends the material, no matter what it is. That it by itself raises the thing observed into a rarer field.' The comment is relevant to the material of Neil Gunn's novels, yet the impression made by the earlier novels such as *Morning Tide* and *Highland River*, is that they are the servants of truths that are in the lives that the novelist describes, that he has made articulate what was there but what had not been previously expressed. To have achieved this in the 1930s in the form, largely, of the popular novel was unexpected. Rightly, I believe, the novel was under suspicion on account of its commercial exploitation and its incapacity to take account of the complex psychological situation of those disinherited from their past by the destruction of traditional ways of living and of belief. What required restating, or rather stated in a new way, was that though the experiences which Neil Gunn described in the novels referred to are peripheral to urban society they are not peripheral to life. Not that I consider it is advantageous for a novelist to work in a mode which does not

H

take account of new developments in ideation and techniques. The Scottish novel was still suffering from the blight of the Kailyard, while the pabulum of the majority of Scottish readers was that bathetic offspring of the patch, the stories of Annie S. Swan and her like. So far from the material of Scottish life being transcended it had been traduced. Lewis Grassic Gibbon's rescue operation was achieved by what amounted to a confrontation; Neil Gunn's as if the quality and character of the life was simply waiting for recognition. The form and style of *Morning Tide* and *Highland River* seemed to grow out of the material as naturally as leaves to the tree. The cases of *The Serpent* and *The Drinking Well* are different.

The titles of those books indicate symbolic intentions. Whereas Neil Gunn recognised that symbolism was implicit in the ebb in *Morning Tide* only after he had written the book, symbolism relates to the construction of *The Serpent* and *The Drinking Well*. Yet the stories are more in line with the popular novel of the day. In both a young man leaves his native village for the city, Tom in *The Serpent* to work in an ironmonger's shop in Glasgow, Iain in *The Drinking Well* to be a law apprentice in Edinburgh. Both have love affairs, both return to their native places, and both have strained and tragic relations with their fathers. Without the symbolism one might have felt there was enough in the stories to make a novel, but the novelist is not content to create a sense of place and persons —which he does justly in country and in town. He requires a measure, a perspective on the events which he depicts. The symbols by themselves will not be this but they are indices of the abstraction from the flow of life, which may give a frame of reference for the happenings. Yet the word

' abstraction ' may be misleading, for the judgements on the comings and goings of Neil Gunn's people that are wisest and are most meaningful are made from within. In *The Serpent* there is an event as symbolic as the title, one which is more germane to the purpose of the novel and which inevitably provides a structure and a stance for the novelist—Tom's ascent of the hill, whereon he recollects his past and comments on it with the wisdom of his years. This is one of the means whereby the novelist ' transcends the material ' and ' raises the thing observed into a rarer field ', one of the means because this is a novel of comparatives, one area of life being set against another, the deepest wisdom coming from the woman who has learned by suffering and who belongs to a continuity of experience that does not change with changing society.

As Tom ascends the hill life spreads out beneath him. The device allows for his observation of the changing village below, of his increasing detachment from it, of the new dimensions entering the novel as one experience is set down alongside another. Unity encompassing diversity is achieved without any sense of strain and yet I have to admit that at the point when the symbolism of the title is made explicit, when at the top of the hill the serpent slips up the sleeve of the resting old man and he dies, I sense a contrivance. Not that the event could not happen. One knows that whenever Neil Gunn strains credibility—as in the size of the salmon Kenn caught in *Highland River*—the impossibility actually happened. Many times Neil Gunn, when a boy, had seen the head of an adder appear unobtrusively a handsbreadth away beside a rock on which he sat in the Strath of the Water of Dunbeath. It could well have entered the sleeve of a sleeping old man. Further, the novelist does not suggest that he died from the bite of the snake. He was an old man. He might have died from shock. With characteristic tact the matter is left open, and the focus shifts to the shepherd who has, in the course of carrying on his traditional occupation, found Tom dead. Tom had been a mender of clocks, the mechanical instrument that registers the passing of time and so change. The shepherd belonged to the near-unchanging occupation that goes back to the tap-root of human existence. This is true, a beautiful ending to a novel of rare quality. Nevertheless I draw attention to the tightrope a novelist walks who wishes to extend experience at a time when the actual does not readily yield the symbol. Tom had, at one stage of his life, been called Tom the Serpent. The serpent is to be found in Gaelic mythology—it is healer and destroyer. All these seem to legitimise the use. Perhaps my suspicion is unwarrantable.

It is the case, however, that *The Drinking Well*, which relies more heavily on the explicit symbol of the well which contains the never-ending water of life, is less unified and has a less defined perspective throughout than *The Serpent*. Both symbols point to the ending of a traditional way of seeing life. Neither generates the idea of symbolism immediately, and therefore they do not act in the mind at both levels unconsciously. In *The Drinking Well* the well is associated with ' mad Maraig '. The concept of the old woman who is outside society and has special insights, had been previously splendidly realised in dark Mairi in *Butcher's Broom*. Dark Mairi was central to the story and she belonged to the ' productive processes ' of her day. Her wisdom was accepted by the traditional society of which she was a member. The society which rejected her was that which drove her and hers from her home. She was first and foremost a mother and wife. The problem of depicting mad Mairig begins with her not possessing a valid verbal currency. One is aware of a Gaelic background to the speech, and Neil Gunn with his fine ear catches the atmosphere but not the natural vigour of speech. Towards the end of *The Drinking Well*, when Mary is hoping desperately that her lover will seek her out at Maraig's cottage, Maraig says:

> " They all come back, one way or another. But his feet were heavy feet, and Nancy heard him going to the well. I found him there. Wasn't it clever of me? "

The brief quotation suggests the risk of working on the margin of social experience, where there is no longer the society to provide the collaboration which renewed and gave validity to the art of the Irish dramatist, Synge.

What is remarkable, however, is not that *The Drinking Well* is flawed, but that in this novel of the 1940s vivid imaginative writing made out of traditional attitudes to life, when placed alongside carefully observed experience of social and legal life in Edinburgh, becomes the measure of the Edinburgh experience. Not that the novelist sets out to denigrate the life in Edinburgh. It is as fairly and vigorously described as is the life in Glasgow in *The Serpent*. Just where the virtue of the novels lies is the concern of this essay.

At the simplest level—the description of what the Philosopher sees from the hillside, the introduction of the direction in which the novel is to go, the picking up of names that are to be of interest later, Huxley, Darwin, Robert Owen, Haekel, the reference to Tom's mother—all this, compressed but with no sense of compression into the opening pages, is an admirable strategic beginning to *The Serpent*. At the same time the author has more significant concerns expressed through this material. The first image that Tom presents is ' . . . the ground around his feet . . .' and he goes on to see that ' The wild roses had just come into bloom, pink roses and white, and the broom was yellow as meadowland butter with an eddy of scent now and then that choked the brain like a sickly sweet narcotic '. The old man is going to die within a few hours, the reader has been told at the outset, and he ascends the hill as spring changes into summer.

Throughout the book change is played off against what does not change. When the Philosopher lifts his eyes he sees distant below him a red petrol pump. There were changes long before this innovation.

> Here, towards the eastern seaboard, the fertile low ground of the glens had been cleared of the folk and turned into great arable farms. Except for those left in the village, the folk had been swept up to the moors to the heights.

The novelist through the mind of the Philosopher comments:

> Changes often appeared to be violent, and indeed were so frequently enough, but it was remarkable how, little by little, change was accepted into the lifetime of a man so fully, so fatally, that bitterness itself was forgotten.

The point of change is reinforced by Tom considering the changes in his own lifetime. Then against the idea of change the novelist states:

> But the village had remained down below, in that wide basin of broken ground, perhaps because here were

gathered together certain indispensable trades and craftsmen, the blacksmith, the joiner, the merchant, the schoolmaster, postmaster, and by inevitable complement, the widowed woman, the old maid, the young girl who went out to service, the young man who learned a trade or went gillieing, or, from carrying a small bursary to the secondary school in town, flowered miraculously into a university student.

Yet it was still attached to the soil, a crofting hamlet, and as he looked the Philosopher saw figures singling their turnips in between the green cornfields on the narrow cultivated lands behind the houses. With their slightly bent heads they moved so slowly that it was easy to get the illusion of an inner meaning or design that never changed.

An effect of distance is to make movements appear slower than they are, so the description of figures moving at their natural business yet giving the impression of going through a ritual, repeating what had been done many times and many ages before, comes from observation. What is seen translates itself into a symbolic act. But Neil Gunn is observing the scene through the eyes of the *Philosopher* and so he comments ' it was easy to get the illusion of an inner meaning. . . .' The observer is under inspection by the novelist. The phrasing is true to the wry scepticism of Tom, who acquired the epithet, *Philosopher*, in mockery. The scepticism is true to the inquiring, practical mind of the man who had gone to Glasgow to mend clocks, had immersed himself in the advanced thinking of the day, had taken part in discussions on the idea of socialism, and who had suffered the arbitrary mishaps of life. This is one aspect of the man, for ' he had taken to the Glasgow life, the life of the streets almost at once and with a real avidity. . . . For a boy out of the Highland country, this may have been unusual, but then he had always had a zest for life, particularly the outsider's zest'.

Neither scepticism, nor irony, has the last word. The presence of both are salutary, as is the zest for life. The complete texture of response is presented in the opening pages—even the judgements which finally place the varied experiences of living that are described in the novel. Characteristically the knowledge that gives meaning to experience comes from the intuitive woman—the mother. Neil Gunn introduces her thus:

> Yet whenever the image of his mother came to mind, at once life moved on its feet, working and suffering. And immediately other pictures were begot—of his father, the fields, the croft work, school days, sunny stretches of countryside. A small stout dark woman, forever busy. He remembered the little scraps of letters he had got from her when he was in Glasgow . . . these scraps, painfully and probably secretly written, had a curious suppressed warmth, though they attended entirely to physical needs. The ordinary phrase ' see and be eating plenty ' could make him laugh and feel awkward, and even, if he thought about it, slightly hot. It was almost as if she had come into the room and spoken to him with others there.

The hints of an inner more durable secret life are there, not associated with marginal aspects of life, as is mad Mairag in *The Drinking Well*, but with the day-to-day necessities, as is the mother in *Morning Tide*—' She was the starting point of a circle that finished in her '—and the mother in *The Drinking Well*. Has any other writer written with such understanding, such delicacy and intimacy, with such a living phrase and with such security about the mother figure? But 'mother figure' is incorrect, for Gunn always depicts different mothers. Each is individual, yet each being subject to the same natural conditions, personal and environmental, is also the mother. In the last resort her wisdom is the wisdom of mother earth, and therefore cannot be made fully articulate. It can only be implied. This Neil Gunn understands. Yet a simple phrase about ordinary needs dismisses to the shadows Tom's hectic encounter with the prostitute in a Glasgow street. Back in his lodgings he takes up his mother's letter again. ' Take care of yerself now and see you and be eating all you can. . . .' The juxtaposition of the elementary condition which in the country relates to living and dying turns the episode to phantasmagoria. And also the movement of the language itself—' Take care of yerself . . .'—has reality written into it by generations of mothers in Scotland seeing their sons off to the big city or to anywhere for the first time. This is the kind of collaboration Synge meant when he refers to overhearing the language of servant girls in an old house in Wicklow. Synge's interest, however, was in the copiousness and colour of the Irish tongue, and Neil Gunn's, in this case, in the naked thew and sinew of the language. Later in the book, where he is presenting his scene of ' recognition '—' anagnorisis '—when the mother has come to look for Tom on the hill, the moment of recognition, and therefore of climax, is registered without direct speech. Then Tom is seeing beyond what his scepticism, what his serpent mind, what the new biology and politics of the city could teach him.

' Unreal city '. But the city has its own validity, and is only felt to be unreal when its terms of reference are put in balance with the language and living of another world.

H 2

There are a series of confrontations in *The Serpent*; Tom
meeting the prostitute—though that is a rout; Tom meeting
Winnie Johnston, the student, and being faced with the
demand to declare his love, and more seriously Tom's
confrontation with his father, and there are others. Running
through them there is the confrontation of reasoning with
instinct or intuition. Tom is reasoning man in Glasgow
welcoming the progressive ideas of the late nineteenth
century, yet more than reasoning man. Neil Gunn puts
the personality into a single sentence: ' At twenty-three
youth can be more positive than age, but there is a sensitiveness, a capacity for pain and horror, for sheer formless
apprehension, that age forgets.' When Winnie asked him
to declare his love, despite his affection for her he found
that ' The reluctance that came upon him was amazingly
strong. Something inside him that would not give way or
be given away '. The attitude does not belong to the
reasoning city man, but he was never a city man, and
because the city, while providing opportunities for enterprise
and friendship, can be no more than itself—a useful ordered
society—no betrayal could happen in it which would
destroy Tom completely.

A parallel episode in the country is another matter
altogether. He could not believe his country girl Janet
would deceive him. Neil Gunn interprets Tom's mind.

> Had he expected something different in the country,
> with its ancient customs and decencies and loyalties?
> He had never really been part of the Glasgow scene.
> He had observed the scene with an extreme clarity,
> taken part in it as far as need be, but something in him
> had held back. . . . This was his scene—here, at home.
> Not Glasgow, known and honest. This.

By implication, here, his country could not be known,
as Glasgow could because there were drives and insights
too deep behind the logic of arranged life to be compre-
hended. Apprehended they might be. If he is sceptic
only, he does not belong to this scene. The exposition of
the dual nature of man, by exposing the returned Tom to
the life that his native place provides, gives a reading of life
which places the book at the centre of Neil Gunn's achievement, and makes it mandatory reading to all who profess a
knowledge of twentieth-century fiction.

One notes how Tom becomes involved with Janet.
There is the chance element in the recollection of the
beginning of the episode. The Philosopher is on his way
up the hill.

> At once, as though he had been climbing strongly, his
> breath quickened and a dizzying shadow passed before
> his eyes. His mind quickened, and the orgy of sex and
> of the earth that had overwhelmed him here long ago
> touched his body so that it momentarily weakened into
> the living effluence of the past scene. Then, looking
> up, he saw the goat.
> The long, narrow, dark pupils in the pale yellow
> eyes, the air of indifference that was yet watchful, the
> slanting measuring look of the antique world.

There follows the account of the goat being dropped down
the chimney—' a great hole in the roof'—of Margad's
cottage, where some girls from the village were celebrating
Hallowe'en. ' Panic fear ' takes over—the phrase was Neil
Gunn's in a conversation—and Tom runs after Janet, whom
he does not recognise. The writer links the Scottish
festival, held on 1st November, All Saints' Day (and also
the date of the Celtic Festival of Samhuinn), with Pan—half

man, half beast. Hallowe'en itself was a mixture of
Christian and pagan ceremonies. The episode ended for
Tom in tenderness and concern because the girl was afraid,
but it also brought him into closer touch with the loyalties
and modes of feeling which took him beyond the rational.
The comment runs:

> On that Hallowe'en his intellectual assurance had been
> dealt one of those invisible blows that scatter elements in
> a bewildering fashion. Dealt not by known Gods,
> whom the anthropologists and the religious analyse
> with so omniscient or reverent a care, but by some dark
> fellow who simply lets out a wallop! As a boy gets a
> sudden wallop on the side of his head from his father
> and sits down among the ruins of his pride yelling blue
> murder.

I find the dismissal of the anthropologists and the religious a
little facile and the substitution of ' some dark fellow ' and
the word ' wallop ' as explanations fails to reassure me that
the interpretation of the events is adequate. The fault, if
I am correct in my assessment, is less in the writer and more
in the condition of the medium. ' The language of the
tribe ', to use Pound's phrase, is in poor shape. To be
explicit about certain heightened mental or emotional states
is to be at risk. When, on the other hand, Neil Gunn works
his meaning through the object, and the object that presents
itself to him may come loaded with meaning, then those
areas of experience that are not readily accessible make their
presence felt in a credible way. The hysteria of Hallowe'en
is given a context in the opening of Chapter VI when the
goat is about to take leave of the Philosopher:

> . . . then reluctantly making up his mind about it,
> walked on his delicate nimble hoofs in between two

junipers and on and in among yellow-flowered broom. But he was not done with the Philosopher yet for his head, rising above the fragrant broom, turned, so that there was the head alone looking at the Philosopher out of the long narrow pupils. It had the stillness of stone, symmetric horns curving backward, the carven head of an antique world.

In his essay ' Passion and Hysteria in Modern Drama ', Professor Ralph S. Walker remarks on the tendency of hysteria to act as a substitute for passion in plays written within the past twenty years or so. He gives several reasons relating to conditions in contemporary society. One is the absence of an appropriate context for feeling. Without a context of time, or a sense that at least a civil order exists, there tends to be left as final expression nothing more than a scream. The oblique Greek reference in the appearance of the goat, which is presented with good humour rather than with irony, suggests that the events of the story are within yet another context than that of Tom's mind.

At the beginning the reader is told that the tale ends in the tragic death of the hero. He is an only son who returns home to destroy—by the betrayal of traditional beliefs— his father. His understanding of the nature of life is a reversal, peripeteia, of the principles he holds when he sets out. The understanding comes largely through the ' recognition ' of his mother. The parallel must not be pressed, but two expressed points relate—the predestined tragedy, the events being therefore fated, and the idea of traditional ways of living being part of a ritual. The latter idea is conveyed in hints, sometimes no more than the suggestion that people in certain situations are unconsciously repeating age-old patterns. There is never at any moment the suggestion of a concept being imposed on the novel, but the strongest and most dramatic moment is not in the descriptions of the extremities of feeling, such as Tom's frenzy after the death of his father, but when he sees his mother on the hillside, when she has become the healing mother earth. Deep feeling amounting to a passion for life is conveyed largely by describing what Tom sees. The success is in relating the actuality to a productive field of reference. In the parallel crisis, the death of Tom's father, the novelist has to be more explicit in creating a context, but the symbolic allusions rise directly from the developments of the story. They are art and part of it.

First it is natural that Tom, called home to help on the croft on account of his father's illness, should wish to use the craftsmanship he has learned. This leads to his attempt to set up a shop and to his father's claim that crofting was good enough for him; why not for the son? Tom has become, to his father, modern man who would change the old ways and deny God. Tom, therefore, is the serpent. He is named as such by William the Elder in an argument on the authority of the Bible. "For I see the serpent within you," shouts William. "I see its evil coils twisting in your body and brain." Tom's father enters.

> The grey face, the grey beard, the blazing eyes, the silent pursuing face—it had come at last. The power of the father created in the image of God. The tribal power, the unearthly power. Each felt it and Tom could not move.
>
> The father gazed upon his son with a fixity of expression more terrible than all words. In silence he groped for William's staff. He took a slow step nearer to his son, and, in the short pause that followed, the intention of the chastisement gathered in a concentration

horrible to behold. Then the hand with the staff went up, not quickly but with deliberation. It rose, until it rose high above his head, then in a moment the stiffness of the arm slackened, the stick fell, bouncing off Tom's chest, the arm wavered down, the body sagged, and with a deep soft grunt it collapsed upon itself, pitching forward slightly before Tom's feet.

In the passage the issues are simplified and narrowed. The father in the name of God will kill the serpent, his son. Appropriately it takes on the hieratical tone of the Old Testament in such terms as ' chastisement ' and ' horrible to behold '. Then again the father moves as a priest might, performing slowly and deliberately a ritual killing. One notes the contrast between the stiffness of the arm and the body sagging ' with a deep soft grunt '. The assertions and affirmations become a soft grunt, and at that moment there may be a hint that the issue is not simply between the tribal god and the new man, but more accurately between a particular institutionalised kind of religion, which has its own rationale, and which it is possible to affirm or reject. Tom had entered the debate on those terms. The death of the father occurs within those terms, but they are not the final terms of reference of the author. Despite the observations of a kind of ritual, its connotation is limited. There is no reverberation beyond itself, as there was when the Philosopher looked down on the ' figures singling their turnips ' with their slow movement giving the impression of ' an inner meaning or design that never changed '.

Tom's enlightenment comes through the acceptance of life through suffering. But first all that he treasures must be destroyed. Janet betrays him and dies. He is suspected of being the father of her unborn child and of murdering her. Distraught, he takes to the hills. Then comes the climax of the tale:

> As the sun was touching the mountain, he heard a cry far down the slope on his left, where boulders and bits of scrub littered the ground before it began to rise again. He looked and saw a squat human figure get up and stumble on. Then it stood, and he heard again its forlorn cry: " Tom! "
> It was his mother.
> . . . Though she moved slowly she had the appearance of going with earnestness and haste, as a dog seeking the scent of its quarry. Now she leaned with a hand against a boulder, stooping slightly, like one drawing harsh laboured breaths. Then on again; but the ground was broken and her exhaustion must have been very great, for, when she stumbled and fell, she drooped in upon herself, like one of the boulders, and, listening acutely, he heard the dry whining of her distress.
> He got up and slanted down the hillside towards her. But while he was yet a little way off, she got to her feet to continue her journey towards the horizon she had set before her. As he drew in behind her on her right side, she became familiar to him as his mother, in her body and its movements and its laboured breath. The familiarity touched him sharply and in order not to startle her too much he called from twenty yards: " Mother! "

This surely must be one of the purest passages in English prose. Gunn, using the most direct and economical means, conveys with a kind of vibrating accuracy the whole changing scene, the outward changing perspective and the intimate inward movements of feeling. The mother is all feeling yet turns to stone, becoming momentarily mother earth while the son listens acutely and hears ' the dry whining of her distress ', as if a contact on a frequency beyond normal human hearing had been made; then ' she became familiar to him as his mother '. Into the phrase is gathered the tenderness and dignity of a man's love for the whole being, the body and the spirit. And in the phrase ' But while he was yet a little way off ' the tenderness of the New Testament is echoed. ' But when he was yet a great way off ' is the expression of recognition of the son by the father in the Parable of the Prodigal as it is told in the Authorised Version. Righteousness and wrath, emanations from the jealous God of the Old Testament, that which separates, are the base for the drama of the death of the father. It is the tone of the New Testament that is taken into the drama of recognition—thereby bringing Greek and Christian traditions together—of mother and son. It is not by chance that the Philosopher, in a reflective passage that follows the death of his mother, refers to ' the solemn tenderness of Christ '. The journey of the Philosopher is a kind of pilgrim's progress, but one in which tenets and props are discarded as the way becomes harder, but where whatsoever gives understanding of life is accepted. Alongside the heightening perception is the humbling knowledge of how little can be conveyed in words of finer human experience. At the end of his journey Neil Gunn writes of the Philosopher: ' The Philosopher's thought, now entering into its ultimate region, assumed the extremely tenuous condition, wherein it distinguished subtleties that no pen could record. . . .'

This is dangerous doctrine for a novelist. It returns us to the question, how much has Neil Gunn said? The passage on the ebb in *Morning Tide* has been rightly praised for conveying the small scale of the boy intimately on the wide beach, but in *The Serpent* the place is conveyed as the great wilderness that is the earth and the persons desolate as the place coming together in the warmth of their being.

The wilderness is also a place of riches for those who have gone along the road to understanding and this serenity and gaiety is in the narrative of the Philosopher as he ascends. The novelists notes: ' The wealth of wild flowers was familiar to him and he began nodding here and there to tormentil and eyebright, cuckoo flower and primrose, milkwort, pink campion, lady's mantle, stone crop, petty whin, trefoil, herb Robert and buttercup.' In the Philosopher, Neil Gunn created a character who could speak for himself exceptionally, so that the comment is dramatically and biographically correct. The generosity of spirit in which the ordinary people are perceived, as in the depiction of the Fiscal who examines Tom, is the Philosopher's at the end of his story and the novelist's. " Love," says the Philosopher. " Well there was love. Just as there was suffering. Suffering by itself brutalised. But suffering transformed by love—than that man knows nothing more profound."

But love must have an object, in which it is planted and out of which it may grow. In *Morning Tide* and in *Highland River* the boy is the unconscious expression of the ideal relationship to life of a community. In *The Serpent* Neil Gunn refers us to the source in these words, as the Philosopher looks on the landscape:

> It has a gladness about it, he thought, as he faced the moor. Not altogether the sort of joy that is next to godliness nor yet the solemn tenderness of Christ. But a gladness that is part of the old human gaiety. Pagan is hardly the right word, not exact enough. It is the

ultimate gaiety that comes from a knowledge of loneliness. It is a gaiety that knows the wind and the grasses and the sunlight and moves with them. It is the gaiety that is lost in the crowd, and lost to oneself when too concerned with the crowd. It is a final individual bubbling up of the spirit of positive life.

The Serpent created the opportunity for rising into an area which is usually associated with the idea of poetry. In the intensity of the apprehension of the passages quoted one may forget how assuredly Neil Gunn writes at another level. A little less than a third of *The Drinking Well* is set in Edinburgh. Here Iain Cattanach has come to serve an apprenticeship in a lawyer's office and to attend the University. The situation is to some extent the reverse of that in *The Serpent*. Iain did not wish to leave home, but his father says there is no living in the land for him and he must go as others of the family have done. Yet the novelist does not play up the difference in outlook dramatically, and the picture of Edinburgh that is given through the mind of Iain establishes itself as genuine. The company of lawyers, clerks and law students is dealt with fairly, though it is a world of competing for place that is registered. It is as real as it can be in so far as it does not measure itself against the ultimates of life and death as a countryman or seaman must do. But Edinburgh is more than a professional city, and its history as it is embodied in the castle on the rock and in the palace of Holyroodhouse is vividly presented through Iain's mind. There are, however, other perspectives on those events.

I do not think the story fully provides the perspective, even though there is a kind of correcting truth to the idea that all virtue is in country people. Iain's financial difficulties are resolved by his connections with the people of the city. But the romantic events and the mysteries of the drinking well do not belong to the inevitable cause and effect sequence of the events as in *The Serpent*. Yet the same deeper reading of life is in *The Drinking Well*. The episodes are not so strategically placed but the observations of the inexorable movements of traditional life are there. I select three, each working at a different level and in a different way, yet all bound together by the organic demands of nature.

The first does not lend itself to complete quotation for it spreads itself over the page in the slow-paced manner it should. Iain's mother has been to see Major Grant to find out if he can help to get Iain into a lawyer's office in Edinburgh. The mother has told her husband, Duncan, that she would go to the mansion house, but he had not deigned to reply to the proposal. Yet he was out on the road with his cart at the appropriate time, his eyes searching the distance for his wife. He does not see her, but she, sitting at the roadside, sees him. The comment runs:

> An understanding of his veiled concern came into her face in half-amused derision. He would not like anyone to think that he was looking for his wife—least of all would he like her to think it. Openly to come for her in a cart! . . . so he would just be passing, as it were. . . . Presently she turned. "Is it you?" she said.
> He drew up. "You've got back?"
> "Yes. Where were you?"

She forces him to pretend that it was chance that he was on the road, but she is compelled to ask him to ask her about her mission.

Here 'The bird flies in the mind and more than bird'. The effect transcends the material. Behind the cryptic dialogue are depths of concern that would be indelicate to expose. There is also the wariness of old people who know how untrustworthy is life. This building of the texture of their lives so that one can feel in their presence and in the presence of their past, provides the ground for the moments of crisis in the novel. It also makes us aware that the high drama of history, as Iain saw it in Edinburgh, does not tell the tale of human history, as do the unrecorded events of ordinary lives.

So many of the rarest effects in Neil Gunn's writings come upon the scene unexpectedly and yet as if they had been there implicit in the events or characters all the time, but waiting to be called, that one feels they get on the page because of some special characteristic in the man. I might call him a listening man. He is forever being surprised by the new thing that is disclosed to him. In his autobiography *The Atom of Delight* he remarks on ' the moment of happiness in life that comes not to order but unexpectedly '. And in his last novel *The Other Landscape* he remarks, ' What has been unthinkable is in a moment apprehended '. If he gives the impression that he has come upon the event by chance, once perceived there is no doubt of its reality. In fact the two aspects are related. The man who is patient in suffering is open to the possibility of joy. And having suffered and loved, then he may see things in a new way. When Iain after much illness and trouble goes to the lambing again, Neil Gunn expresses his feeling thus:

> Heaven knows he had seen enough lambs in his time, but never a lamb like this lamb, newly born, swaying on its stilts, but hardy, for when he went a step or two forward out came its thin bleat and waggle went its tail with energy. . . . The whole scene etched itself on

his heightened mind. Such conjunctions of the seen and heard were normal enough. But as he took a step or two away, looking back, the face of the mother and lamb came through that arrested time and place.

When the concept is articulated in such words as ' arrested ' and ' etched ' I feel the writer has moved away from the sources of life, and the writing is less compulsive. It may be that this passage does all that is required of it in its context, but when Iain is on his way, wholly unconsciously, to an acceptance of life, shortly before the death of his mother he overhears his grandmother and his mother:

> Sometimes, too, he would hear the two women talking away. Occasionally his mother's voice would lift and crack, but his granny's voice was always sensible and calm. It's not that his granny's voice was humouring his mother's fancies. It was more than that, and it was the ' more ' that searched him out. She was the mother talking to her child, hardly listening at times, because her hands were busy; chiding now and then, but prepared to explain over and over. There was something so normal about this, so assured, that it gave Iain a conception of women which he never afterwards forgot.
>
> At the beginning of life and at its end, they were there, handling the unbearable with competent hands, doing little things, material things, with knowledge in their eyes, moving about, silent or speaking as the need demanded. They were there, with the awful progression of minutes in their hands.

The disclosure of the dignity of living in the midst of indignities is a very honourable achievement. To look so closely and with so much human kindness, and to bring out of desolation a kind of richness, gives Neil Gunn his unique place in the history of literature.

Comedy and Transcendence in Neil Gunn's Later Fiction

FRANCIS RUSSELL HART

During the Second World War, with the mythic dystopia *The Green Isle of the Great Deep* (1944), there occurred in the fiction of Neil Gunn an expansion or a displacement of theme into urgencies of the mid-twentieth-century world. They are anticipated most clearly in *Wild Geese Overhead* (1939), a first novel of violence, physical and intellectual, in a modern urban setting. Two later variants of the same 'fiction of violence' are *The Shadow* (1948) and *Blood Hunt* (1952). It appears, as well, in two novels that use popular and contemporary 'suspense' or intrigue motifs, *The Key of the Chest* (1945) and *The Lost Chart* (1949). But Gunn's ultimate form was the one Edwin Muir recognised and admired in *The Silver Bough* (1948), and we see it likewise in *The Well at the World's End* (1951) and in *The Other Landscape* (1954). It is the ageing modern intellectual's quest into primordial place and atavistic time for his own renewal, his search for the displacement that enigma can bring, bewildering him onto 'The Way' or giving him divinely comic nudges onto the 'other landscape'.

This is not to impose an arbitrary barrier between 'early' and 'late'. The great 'historical' novel *The Silver Darlings* (1941) magnificently recapitulates the earlier books, just as *The Green Isle* meets new challenges, and yet, young Finn of the first belongs with Young Art, whose two stories follow his. In his story, comedy's ultimate invasion has begun, and a legend of triumphant and archaic individuality prevails over a novel of regional history. But the new challenges are none the less real, and new levels and intensities of response justify this separate look at Gunn's later novels, novels that should have considerable appeal for a generation newly sensitive to the survival of mythic pastoral values and devoted to the fiction of Hesse and other more whimsical Western pilgrims to Zen.

The new challenges came in Naomi Mitchison's response to *Young Art and Old Hector* (1942). Was this not a persistent escapism? Was his art restricted to the reinterpretation of Highland values, the translation of Celtic legend into terms viable for modern Highland pastoral? Could his fiction cope in the 1940s with the growing complexity and murderousness of the modern world? The challenges in themselves are somewhat prejudicial, and Gunn's later novels have not met them so much as shown their limitedness. But a first response came in the dystopian parable, *The Green Isle of the Great Deep*. Troubled by reports of totalitarian brainwashing, Gunn decided to send river-bound Art and Hector by accident into a Celtic legendary version of Huxley's *Brave New World*. The result combines the wise whimsy of earlier Art-Hector episodes with the awesome scope of Edenic myth temporarily perverted into totalitarian nightmare.

Tangling with a salmon in a pool, Art and Hector fall through the pool's bottom into a collective dream. Together they become Utopian voyagers. The 'strangeness' of discovery is essential to the voyager's ambivalent vision of paradise; Hector becomes a deeply troubled 'stranger in the Perfect Place ' as the horror dawns on him. He becomes a hopeless ' insider ', and through his capitulation to the behavioural engineers, we see a paralysis of will analogous to the somatose infantilism of *Brave New World*. In his interview with the Dostoevskian Questioner, Hector finds little interest in his sins but much curiosity about his happinesses. The ' atomic ' psychologists benignly remove the anarchic factor from man's spirit: for Zamiatin the fancy, for Huxley mature self-awareness, for Orwell memory, and for Gunn the will. The remnant is a shell, all that is left after ' the exciting game of teasing the human mind into its strands, and leaving them knotless and gleaming and smooth over one's arm or the back of a chair '. It is ' all being done for the best ', Hector concedes, in the true anti-Utopian pathos.

Art reacts differently. Like Finn, his essence as young hero is to resist with devious fury or dumb flight any threat to his intact self. Repeatedly he escapes the authorities until his power of flight assumes the force of legendary magic. The legend of Art reaches an absentee God, and like the Good Landlord hearing of his evil factor, or Shakespeare's ' duke of dark corners ', God returns to paradise and returns paradise to itself. The hunted, Art and Hector, become the hunters, the ultimate threat to the urbane Managers, who have been so intrigued by the indestructible bond between old man and boy. ' An interesting form of atavism ', they call it; it is too profoundly natural or primordial a loyalty for the analytic Hunters ever to ferret out.

Reflecting on artistic and philosophical defect in *Brave New World*, Huxley concluded that his work had failed to provide adequate rational alternatives. His criterion recalls the humanistic origins of Utopiansim. The anti-

Utopia as we know it has repudiated not just Utopian visions in particular, but Utopianism itself, thus rationalising the *status quo* and denying even hypothetical existence to rational alternatives. This is the anti-Utopianism Paul Goodman deplores and David Riesman traces to our ' disillusion with all systematic thinking—ideological and Utopian alike '. Anti-Christ alone is an able dialectician, and the good man, Christ or Billy Budd, can reply only with a stutter or a silent kiss. Has Gunn offered only a choice between the rigid pseudo-intellectualism of the Questioner and the sullen evasiveness of a primitive poacher? Hector is a far wiser norm than this. But it is the folly of the misguided Utopian Questioner that is central to true anti-Utopian satire. Gonzalo would have no sovereignty in his commonwealth, and yet be ' King on't '. However diabolical his delusion, the Utopian projector is a fool. But in contemporary anti-Utopia only the diabolism remains; he is now the evil centre of a tragic vision. ' A utopia,' says Richard Gerber of *1984*, ' cannot bear such tragedy. A Utopian tragedy tends to be hysterical or sentimental.'

The Green Isle avoids both by returning to the comic origin of anti-Utopianism. ' Tragedy can take us no farther,' says Northrop Frye, ' but if we persevere with the mythos of irony and satire, we shall pass a dead centre, and finally see the gentlemanly Prince of Darkness bottom side up.' The Managers, foolish rather than evil, reach their normal limits when God baffles his vicegerents at their own game of dialogue, not because they are dialecticians, but because they are nothing more. Divinity reconquers knowledge with wisdom and magic. It was Huxley who made a title of the *Tempest* tag, but it is Gunn's Utopian fable that, like Shakespeare's play, finally transcends the bitter irony of Miranda's *naïveté* with the divine comedy of a triumphant innocence in an anti-anti-Utopia both brave and new.

Here, then, are the lineaments of Gunn's comic vision, beyond the tragedy of history, surviving in the indestructible whimsy of wise age and defiantly fugitive youth. The issue of escapism is seriously broached, and the related issues of primitivism and anti-rationalism, and Gunn typically discriminates true escapisms, primitivisms, irrationalisms, from false ones. Such are the concerns and manœuvres of his later novels. To trace them in groups, let me go back a bit.

After *Highland River* (1937), his most sophisticated treatment of Highland boyhood, Gunn turned in *Wild Geese Overhead* (1939) to the very different world of the urban adult and a city reporter's efforts to validate his own escapist impulses. Structurally, the novel is akin to its predecessor, specifically in its initial focus on a single momentary experience of transcendence. The sudden struggle with the great salmon has become the sudden lifting apprehension, in a suburban road, of ' wild geese overhead '. The setting is the intellectual-Marxist 'thirties. The problem is the validity of modes of thought and feeling that the Marxist finds absurdly pre-scientific. Will, the aptly named hero, seeks to recapture a moment of transcendent delight, to measure ' that uprising of the deeper self into freedom ' against other insistent realities of urban violence and despair, to understand why the modern world finds such menace and betrayal in the mood of secret delight such moments bring, and to persist in ' a lingering animosity against those who took life's central purpose of delight and smothered it, out of fear and self-importance and egotism, and the devil's thrill of power over others '. This effort is to be the motive force of the later fiction.

Will's newspaper friends find him an absurd, romantic escapist. His chief antagonist is the Mephistophelian figure we have seen in the caustic destroyer of *Second Sight* and the Managers of *The Green Isle*. Yet Will and the compulsive nihilist Mac are drawn to each other, hunter to hunted; each is the other's shadow self. Will is imbued with his creator's archetypal vision to see his story as an incessant spiritual warfare: ' Out of humanity in the reaches of time appear figures like Christ the saviour, Nero the destroyer. . . . In every little circle, in every village, town, country, walked the individual saviour, the individual destroyer.' Will has the double vision of the ' other landscape '. What makes everything come ' rounded and alive, with depth and, above all, an extraordinary amount of light ' is a stereoptical habit of seeing. Will sees the city, as the remembered stereopticon of his boyhood saw every-thing, in ' an oddly double way '. The visionary sense of reality leads away from personality; in true vision, ' the ego was lost in the calm uprising of the second self, the deeper self, into conscious freedom '. The condition of self-transcendence is comedy, laughter, delight. The reward is love and wholeness.

Such a novel can have only limited plot value. In the novels of 1937-1940 (*Highland River, Wild Geese Overhead, Second Sight*), Gunn was too preoccupied with finding his modern themes, probing impulses or experiences for their archetypal truth, to attend much to values of narrative pattern. In the novels after *The Green Isle*, he has found the plot conventions that best serve these serious purposes.

We can see the extraordinary change made by a decade in another novel of modern urbanity turning on the issues of escapism, *The Lost Chart* (1949). The title, like *The Key of the Chest* (1945), suggests the structural idea: the dangerous quest for the lost paradigm or 'key', set in a world of modern violence, yet displaced in the protagonist's vision and ours onto the 'other landscape' where all stories are one story and all times one. The hero is a young shipping clerk; the urban setting is an unnamed Glasgow. The hero is involved not with city cynics and socialists, but with Highland Fifth Columnists in the Cold War. The plot turns obsessively on time—time is of the essence—the time is a day of crisis—the times pervade all thought and feeling, proclaiming another Dark Age. The question of escape arises with a horrible new urgency. The 'lost chart' which is stolen from Dermot and which, in an exciting battle in a sea-loch, he finally recovers, is a chart of sea approaches to Cladday, a remote Hebridean island.

Its location, like that of Mackenzie's Todday Beag, makes it of strategic importance, but for Dermot it is a pocket of salvable humanity where life may reassemble and go back to its sources when the missiles hit the city. The hunt for the real chart becomes the hunt for a mental chart of the 'other landscape', the one humanity has lost. The other chart is the power of vision; humanity must 'go back' to find that power or that way, and the book discriminates between 'the two kinds of regress', the 'drawing back' of the totalitarian and the creative atavism of the artist. The painter, Joe, and the Gaelic singer, Ellen, are the true image-makers in a world seeking imaginative renewal. It is Joe who defines the test: 'There cannot be a regress when you're searching for light.' It is Joe who

sounds the triumphant comic theme of all the later novels:
' The darkness creates drama ready-made for man; but
man has to create his own drama of the light.' To do so is to
' go back ' for the lost way, to find oneself mythically.
' Man must forever move,' says *The Key of the Chest,*
' like a liberator, through his own unconsciousness.' He
does so by the gesture Gunn has likened to the fisherman's
backward cast, by what Mann calls the ' archaizing attitude '.
Such is the ' drama of the light ' enacted on the ' other
landscape ' of Gunn's post-war novels.

Let me recapitulate what I have said elsewhere of three
of these novels, three that evoke the murderousness of the
modern world in acts of individual murder and their
impact on traditional Highland community.

For Gunn, as for Conrad's Marlow, ' the meaning of an
episode was not inside like a kernel but outside, enveloping
the tale which brought it out '. The episode of *The Key of
the Chest* (1945) is the death by strangulation of a Swedish
seaman during his rescue from a sinking freighter. His
rescuer, Charlie, is suspected of murder; Charlie's brutish
shepherd of a brother is suspected of stealing money from
his chest. Like other Gunn protagonists, Charlie and Douglas
live spatially and morally on the outskirts of their community. They are in longstanding conflict with the minister, a spiritual despot on whom life has taken its revenge
by arousing a love for his daughter both incestuous and
idealising. Charlie is his rival; the minister sacrifices his
whole position in a death hunt to drive the brothers to
destruction. The lovers are rescued, and the minister is
chastened. The ' key ' is to be found in the mystery of
the bond between the ' dangerous personal ' and the
' universal '. It is a way of seeing. But the key is also in

the mysterious bond of the brothers, reflecting the brotherhood of the sea, and given its universal significance by a
texture of allusion to Cain and Abel. Both brothers are
accused of wearing the mark of Cain. The novel explores
Cain's query: how *can* one be one's brother's keeper?
Ironically the Cain-like Dougald supplies the answer—
by instinctively knowing how to defy the destructive forces
that threaten his brother, with the unobtrusive, practical
helpfulness of traditional community. Brotherhood requires
the most delicate tact, the operative vision of individuality
without which brotherhood will violate individuality.
This is the ' key '.

The structure of the book is complicated, its image of
community large, its centres of consciousness numerous.
The doctor, a focal figure of humane concern in the community, serves well as a centre, intellectual, yet urgently
practical, bound to his people by instinctual ties, yet
drawn to sophisticated outsiders, the energetic young hunting laird Michael Sandeman, and his foppish but kindly
pedant of a guest Gwynn, whose own hunt for the key to
modern ' primitivism ' in art has brought him to the
traditional community and made him spokesman for some
of Gunn's serious attitudes. The doctor retreats into silence
from their aggressive curiosity and rush of words. This
mechanism for dialogue is a fine means of sorting views of
primitive and pastoral values, with the doctor as an ironic
control on the tendency to lose human reality in academic
discussion. The ideas are pertinent, yet an expository
excess is an integral problem of the narrative's meaning.
The key of the chest is to be found not in words, but in
personal and archetypal vision and in operative brotherhood.
The novel is perhaps Gunn's most ambitious and successful

fusion of narrative complexity and ideological fullness.

The title of *The Shadow* (1948) refers to the shadow cast by the robbery and murder of an old hermit. The episode occurs during the convalescence of a young woman who has suffered nervous collapse during the London blitz and comes to her aunt's Highland farm for peace and rest only to have ' the living figure of destruction . . . come away from the city where he has been impersonal and many-shaped, shapes flying across the sky, come at last to the country, to the quiet countryside, to prowl around on two feet and smell out a poor old man and murder him for his money '. The result (the second of three parts) is ' Relapse '. The third, ' Recovery ', is the outcome of a complex inner war, her own ' drama of the light '—and of an outer war among friends, relatives, lovers, who claim her spirit on behalf of their conflicting visions of her illness and of the world's illness it embodies.

> The child, wandering up through the daylight fields, trying to clean the shadow from the world. . . . The thistledown, the soft eager balls, seeds on the wing— changing into the grey steady eyes, the searching eyes of the policeman. Changing, in his turn, into the youth with the tommygun on his knees and the cigarette in his mouth, while love in its naked family waited in the trench; he mowed them down as a pernicious corn.

Nan's lover Ranald, descendant of the Green Isle Managers, is, like Michael Sandeman, potentially one of Gunn's intellectual destroyers. In argument he ' gets pale . . . and logical in a remorseless way '. He enjoys tearing his opponent's ' mind into small bits '. Aunt Pheemie sees a ' remorseless white face, like Ranald's face. . . . It's the slayer's face, thought told her in silence '. But

NEIL GUNN with his wife, 1935

JAMES BRIDIE   NEIL GUNN
J. M. BARRIE   ERIC LINKLATER

('Authors in Session' by Stanley Cursiter)

The moorland above Dunbeath, with the
Caithness mountains in the background

Entrance to Dunbeath Strath, with the
'House of Peace' on the left

the point of the book is that Ranald must be saved, not rejected; through Nan's recovery he must be made whole. Self-transcendence is never self-surrender to the irrational forces of ' blood ' or darkness. Wisdom is never gained by an abdication of reason. Nan's cry sums it up: " We have to rescue the intellect from the destroyers. They have turned it into death rays, and it should be the sun." The destroyers pervert intellect into ' Reason's noise. One who makes too much noise will never see a fawn in a glen. But there are fawns in glens '. ' Reason,' Gunn continues (in *Atom of Delight*), ' has tended to collar intellect in our time.' And what the ' Old Schoolmen ' knew as intellect ' reason calls non-rational '. To save reason from itself, then, is ' not to disparage reason or intellect and opt wholly for the dark gods, the irrational flesh '. Gunn is consciously anti-Lawrentian. Like Thomas Mann, he moves only experimentally among the anti-intellectuals.

Seeking to recover life, Nan is the hunted animal, fleeing from violence, but also from the disintegrative rationalism that labels her neurotic. Her flight carries her too far, and she gives instinctive, self-meaning allegiance to one she thinks the murderer, the strange young hunter in the woods, appropriately named Adam. Her allegiance is the attraction of a newly awakened anti-intellectuality to the ' dark gods '. But she derides the talk that ' Nan is going all D. H. Lawrence '. She must work her way through the allegiance (like Dougald in his allegiance to his brother and old Sandy, in *Bloodhunt*, in his allegiance to the murderer). With the reawakening of her love for the ' real Ranald ' comes what is almost a second murder. The fight is the clash of instinctual man with the logical utopian. Adam is the ' fighting wild thing ', ' his eyes wary as a

I

stoat's '. Ranald is one 'who knew he would kill at his leisure, but needed first to dominate the mind in front of him, to frighten it into gibbering bits'. No one wins. Adam slips into the river, but survives. Ranald goes back to Nan exhilarated by a rare surrender to instinct. We must learn why no one can win, and why Nan cannot choose Adam but must work for Ranald's redemption.

Bloodhunt (1952) as narrative is simpler than *The Key* and *The Shadow*, but its parabolic simplicity carries the same symbolic burden. A likeable young man has killed the rival who got his girl pregnant. The bloodhunter, a policeman, is the murdered man's brother. An old retired seaman, Sandy, living in peaceful isolation on the edge of the community, is destined in spite of himself to become ' secret sharer ' of the guilt of his young friend the murderer. Sandy carries on tragicomic intrigues to hide and feed the fugitive, resists the invasions of a ' well-meaning ' Widow Wadman from the next farm, and finally accepts and protects the pregnant girl. The hunt goes on. The hunter is brutalised; the fugitive is caught and killed. Sandy, knowing all, remains silent, calling an end to violence, and finds new life in the girl and her baby, born in Sandy's barn. As Sandy sees them, the events are a ' sacred repetition ': ' The manger and the hay and life's new cry; beyond it, that hunt. Of all the stories man had made only two were immortal: the story of Cain and the story of Christ.' Sandy chooses his story and enacts his own ' drama of the light '.

Menzies the policeman, like Spenser's Malbecco and Milton's Satan, comes to personify his obsession. Beginning as his brother's avenger, he wears at last the mark of Cain. His face becomes ' not only thinner but darker. . . . He had taken the night in with him'; he lives in a 'dark inner world'. In the 'secret country' of Sandy's mind, too, a war goes on between dark and light, the tribal law of vengeance and an older law, 'the warm feeling at life's real core'. In his own secret country every man is hunter and hunted; Sandy is hunted by life and his futile flight is the comic momentum of the story. Life is participation in life; Sandy finally accepts the law of love and rejects the law of Cain behind it. It is remarkable how wide a vision of human alternatives is embodied in this parable, how much is implied in the shift of Sandy's allegiance from the fugitive murderer to the girl and her bastard, while outside in ritual circles the hunt draws to its own destruction. This, the next-to-last of Gunn's novels, is unquestionably one of his most perfect as story and myth.

Let me suggest, however, in a last grouping of novels a final development beyond narrative itself in the direction suggested by *Highland River*, the direction of philosophical comedy and dialogue. Three of the last novels share the impulse: *The Silver Bough* (1948), *The Well at the World's End* (1951) and *The Other Landscape* (1954). The three protagonists have much in common—all are academics, an archaeologist, an ancient historian, an anthropologist— and all are in pursuit of the essentially primitive. All are questers in words, and all discover the nonsense of their academic categories in the deviously learned talk that is Gunn's highest humour. All three engage in humorous dialogues in caves, caves explicitly, if whimsically, associated with archaic man's sources of magical power and with the spirit secretly made there. In *The Well at the World's End*, the cave is a smuggler's bothy where the professor has a wondrously alcoholic blether with the proprietors of illusion and earthly paradise. In *The Other Landscape* the cave is dual. At the hotel, nightly talks with the nihilistic old major take place by flickering lamps, and the major's heroically anachronistic dependence on a chest full of embassy candles out of his diplomatic past leads to a night of infernal humour when the place almost burns and the major's hellishness is doused. In the sea cave, Menzies, the major's spiritual opposite, keeps his cask of shipwrecked rum. The talk there becomes a form of magic; the mundane academic has gone underground into the world of the gods.

The Silver Bough opens the way. The bough of the plot is both story and song and talismanic child's toy; it functions as means of entry to the underworld and as the prize for which a foolish king temporarily traded his wife and child to the king of the sea. The 'foolish king' is the landowner who, sickened by war violence, has never married his 'wife' and has disowned her child. He is male counterpart to Nan of *The Shadow* (also 1948). The horrors of jungle warfare have turned him into a blood-hunter, and he must be rescued: such is the unwitting mission of the archaeologist's voyage to the underworld.

The Well at the World's End is another novel of rescue, chiefly the academic protagonist's own, from the perilous doldrums of domesticated middle age. His climactic perils follow a great sea rescue, when alone among the mountains he is almost killed trying to rescue a lamb trapped on a cliff. Wounded, he fights against the will to die. He seeks in vain the help of a local 'wild man' or primitive, only to learn the man is dead. Yet, mysteriously at night in the wild man's cave he is visited by the man's spirit, becomes the man reincarnate, and is reborn in the will to live by

virtue of the kinship. This is the ' something ' in the well
at the world's end, not a source of cultural renewal (as in
The Drinking Well) but a source of personal power and
archaic reanimation.

In *The Other Landscape*, too, we are concerned little with
cultural renewal. The vision of *The Grey Coast* was double,
but the real local landscape had fashioned the habit of vision
by which the ' other landscape ' was seen. Vision is no
longer cultural, but has become a universal creative force
both artistic and religious. The question is of the rescue of
modern man; he, not the nearby traditional community,
is the one needing rescue. The rescue of Douglas Menzies,
the withdrawn composer living on the cliffs, the alcoholic
widower, turns ironically about as Menzies literally becomes
the hero of the cliffs, the rescuer, and then is released to his
own death, as he repeats his daring climb down for rum
to give the old fisherman he has rescued. He has rescued
himself, though he seems at last to have drawn on powers
preserved in traditional community: love, brotherhood,
communal art, humour.

The three novels share a stress on humour. Humour
inheres in the incidents of *The Silver Bough*, yet the background to humour is the same modern murderousness of
books already discussed. What was lost and found in *The
Key of the Chest* and *The Lost Chart* was of solemn urgency;
what is found, lost, and sought after in vain in *The Silver
Bough* is a crock of gold, stumbled upon by the archaeologist-
hero and stolen by the village idiot: ' All this he had done—
to be foiled by the idiot of prehistory.' The story of
Martin's recovery is solemn enough. But the archaeologist's
confrontation with the idiot is ' damn funny '. The earth
about him seems filled with the humour of life: ' The

grasses flattened themselves, wiggled, in a green mirth that held on. The rowan tree was a more solemn riot, full of convolutions of itself and high bursts of abandon, but sticking to its own root at all the odds '—a fine description of the dialogue in these novels. The protagonist's own self-discoveries evoke laughter: ' the more he penetrated, the more he discovered of himself, *the nearer he drew to the crock of gold.* That was no myth: it was simple fact. In a momentary wonder that it should be so, he laughed '.

The Well at the World's End is a middle-aged academic's holiday of picaresque humour, off and away from his wife and his serious thoughtful self, in search of the sources of eternal youth. It opens with an empty teapot and a visit to the well that appears empty but never is. Nothing is seen there but something is there indeed. The professor's adventures take him into the well of man's illusions, his lingering superstitions, in quest of the ' something ' that is there when ' nothing ' is seen. The pattern is episodic. The form is a complex, ambiguous circling, back to his wife and his own beginnings. At each new revelation, a humdrum Highland world uncovers the exhilarating, ludicrous magic of rituals supposedly lost. The climax comes when, near death from his fall, Peter Munro nurses voraciously at the udder of the bereaved ewe and gains nourishment for survival. This, unquestionably the most extraordinary incident in Gunn's novels, hovers beautifully between the grotesque and the archetypal, with the humour of the drop that is poised precariously on the old woman's nose as she pours Peter's cup of tea. We have had the ' prank ' at the haunted cottage, the night of wise hilarity in the cave, the enchantments of Cocklebuster's erratic dog, the archaic magic of marital renovation, the wild

street fight at the country-town dance, the heroic confrontation of old self-reliance and new welfare in a coastal
storm, and finally the accident of the lamb and the battle
for life in the wild man's cave. What matters in all of it is
the humour of which legend is born, and all that avails
when Peter faces the grey nihilism of the visionary cerebral
he-goat of modern life—is laughter: ' And the more he
couldn't laugh, the more he knew that laughter, deep
laughter from beneath the belt, was the only specific for
the goat, the sole charm against its evil eye, its whole
spectrum, its spectral tee-totum.'

The humour of *The Other Landscape* is most pronounced
and most difficult. The book jacket speaks vaguely of ' that
rarely reached point where tragedy and comedy meet and
something else is added which nobody knows how to
name or define '. Menzies's wife had died the night of a
storm because he could get no help. Since then, he has been
on a lonely search: ' I saw this search by Menzies as more
than a search for Annabel, though it was primarily that. I
saw it as a sort of warfare into these regions which (to call
on the image) the Wrecker inhabits. There could be only
one end to that search, that warfare: tragedy.' But the
end is beyond tragedy.

It transcends tragedy by the closely related features of
the protagonist's archaising vision: legendary recurrence
and humour. The feature that for George Eliot makes
human destinies tragic—recurrence—for Gunn lifts them
beyond tragedy. An old Gaelic air can tell of a human
tragedy ' so winnowed by the generations that it could be
sung, hummed, as a lullaby to a child. I know of no
essentialising process more profound than this '. Tradition
winnows the rhythms of life ' as the crofter's winnower

eliminated the chaff. What was left was cleansed of the personal in the sense that all great art is impersonal and thereby achieves the ultimate expression of the personal. At this point only paradox is left; paradox and the urge to give it form or shape in myth or image or symbol'. Humour enlivens the rhythms. Destruction is part of godhead, but there is more to it, and the more is humour. ' There is a grey humour in the eyes of God when he is not the Wrecker. The morning of the earth has pointed ears. The Wrecker, the bloody Wrecker, has only the one trick.' Face the tragedy, and there is always *something more* —and to sense this something more is humour:

> Presently I found myself sitting again like a fool in the twilight. I could not help laughing under my breath at my astonishment, and when I realized I was laughing I had a look around. . . . It was laughable and delicious; like imps of the night dancing in a ring. Nothing was quite real. There was *something more*.

And always in his debaucheries of talk with Menzies, ' there was a smile in his eyes and the outer corner of his left eyelid quivered very slightly in a critical, understanding humour '.

The negative side of the humour is in the major, the despotic retired attaché who stays in the hotel, goading his gillie, doubting the locals, seeing in Menzies only a man drinking himself to death. He is recognisably the nihilistic destroyer of Gunn's earliest novels, but in a humorous version. And there is something more: he is ' jealous of Menzies. He knew that Menzies was the only one who could stand beside him at his utmost reach—and then go beyond '. The major, his mouth full of Fitzgerald's *Rubá'iyát*, has ' assured himself that there was no beyond '.

He believes in hell only. The limits of his belief are humorously exploded when his hell comes to pass, his embassy candles set his room afire, and amid the comic inferno stand the tormented gillie and his equally tipsy friends, drenching the major and his hell with the hose. The major is chastened, and following the death of Menzies he does not return to the hotel.

For the major there is no place left. For Menzies, this remote Highland place means reunion at last in death with his Annabel, and we realise with a shock that Gunn's other landscape has become Brontësque, that regional locality has become insignificant. The issue between Menzies the Lowlander and the English major has nothing to do with crises of Highland culture. The problem of evil is no longer psychological and cultural, but metaphysical. The novel shifts to a new level of concern, from magic and science to religion and art. Menzies and the major hold opposed conceptions of godhead; the Wrecker is a part of divinity, not humanity: there can be no absentee Jehovah to set things right, as in *The Green Isle*. The questing narrator's search for the 'primitive' is lost in Menzies's search for the ultimate mystery. For these reasons, *The Other Landscape* remains a puzzle—a startling new departure for a final novel—and in fact its author's *least* ' Highland ' book.

But enough remains to remind us of the continuities of Gunn's fiction and to suggest the lineaments of its greatness. His vision is as unmistakably his own as his language and his humour: a humour that transcends the tragedy of history, gives birth to legends, and so rescues from the destroyers the delight that is always at the bottom of life's well, the heart of its circle.

I 2

The Well of Delight

STEWART CONN

None of Neil Gunn's novels is more intimate and self-revealing than *The Well at the World's End*. Its opening scene precisely depicts something that happened to Gunn and his wife while on holiday. The central character's subsequent pilgrimage is so personal, and the values he calls in question so fundamental, that I do not see how he can be dissociated from the author.

The Well at the World's End also contains (despite my affinities with *Highland River*) the single chapter which most profoundly moves me: the description of the storm at sea. As a self-contained unit, and within the framework of the novel as a whole, this episode has intense dramatic quality. It brings me perhaps closer than any other to what I recognise as the pervading spirit of Gunn.

Peter Munro, a professor of History, sets out with his wife Fand on a camping tour of the Scottish Highlands. They are directed by an old woman to a well. Due to a freak of the light, the crystal water is at first invisible. That night, as he lies in his sleeping-bag, the experience sticks in Peter's mind:

" That was odd—about the water in the well," he said.
" Yes."
"What's that old legend about the well at the world's end?"

" An old Gaelic legend—with a tragic end."

" Tragic? "

" Yes. It's about a goddess that went off to find the well in the land beyond ours, the Land of Youth. When she found it, she couldn't have done the right thing—though what she should have done we don't know. The water in the well got angry and rose up and drowned her, for her body was found on the bank of the river that flowed from the well."

He was silent for a little while. " What did she expect to find in the well? "

" Knowledge and poetry. There are hazels above the well, and they burst into blossom when you find it, and inspirations and wisdom fall into the well, and the well surges. You'll often find mention of this well in the old legends."

Here are echoes of Kenn's river of life, in *Highland River*; of Young Art and Old Hector stretching across the salmon-pool, at the opening of *The Green Isle of the Great Deep*. But Peter's musings take another direction:

That extraordinary moment when the invisible water moves in the well—is it as rare as all that? Do people, ordinary folk, ever stand tranced before some wonder that not only takes their breath away, but for an instant, the human boundary itself away?

The quest Peter embarks on is to be taken on several levels. There are the immediate allegorical implications of the hazel-nuts—the nuts of the knowledge of good and evil—and of the well itself. There is the reference to legend, to the goddess. There are also parallels with *The Silver Bough*, very much a companion volume. Both titles are from fairy tales. Each novel has its reminders of the past:

the Picts' houses, and the Neolithic cairn; Peter's exploration, Simon's archaeological dig. In each instance, references to knowledge confirm the spiritual nature of the search. Indeed *The Silver Bough* is explicit in its mention of the Holy Grail.

The pattern of *The Well at the World's End* is nowhere more discernible than through Fand. She not only recalls the magical well, and hints at the hazards of the quest. Her origin is in Celtic myth. In the ' Sickbed of Cuchulainn ', the hero forsakes his wife Emer for Fand. As poet (and warrior) he comes under her spell: she is his muse. When Emer comes to reclaim him, Fand renounces him. He has not measured up to her:

> Emer, noble wife, this man is yours.
> He has broken away from me.
> But still I am fated to desire
> What my hand cannot hold and keep.

The marital complication is not retained. But Peter's is a moral test, to determine whether or not he ' measures up ' to himself—and, through himself, to Fand.

Needless to say, the novel's tone is not of gravity or mystic opacity. It is brilliantly entertaining. The characters, picaresque and picturesque, are among the most memorable and comic in Gunn's output. There is Phemie Bethune with her cat and her hens, her hands like old leaves and a drip at the end of her nose: a drip Peter knows is destined to fall into his cup! There is Alastair the Shepherd, who speaks of his own ' boundaries ' up in the hills— and who proudly remembers Peter's father. Above all there is the magnificent Cocklebuster, whose spaniel Sally so mysteriously loses her scent.

In Cocklebuster's pine forest, conversation jumps from Confucius to M.I.5. Peter loses Cocklebuster and Sally. Hilarity and dream merge. His universe is permeated by the enigmatic nothingness of a Sibelius symphony. Later:

> Peter twisted round . . . and saw to the right of the spreading beech, across a hollow with a trickle of water, the trunks of trees, bare trunks, and between the trunks and beyond them, he saw the gleam on the far side of the wood like a golden light in a lattice window. Whether from the angle at which the afternoon sun hit distant grass or leaves or what not, the light was golden . . . paradisal . . . warm.

The music is not merely in the background. It, and its absence, are orchestrated to Peter's state of mind. Similarly, throughout the novel, the quality of light and its transitions mirror what he is experiencing. They are a counterpoint, a heightening of emotional expression. Individual moments, and objects, are transformed: as when Mrs Douglas, *la belle dame sans merci*, slants like a phantom through the mist in search of the purity-restoring *mothan*. In the storm scene, the elements themselves are active participants.

> Peter was wakened by a loud knocking on the door and at once knew something was wrong. "Come in!"
> Mrs MacIver entered. "Oh, sir, it's a terrible storm. They're on the sea."
> "Who?"
> "Willie." Her eyes, which could gather concern quickly enough, were now tragic. "He's with old Malcolm and his son Angus. The three of them. I'm just back from the harbour again. They're going to launch the lifeboat." Suddenly she was overcome and went out.

He heads for the harbour.

> The tide was on the turn and smashing along the shallow
> bar. The churned water blew its froth into his face.
> The wind whistled. Knots of men and women, girls,
> running boys; some figures towards a headland away to
> the left.

As in *Morning Tide* the watchers on the shore are ' like a
group caught in a grey dawn of history, or legend, their
separateness from the men fateful and eternal'. Here
however it is more than a struggle between men and the
Sea:

> It was not that Norman, skipper of the lifeboat, and
> Malcolm were political opponents, with Norman all for
> the new way of life, complete with Government
> assistance, and Malcolm for the old individualism; that
> kind of political warfare enlivened many an evening
> and no harm done; it was that the old man should be
> caught out in his sea lore, that he should be wounded
> so deeply in his sea pride, that he should be saved by
> Norman of all people. . . . The climb down was not
> going to be easy.

The lifeboat comes alongside the *Rose of Sharon*, and heaves
to:

> Every face took on a strange smile and Willie felt a
> shiver of wild mirth go over him.
> " We've come for you," roared Norman.
> There was always something authoritative in
> Norman's voice beyond perhaps what he intended.
> " Who sent you? " shouted Malcolm.
> " Common sense," shouted Norman.
> " Thought you had parted with it to the Government
> long ago," called Malcolm.

There was a laugh, for the conversation was shaping well. A few more jokes of the sort and Malcolm and his crew might climb aboard the lifeboat with reasonable grace, giving nearly as good as they got.

But Norman had to show his hand. . . . " Stand in to come aboard! "

The order is too direct. A rope is thrown. Malcolm takes his decision: he is going home under his own sail in his own boat. Norman tells him, if he cannot think of himself, to think of the crew. Malcolm asks his son if he wants to board the lifeboat:

Angus could not meet his father's eyes. He glanced here and there with a congested petulance while the drawn skin whitened round his mouth. " I think we should," he said and gulped, and his blue eyes suddenly flashed a sort of dumb wrath.

Malcolm recognises fear. Willie realises it will destroy the old man. Malcolm tells Angus to take the line. Angus does not move. A bleak deadly smile comes to Malcolm's face:

" There are times maybe when it's better to drown." Picking up the heaving line, he methodically coiled it as far as he could and pitched it into the sea.

The *Rose of Sharon* heads for a narrow swing of unbroken water marking the deepest part of the channel. Malcolm must hit this if he is to have a chance. Many a boat has broken her back on the harbour bar. She comes at speed. The lifeboat follows her in. She is flung like flotsam. It seems Malcolm has misjudged it. But no: the *Rose of Sharon* makes it.

A high sound like a drawn-out sigh rose up from those strung along the edge of the quay; here and there a woman's voice broke; and Peter saw that there were no words for the wonder that had come upon them, for the relief and joy, for the gallantry of this old man of their blood who had fought death and conquered.

The battle with the Sea has been won. Human tensions remain. Gunn resolves these with three masterly brush-strokes. First comes the exchange between Malcolm and the harbour master—with the brand of bantering under-statement typical of such a community:

" Aye, Malcolm, I see you have a good fishing."
It was the native stroke, and relief ran along the wall as if a trigger had been pulled.
Malcolm straightened his back and glanced up. " Fairly good," he admitted with a faint smile.
" We thought there was a bit of a sea running. . . ."
It was the kind of humour they loved. It was the way their legends were born.

Willie sees Peggy on the shore. Suddenly he understands why Angus acted as he did:

" It was Norman. Angus did not want to annoy Norman. That's why he said that he wanted to go on the lifeboat. Have you never heard that Norman has a daughter called Peggy? "
Willie saw Malcolm's lips come slowly adrift.
" Angus and Peggy; they're walking—and dancing when there's a dance going. I confess I could not understand the lad out yonder for he has your blood in him. Lord Almighty, he would sail us both under and not notice it! Didn't you know? "
Malcolm stood still for a little; then he sat down as if his legs had weakened; and Willie for the first time in

his life saw the forearm that had held the tiller shake.

Willie bunched the fish, so that watching eyes might be misled as to their talk, then he added quietly, " You'll go and thank Norman."

" Yes."

" I could dish out the fish as a present to the lifeboat men, if you like."

" Yes."

" I could give Norman the turbot," said Willie, his wild humour mounting dangerously in him.

" Yes, do that," said Malcolm, all with the solemn wonder and simplicity of a child; and it was only then that Willie realised how deeply this man loved his youngest son, the only one of his three boys who had followed him in the ways of the sea.

Literature has made recurrent (often brutal) use of the father-son relationship. I have come across no instance more blinding than this. It illustrates perfectly Gunn's gift for handling the virtues of tenderness and love without sullying or sentimentalising them. What must follow is the confrontation between Malcolm and Norman. They meet on the path from the shore:

> Simply and sincerely, in a clear voice heard by all, Malcolm said, " I have to thank you, Norman, for standing by us." Then he put out his hand.
>
> Norman looked at him and looked away, as though not seeing the hand.
>
> All those who had lived through the desperate hours stood utterly still in that hollow of shelter behind the headland, watching Malcolm holding out his hand, and suddenly Peter knew, because of the greatness of the sea that was in the man, that he would neither withdraw his hand nor drop it, until Norman decided on his course.
>
> And with an austere sense of justice, some of the older men, aware at last of what had happened under the lee of

Rock Island, knew that Norman was entitled to his moment—if to no more. It was in their eyes.

Norman's face came back to Malcolm's, and something of the grave peace in that face, with its friendly smile, must have touched him, for his hand came out straight, and there and then their two hands gripped openly and strongly.

Instead of a cheer a deeper silence ran through those who were watching, before they turned their heads away, their eyes shining, as though they had been witnesses to an ancient rite.

This *deeper silence* is akin to that experienced at the end of a superbly played symphony, or mass: an interval of no-sound, of spellbound suspense, before release. The same cathartic principles apply. Malcolm's courage is a means, not an end. Through it we, the watchers, are cleansed.

Peter, on shore, has not overheard the exchanges aboard the *Rose of Sharon* and the lifeboat, or between Malcolm and the others. But Willie later tells him, in detail, what had happened. It seems fair, then, to treat the entire episode as impinging directly upon him. He has not only witnessed but been involved in a trial of strength—physical and moral. The struggle has confirmed the fibre of the fishermen. In the scene's ritual context, something of this has been absorbed by Peter. That is to say, he is the better armed for what lies ahead. The strengthening factor is not merely knowledge, but *self*-knowledge. This is substantiated in *The Silver Bough*: the archaeologist, asked what sort of knowledge is extended by disturbing the bones of the dead, replies: *knowledge of ourselves.*

Such apprehension comes in glimmerings. These are the moments when ' the invisible water moves in the well ':

the moments that pervade Gunn's novels and which he elucidates in the autobiographical essays of *The Atom of Delight*.

On board the *Rose of Sharon* Willie ' felt a shiver of wild mirth go over him '. This is one of Gunn's exquisite and infinitesimal equivalents of a sonic boom; a boundary being broken. Such moments are a chiming in the mind, and cannot be grasped or graphed by the intellect alone. The *shiver* is a *frisson* of the spirit; one of the atoms of delight that comprise our psychic identity. Think of Peter's response to the ' ancient rite '. Remember what he experiences (or experiences himself experiencing, so detached is he) in Cocklebuster's pine forest. At such moments, the self is at one with reality. Nor does it impose itself on externals. It is subsumed by them. The process is one not of domination, but of liberation.

Intellectual content is not wholly absent. Keats's urn comes to mind. The poet conceived it, and perceived it. Not only that: he totally identified with it. The key is in the fusion of projection and empathy. This is what makes the little town, the suspended kiss and priestly sacrifice paradoxically perpetual. As the urn is ' immortal' so is the sweetness of unheard melodies, the arrested symphony, the handshake between Malcolm and Norman, the silence of the watchers on the shore.

It is a tiny jump (and one uppermost in Gunn's mind) to the Zen master and his pupil watching the wild geese fly overhead; to the pupil's remark, and the master's instant rejoinder (complete with nose-tweak) that " the geese are *not* gone ".

The essence of Gunn is that these moments of enlightenment contain the ingredient Delight: we recognise them, through our exhilaration. This equation of Reality and Delight may seem even more difficult to sustain than Keats's of Truth and Beauty—which can at least be related to a specific or 'character' context. What really matters is Gunn's claim that the hunt is worth while. The glimpses, he says, are worth seeking. His work, in other words, amounts to an affirmation of the spirit.

This is markedly out of keeping with the times, and with recent literary trends. Gunn pinpoints Delight, as against Despair. He sees a pattern in the whole. Rather than be reduced to fury or cynicism by apparent absurdities, he relishes them. He allows for exercise of the human will.

Against this set Beckett's void, Heller's merry-go-round, the bloodbath of Bond and others. The work of these writers, however varying their stature, is representative of the age in which we live. Mankind's potential for self-immolation is greater than ever before. Society is undergoing a transformation difficult to distinguish from fragmentation. On all sides is evidence of the break-up of the individual psyche. Man's nature appears deterministic, his function arbitrary. Even in the face of this, however, I am not persuaded that Gunn is totally invalidated.

One can no more impose a 'non-affirmative' than an 'affirmative' tone on a writer—without usurping his function. He must be free to fight his battles, in his own arena. His conclusions must be truthfully based on a response to his own experience. Wider validity depends on the extent to which he reveals something applicable not only to his predicament but to that of his fellows. Moreover, he is entitled to apply himself to areas of activity, to elements in man's nature. Granted that literature must face up to absurdity and mortality, need this preclude its remaining, in Pound's phrase, ' an incitement to living '?

Even if (as is on the cards) our world goes up in flames, I cannot see this as a total refutation of Gunn's values—any more than of the human spirit itself, which has produced a Beethoven and a Rembrandt and latterly (more relevantly) Muir, Pasternak and Solzhenitsyn. It will mean simply that their dark counterparts have had, in the final stages of a battle that has been engaged from the start, more devastating machinery at their disposal. This is a subjective judgement, in that it introduces a question of basic (if desperate) belief. What I find heart-warming about Gunn's work (as about the man) is that it goes towards providing a stepping-stone to such belief.

This does not presume, even in myself, an easy acceptance of Gunn's viewpoint and values. For one thing it could be argued that there are crucial contemporary pressure areas which he ignores rather than acknowledges. For another, his quest is for something (like innocence) so elusive that its very existence is a hypothesis. His uninhibited philosophical zeal may thereby appear rarified, over-selective (or reductive) in its terms of reference. His stature as a novelist rests, however, not on such abstract matters, or in ' making them new ', but on his ability to relate them to real life and experience.

However ordained Malcolm's role, however dominant the viking in him, he could not be more down-to-earth. Fand's saving grace is that she is flesh and blood. In *The Atom of Delight* it is ' living passages ' to which Gunn keeps returning. Similarly his animism is a function of real terrors and guilts. Peter in the pine forest, seeing a troll's face peering at him, deserts Sibelius and flees back to his youth, to ' an *actual* wood of his boyhood . . . an *actual* experience ':

> It was a very strange gleam, like a gleam at the end of the world, and suddenly he knew that through it, towards the wood where he was hiding, would come the old man with the beard, the man of authority with the power of the courts, the man who could put terrible shame on him, the old gamekeeper.
>
> Lying here now in this pine forest, Peter actually began listening for the gamekeeper as acutely as he had listened when a boy.

We are back with Kenn at the Well Pool; with Hugh in *Morning Tide*, fastening a hook to a hazel wand; with the boy Gunn himself. For he is Young Art and Old Hector, in one. And his vision of the past has not only clarity but honesty. After all, half the salmon went on a pair of new boots; and while the grilse was being caught, a mother lay dying.

Nor are these moments rooted only in people and their actuality, but in the community and ancestry and primal force that have given them their being. To attribute this to mere skill is to miss the point. There can be no accounting for it, but genius: Gunn's own, and that of his race expressing itself through him. By him our literature and we ourselves are inestimably enriched.

The Quick Movement of Affection : Neil M. Gunn's Short Stories, Plays and Essays [1]

JAMES AITCHISON

In the radio programme, ' In Search of Edwin Muir ', broadcast in April 1964, Neil Gunn spoke of that particular aspect of Muir's vision, the paradox of his simultaneous detachment from and involvement in the human situation. As Gunn explores this attitude, he realises that he and Muir share the same vision, and he clearly identifies with Muir—as he does at several points in the broadcast—when he says:

> He will become detached and, whatever the situation, he will see it objectively with immense clarity. Then this process happens where he and the object fuse and he understands it now as he never understood it before, which I think may help to explain why it is that some of the great figures in history, and in religion, came back and understood their fellow humans and had humility and had, over all, particularly forgiveness because they understood.[2]

The combination of detachment and fusion, separation and involvement, leads to a heightened awareness and an unprecedented understanding of the situation. Objectivity alone is not enough; the new understanding is born of objectivity and involvement, an imaginative participation in the situation, a creative interplay between the situation and the mind of the writer. And Neil Gunn is led to speak of the great figures in religion at this point because this attitude is essentially a religious one in which ' understanding' means an acceptance and enjoyment of the world. In the same statement Gunn continues:

> When you come back now after having had experiences of that sort, you are not escaping from your fellows. On the contrary, you come back to them and you talk to them and you see them as never before, and you forgive them. You can understand what forgiveness means. The person who can't forgive at that point is the person whose ego, whose own ego, has never been vaporised.

As Gunn speaks, his pronoun changes from ' he' to ' you ', reflecting exactly the movement from detachment to involvement. A further change is that the language of religion is modulated to the language of psychology, and in Gunn's vision of life there is no division between the two disciplines, the two complementary ways of looking. Forgiveness is possible with the vaporisation of the ego, and in saying this Gunn is not acquitting or exculpating his fellow-men. For Gunn as for Edwin Muir forgiveness begins within the self in an acknowledgement of the inadequacy of mere ego-personality and an acceptance of the greater self; this attitude of acceptance radiates outwards from the centre to include his world and his fellow-men, so that in Gunn's vision of life forgiveness is not an act of judgement on his fellow-men but an act of communion with them, a celebration of life in the quick movement of affection. It is this vision of life—a vision that is confirmed and extended in *The Atom of Delight*—that underlies and illuminates the short stories, the plays and the essays in *Highland Pack*.

Gunn's themes in these works are essentially the same

as the themes of the novels: childhood and the kindling awareness of life; love and the growth of love from an interpersonal and yet asexual relationship into a widening circle of affection; death and the acceptance of death as part of the pattern, part of the cycle of existence; man's relationship with the land and the sea, a bond that outgrows geographical and temporal limits and becomes a search for a greater harmony and reconciliation.

Childhood, perhaps surprisingly, is a minor rather than a major theme in the short stories. The process of growing up is explored so completely in *Morning Tide* and *Highland River*,[3] the innocence of childhood is expressed so fully in *Young Art and Old Hector* and *The Green Isle of the Great Deep*, and the joys and anguish of adolescence are dealt with in such scrupulously intimate detail in *The Serpent* and *The Drinking Well*, that there seems to be nothing left over for the short stories; or almost nothing. But in three of his short stories, ' Whistle for Bridge ', ' Paper Boats ', and ' Dance of the Atoms ',[4] Gunn looks at childhood from a different angle.

In ' Whistle for Bridge ' Gunn captures one of those awkward, vulnerable periods of childhood when the innocence of the child is breached by a glimpse of the adult world and by a new fallen consciousness. The nine years old Donald cannot understand the discussion of psychology in which his father and a friend are engrossed, nor can he understand the quarrel between the two men he passes on the bank of the Caledonian Canal. And when he sees a salmon in the water—that complex and ambivalent symbol that runs throughout Gunn's work—he feels vulnerable and haunted by the image: ' Donald could not move because he was rigid with fear of this beast that was not a beast but an apparition.' He cannot understand why the swing bridge does not open when he whistles at it, since the board beside the bridge clearly states: ' WHISTLE FOR BRIDGE '. Then he is told that it is the passing boats that must whistle for the bridge, and Gunn writes: ' Revelation caught Donald in a flash of light and he went hot with secret shame.' The revelation is more than the new item of knowledge about whistling for the bridge; and the secret shame is more than Donald's misunderstanding of the notice board. Behind the apparent simplicity of the notice there is the sudden vastness of new knowledge that the child cannot assimilate; the ' revelation ' is that the simplicity of childhood is being replaced by the beginnings of adult consciousness, and the embarrassment of that moment is intensified to a ' secret shame ' because Donald realises that he has stumbled from a primary world of innocence to the edge of a new region of conflict and confusion and guilt. ' Whistle for Bridge ' captures one of those critical turning points in childhood when the young person experiences an intimation of mortality, the instant of perception that the adult tends to dismiss as being impossible in a child.

The delicately oblique approach of ' Whistle for Bridge ' gives way to what seems to be a self-explanatory situation in ' Paper Boats ' when Hugh's paper boat outsails George's. But George's boat had been perfectly fashioned, shaped with care and craftsmanship and concern while Hugh's had been clumsily botched; and through this the boys have their first intimation of chance, of the arbitrary element in life. And the story, expressed in terms of child's play but making a deeply serious observation, is an expression of conflict, the conflict between man and the sea and that other conflict between man and man. The story ends: ' All the world grew silent as though a shining finger had been laid on it. Hugh got up and went away, smiling secretly to himself.' And the source of Hugh's secret satisfaction is his first taste of victory in these two areas of conflict.

Gunn explores another critical turning point in childhood in the chillingly effective story, ' Dance of the Atoms '. Eight years old Charlie wants to be a scientist, a wish that is indulged by the boy's father but gently opposed by his mother, and in this affectionate tension between the parents Gunn expresses, without being didactic, the opposition of the masculine element and the feminine, the rational and analytical as opposed to the imaginative and creative. The tension is expressed playfully in the argument about Charlie's reading material; Dorothy, the mother, suggests fairy tales while Charlie is actually reading *Shooting Electrons*. Dorothy's anxiety is justified because her son's interest in science is obsessive, and his need to prove some scientific point—for example, the carbon monoxide experiment— takes on an urgency that is a barely suppressed hysteria: ' A craving to make atoms perform, as he could make locomotives and coaches perform, began to get a feverish grip on him.' And Charlie makes the atoms perform: he takes the family's pet dog to the garage, starts the car's engine, and leaves the dog there to die; later he hides the dog in the shrubbery. Young Charlie makes the discovery that every child makes when, in a moment of morbid curiosity, he pulls the wings from an insect, as young Finn does with the butterfly in *The Silver Darlings*. But in ' Dance of the Atoms ' the discovery is prompted by a feverish urgency and is acted out in strikingly modern terms. The new consciousness of mortality and guilt is the intimation that touches every growing boy, but here it is also an intimation of the poisonous effects of an obsessively mechanistic world.

In the novels childhood is seen mainly but not exclusively as a state of comparative innocence and timelessness, and if the child is seen as a primitive rather than an angelic creature, then he is a primitive who still inhabits the paradise of unconscious and unfallen childhood. In the three stories discussed above Gunn concentrates on those moments in childhood when the paradise is breached, when the unconscious gives way to a new consciousness, when the innocence is stained by guilt. But when Gunn turns from a minor to a major theme in the short stories, from childhood to love, then he rediscovers a whole new area of innocence.

That so many of his love stories should be songs of innocence rather than of experience may leave some readers dissatisfied, and it could be argued that there is an incompleteness in his treatment of the theme since he deals only with the psychology and not the physiology of the relationship between man and woman. One simply has to accept that Gunn is concerned to recreate the tenderness, the delicacy, the sharpened sensitivity of people in love—a notoriously difficult area for the writer; but one must also accept that he does this with a precision and clarity that never betrays the emotion by reducing it to sentimentality. And in his exploration of these areas Gunn gives an insight into the complexity, the intricacy, the mystery of the phenomenon that one calls love. He accepts that love is ultimately inexplicable and that it is a central part of the total mystery of the human situation; but although it cannot be explained, it can be understood to some extent if the individual is able to acknowledge and assimilate his own experience and to make a sympathetic act of the imagination.

In the short stories as in the novels love is a quickening of the heart, both literally and metaphorically; it brings alternating moments of disorientation and assurance, giddy panics that give way to bewildered and incredulous certainty; it brings confusion in those moments of naïve embarrassment and self-consciousness, and clarity when the presence of the loved one allows the lover to escape from the imprisonment of the self as mere ego-personality; and there are moments when the lovers' delight in each other seems to cleanse their vision of life so that they see the world through a clear lens that reveals something of the original freshness and loveliness. There are occasions in Gunn's love stories when an inter-personal affection outgrows the limitations of the male-female relationship and becomes a love of the world.

This is the case in ' Blaeberries ' and ' The Moor '.[5] In ' Blaeberries ' as in several of Gunn's stories the characters are not named, but this is not, as a recent commentator suggests, a matter of Gunn's ' typical secretiveness '.[6] What matters is not the name but the nature and the identity of the characters, and when the characters are at one and the same time particular and universal, individual and archetypal, then names become almost irrelevant. In ' Blaeberries ' the man sits alone at the edge of the sea and thinks of the woman in these terms: ' She became a figure in desert places; she became a night-wrapped figure of lost dim moorland places; loose-haired, slim-swaying, like a nymph or prophetess.' The woman has a physical existence. and the couple's fierce embrace with which the story closes shows that she is as firmly dressed in resilient flesh as she is wrapped in night. The lover in ' Blaeberries ' like Evan in ' The Moor ' has a double image of woman: there is an acute sense of her physical, objective presence, but there is also an immanent image that haunts the mind like the visitations of a gentle ghost (the image that Jung calls the anima archetype). When the immanent image finds its realisation in the actual woman, when the archetype becomes identified with an individual, then the man's mind is changed, the archetypal image is released and he finds himself in love. In Evan's case Gunn expresses the phenomenon in these terms:

> He awoke to a stillness in his room so intense that he held his breath, listening. His eyes slowly turned to the window where the daylight was not so much fading as changing into a glimmer full of pale life, invisible and watchful. Upon his taut ear the silence began to vibrate with the sound of a small tuning fork struck at an immense distance.

In the intricately effective story, ' Love's Dialectic ',[7] Gunn approaches the situation from the woman's point of view and, although a man can never know to what extent he has penetrated a woman's imagination, Gunn's handling of the situation is totally convincing. The young woman, Anne, admits to herself that the fascination she feels for the man may be prompted by sex, but she thinks— that is, she intuits—her way deeper into the complex of emotions:

> For the first time she saw that you could not diminish a natural force by putting a label on it. In any case,

she knew with complete certainty that this obsessive emotion was something very different from any sex stirrings she had ever had before. She could not even think of him in that direct way. She could only see his face, the slight wave in his brown hair, the movement of his hands, and the expression of his eyes. She felt a craving, a hunger for these features. She wanted to be near them, looking slightly up at them, and the thought of touching them touched the edge of a happiness like a lovely bright delirium.

Throughout this story there is a delicately understated parallelism between the woman's occupation as a wartime censor and her personal attempt at censorship in a mildly Freudian sense as she tries to prevent herself from falling in love. It is when she breaks the professional code of secrecy and reveals the contents of a letter that she is able to acknowledge her love for the man; she kicks over the professional and the psychological traces and finds herself released into a new world: 'She felt somnambulant, walking in a new world, made out of the union of the old night world and old day world. A new world.'

Not all the love stories are as effective as this, and in some of them there is no sense of a release into the new world. In 'On the Stone'[8] Gunn expertly captures the awkwardness, the self-consciousness, and the embarrassment of love between two young people, but the prolonged cliff-hanging episode in which the two are literally suspended from the edge of a cliff wrenches the story from the subtly psychological into the wildly histrionic. There is distortion again in 'Black Woollen Gloves'.[9] Gunn shows two lonely young people coming together through a series of unplanned but deeply wished for meetings, and the story is effective as a study of the two finding their way from their separate isolations to the communion of love. But the Maughamish ending introduces a cleverness, a trivial sophistication, that contradicts the naïvety that is the essence of the situation. And in ' Pure Chance ' [10] the story strains in so many different directions—young love, adventure at sea, mystery and suspense—that it finally disintegrates. But there are other stories in which Gunn handles several elements simultaneously and brings them together in a natural unity.

' The Chariot ', the opening story in *The White Hour*, and the title story [11] show an interaction and interdependence of the themes of youth and age, love and death, the quick movement of affection and the negative vision of life. The doctor, the central figure in ' The Chariot ', regularly visits old Donald Macready as he nears death; at the same time the doctor is in love with Macready's niece, Johanna. They are aware of their love but they cannot express it, not out of respect for the dying man but rather because Macready's mercenary, predatory attitude to life casts a shadow and a spell over the young people's love. The doctor feels this intensely on one of his visits to Macready:

> To the doctor, however, there was in the hollows and bone ridges, in the withdrawn expression, a pathos that affected him, in an unexpected moment of feeling, with a sense of colossal guilt. Not so much his own guilt, as the guilt of all mankind, an incredible and pathetic conspiracy in guilt.

When the old man dies, the doctor and Johanna come together naturally, and in the moment of physical contact the doctor finds a communion that releases him from impersonality and cancels the conspiracy of guilt:

> And the mood that had been growing within him
> these last years, the half-friendly but arid insight, the
> deadly insight, was dissolved, and life ran in a wild
> warm tide.

It is an old woman who is nearing death in ' The White
Hour '. She has felt the presence of death, the palpable,
terrifying nearness that she expresses in terms of " that
terrible white light hurting the balls of my eyes and pressing
long white fingers against my forehead. Pushing me back,
it was, back...." But unlike the old man in ' The Chariot '
who tries to feed on the vitality of others in a last desperate
attempt to deny death, the old woman accepts the situation.
She reaches out of her personal wilderness not to take life
but to give it, and to bring the young man and the young
woman together:

> The white skeleton fingers came out and caught his
> passing hand, and held it. . . . " In the world there is
> no girl like her," was her only saying, and with that her
> hands dropped.

Death is one of the recurring themes in Gunn's short
stories. In his first collection, *Hidden Doors*, published in
1929, it is the subject matter of ' The Uncashed Cheque ',
' Between Headlands ', and ' Hidden Doors ',[12] but each
of these three stories depends to some extent on a formula,
a fateful twist, an element of mystery that is contrived
rather than natural, and one notes that none of the three
is reprinted in *The White Hour*. In the best of his stories
on the theme Gunn sees death as part of the pattern of
existence so that, far from being morbid or depressing,

K

death is seen as a fulfilment and a completion of the human journey.

In 'Symbolical'[13] a sick old crofter wanders across the moor during a spring blizzard; later he is found dead, frozen stiff in the snow. Geordie Acharn's death on the moor is grimly appropriate; the impression that emerges from the story is not that he has been defeated by the elements and the landscape but rather that, feeling the nearness of death, he has been impelled to make a final contact with the land against which he has struggled and by which he has been sustained throughout his life. With his death he becomes part of that landscape, and when a neighbouring crofter finds the corpse it is as if the dead man had discovered, in the very moment of his death, the final stage in his relationship with the land: '... his eyes wide in a fixed stare at the inimical expanse as though they could not get over some final knowledge that had been vouchsafed them'.

This concept of death as a final relationship with the individual's environment is one that Gunn develops in the stories, and as it develops, death comes to be seen as a return to the source of life, a re-entry into the matrix of existence. This is the case in 'Such Stuff as Dreams', 'Down to the Sea,' 'Henry Drake Goes Home' and, allowing for the element of suicide and the aura of necromania, in 'Half-Light'.[14]

'Such Stuff as Dreams' is similar to 'Symbolical'. in concept and structure, but it is more fully and explicitly stated. An old farmer leaves his sick-bed and sets out to rediscover the lochan in the hills that he had known as a boy. He is delirious, and yet beneath the hallucinations there is an urgency and clarity of purpose: he must find the way back, ' a sheep-track so lonely, so lost, that its loneliness induced laughter, a gaeity of companionship. . . .' And it becomes clear that the sleep-wandering old man is searching for a place that is more than geographical; he is being drawn back to ' some magical place known to the heart with an absolute intimacy, with a sense of healing and rejuvenation in its very look '. The old man's walk to the lochan is a version of the *peregrinatio*,[15] the spiritual journey through which the pilgrim hopes to find his place of acceptance, of reconciliation, or even of resurrection; the place where, as Gunn's delirious old farmer knows, ' the burning body could slip its burden, be purged of its fever '. And the fact that the old man has been hallucinating to the extent that he has been walking, not to a lochan in the Scottish hills, but to a water-hole in the Canadian prairie, does not invalidate the journey; instead, it intensifies the sense of pilgrimage because in his hallucinatory state there has emerged from his unconscious mind the archetypal image of the spiritual journey and a vision of man's origin and end.

It is essentially the same journey that is undertaken by Lachie in ' Down to the Sea ' and by Henry Drake in ' Henry Drake Goes Home '. Lachie, a retired fisherman, walks by the sea each evening, and as the story develops one realises that he is not simply taking a stroll; he is drawn irresistibly back to the element from which he had won his living, drawn by his ineluctable relationship with the sea. And this love of the sea is intensified, thrown into a sharper relief because the fishing has ended; the curing sheds are now roofless, the beached boats are rotting on the shore, and the cooperages are boarded up. Life on land is a waking death, but when Lachie looks to the sea: " Ay, the sea, always the sea, restless, full of infinite variety—yet ever the same, eternally changeless. . . ." Whether old Lachie's death by drowning is an accident or a suicide, it is inevitable and strangely beautiful because it is a return to the known and loved and living element. Henry Drake's journey is treated differently. On the outbreak of war Drake decides to walk from his place of exile in the North of Scotland back to his home in Devon, and the official in the pensions office of the northern town records Drake's progress in terms of cashed pension orders and occasional inquiries from the police. The official finds that as Drake continues, he ceases to be a case study and assumes ' lines of a mythical simplicity '. He realises that ' Henry Drake was going back to something deep in him as life itself '. And although Drake dies in Manchester, the official knows that the old man's real journey has been completed.

> They could deal with the body as he himself would now deal with this loose-leaf. The spirit eluded all bureaucratic forms. And the spirit of Henry Drake had gone home to Devon.

Neil Gunn's preoccupation with a sense of place in the short stories is ultimately a spiritual concern, and the journey that his characters make is a form of pilgrimage. In this there is clearly an element of nostalgia, which, like those other concerns of Gunn's such as innocence and tenderness and love, is so frequently mishandled and misunderstood by others that it tends to be a pejorative rather than a descriptive term. Nostalgia is a love of home, and the concept of home that emerges from Gunn's stories, plays and essays is more than geographical or topographical; home is the goal of the *peregrinatio*, the place or the state of mind in which man finds reconciliation; home is the achievement of an understanding of life, a vision of life that makes this reconciliation possible; home is the fulfilment of the human journey. This concept of home emerges clearly from the short stories, but any lingering doubt is removed by Gunn's non-fiction writing, *Off in a Boat, Highland Pack, The Atom of Delight,* and the essays in *Saltire Review* during the period 1958 to 1961.[16] Between the fiction and the non-fiction lie the plays. Here the sense of place is just as profound, the love of home as intense, but the concern is expressed in a fiercely passionate, bitterly ironic way, and with an edge of aggression that is rare in Gunn's work.

The anger and the bitterness is present in Gunn's first play, *Back Home,* published in 1932. The central figure is the young man, Iain Cattanach, essentially the same Iain Cattanach who reappears in the novel, *The Drinking Well,* some fourteen years later. Iain has lived in Glasgow, but his love of the land has drawn him back home. He returns to his origins only to find that he is regarded as a failure:

> You think I don't see? Ah, Granny, I see all right. I am the one unpardonable sin—the man who came back to the land! Back to the land—eh, Granny! You know, that's why the lawyers who are the great politicians—that's why they have to stay in their big houses in the great cities—so that it will be handy for them to shout " Back to the land." And sometimes they come back themselves—for the shooting in the autumn.

Young Cattanach's bitterness is prompted by his awareness of a great conflict and by his inability to resolve the conflict; it is the conflict between the 'great politicians' and the poor crofters, between Highland and Lowland ways of life, and between himself and his father. But the main source of his bitterness is that he came home and was rejected. The decision to return was prompted by ' memories of the glen ', of ' the long quiet hours on the hill ', and of ' a night at the bothy when the cattle are up at the summer grazing '. When he finds that he cannot be readmitted to this way of life, this home, Cattanach leaves again. His departure symbolises to some extent the depopulation of the Highlands, which in turn is like a modern re-enactment of the Clearances; and it is not too fanciful to suggest that the Clearances were a wretched re-enactment of the archetypal expulsion from Eden.

Gunn's second play, *Choosing a Play*, first published in 1935, is subtitled ' A Comedy of Community Drama ', and it sparkles with a vital, affectionate humour. But beneath the comedy there is a deeply serious argument. The search for a suitable play to stage at a drama festival becomes a search for the identity of the Scots, a search that reveals again the ' Caledonian antisyzygy ', the great schizothymic dilemma that plagues the race. The point is made forcefully by Flora, the most articulate and passionately committed of the five characters in the play:

> The tragedy is that you bluff yourselves, that you smear our people with your mawkish sentiment as if they were sheep and you had to disinfect them from life, against living, against all that is fine and splendid and daring. They can't even laugh. They wheeze. They are pawky and canny. O God, canny! The Scots race canny—the only mad spendthrift race in the history of Europe. . . . You sneer at poetic drama— but history has shown it to live and move in the land. The land where Scotsmen—the world's maddest fools—

so often risked all for an ideal—and finally lost all to the canniest nation in Christendom.

Flora's case—and to some extent she may be speaking for Gunn himself—is not chauvinistic or xenophobic; unlike Hugh MacDiarmid, Gunn makes no appeal to anglophobia, and unlike Edwin Muir in *Scott and Scotland* he makes no attack on Calvinism. Flora's passionate commitment is to the Scots and to an uncompromising spirit of life. Appropriately, it is she who has the last words in the play: ' Remember, never give in—or you're lost. Never, never let us give in.'

In total contrast to the urgent search for identity and the impassioned assertion of life in *Choosing a Play*, Gunn's next play, *Old Music*, published in 1939, is filled with such a profound sadness that in the end it is an elegy for the loss of a whole way of life. The central character is old Mrs Ross, and as the play opens her grandson is leaving the small Highland community for a new life in Canada. Mrs Ross sees her grandson's departure as a stage in a continuing process of desolation, and she says:

> It's not only that the fire burns down, till nothing but the dead ash is left: the roof of our habitation is destroyed and the dead ash is scattered and the hearthstone itself lies cold under the sky for evermore . . . and the earth here, our own earth, has become bare as the smooth rocks at noonday in barren places.[17]

Mrs Ross is both individual and archetypal, a sibylline figure who prophesies the loss of a language and a culture and a whole way of life; for decades she has watched and experienced the disintegration of a society until she feels that the society itself has a death wish, ' a terrible, terrible destroying of the spirit—by the spirit itself'. It is at this point in the play that the folklorists, Mrs Smith-Wanders and her nephew Arthur, appear. They have come to record the old music before it finally dies out, and their dialogue is like a black parody of the death rites as Arthur says to his aunt: 'I merely have the feelings of one of those johnnies who used to rob graves.'

Outside the novels, *Old Music* is Gunn's most pessimistic comment on life in the Highlands, and if the depth of his pessimism is an indication of his despair, it also indicates the intensity of his love for the people. In his fourth play, *Net Results*, also published in 1939, Gunn expresses his concern for the country and the people and their way of life in another set of terms. The nostalgia of *Back Home*, the search for an identity and a role in *Choosing a Play*, the bitter elegy of *Old Music*—these arguments give way to the hard economic argument of *Net Results*.

Again the title of the play is ironic: the Sinclair family earn their living by fishing, but the net results of their efforts is continuing debt. The Sinclair parents, Dan and Johan, accept the situation with a resignation that contains elements of stoic dignity and also a pathetic fatalism, but their grown-up children, Meg and Tom, fight back. Meg, with a passion that resembles Flora's in *Choosing a Play*, argues the case on moral grounds; her brother Tom presents the case in precisely detailed economic terms, quoting prices, profit margins, interest rates and insurance premiums, and Tom concludes: 'We have paid far more in bank interest and insurance in the last ten years than the total amount of money we now owe you.' Morally and economically the Sinclairs' case is irrefutable but, although

Jamieson the bank manager is not unsympathetic, he insists that the debt be cleared or the boat and the gear will be taken as payment. The Sinclair family, who represent an industry and a culture, are forced into the position of debtors and beggars, but it is society at large that is the debtor; and the distortions of our society allow the Sinclairs to become the victims of an impersonal, predatory financial system. And here one cannot avoid noting the grotesque extension of the irony of *Net Results*: it took a world war to allow the Sinclairs—that is, the small fishermen of Scotland—a temporary solvency.

Neil Gunn's four plays show his fundamental involvement in the life of his people, but his way of expressing that involvement varies from play to play. In his collection of essays, *Highland Pack*, there is no such ambivalance. The essays were written as ' nature notes ' for *The Scots Magazine* during the war, but they outgrew the genre of nature notes and become something much more. Gunn's vision of life, a vision that is founded on wonder and delight, gives the essays a continuity and a unity. As the book evolves—month by month, season by season, year by year—one becomes aware of man's deepening relationship with the natural world until in the end this expression of an intricate and intimate relationship is a celebration of life itself.

Highland Pack is descriptive writing of the very highest order; on page after page Gunn captures the infinite variety, the colours and textures and contours and movements of the natural world in a radiantly lucid prose that is a recreation of that world. Gunn is impelled to recreate his world because he is constantly astonished and haunted by its beauty. He has a sense of the miraculous, of the

K 2

luminous element in life that gives *Highland Pack* a religious quality, the religion of acceptance and gratitude and joy:

> The sun would pierce through, and all the world would fill with light; brim and tremble and spill over, and off sped the light over the grass and in among the wild roses and glittering across the sea. The sheer freshness of such a moment had surely the spirit of creation in it, a first creation.[18]

The book is filled with moments like this, moments in which Gunn sees the thing itself—the flight of a bird, the intricate configuration of a landscape, the movement of clear water, the quality of light that spills across a skyline—and then sees beyond the thing into a region where all things coexist in a harmony that is beyond the reach of time. Gunn himself anticipates the accusation of ' escapism ' in all this; he is aware that if an individual is determined to deny the mystery of life, to reduce it to an ' explanation ' or pervert it into an ideology, then there is no possible answer to the charge that would satisfy such an individual. But in the chapter, ' The Wilds of Sutherland ', Gunn observes:

> For, after all, from what does one escape—and into what? Mostly from an overdose of mass feeling of sensationalism into the forgotten reality of oneself.

And for Gunn the self is not the ego-personality, not the factors that separate man from his fellow-men and from his environment, but rather those features that unite so that, with the way of looking that he calls ' the quick movement of affection ',[19] man can see that he is part of the pattern of existence, part of ' the totality of mystery '.[20]

Throughout *Highland Pack* and indeed throughout all his work Gunn is aware of the rhythms of life. He feels the rhythms of man; the throb of the human pulse, the beating of the heart and the circulating blood, the tide of breathing; he is aware, too, of the rhythms of the natural world, the sea's tides, the cycles of the days and the seasons and the years, the revolutions of the planet; he is aware of the ultimate unity of these rhythms. He observes the fall of a leaf, and he writes:

> The eye followed its slanting descent, and not so much thought as the blood itself became conscious of fullness, of a natural process completed in all its stages and now falling out of space, through time, slowly, as in a dream. Each leaf had all the lightness of a dream-like motion, a setting out for the last time upon an individual journey.[21]

This movement of affection for mankind and the world, and the corresponding visitations of mankind and the planet in a warm constant haunting, result in a fulfilment and harmony that is a form of mysticism.

NOTES ON REFERENCES

1   *Hidden Doors:* Edinburgh, Porpoise Press, 1929; *The White Hour:* London, Faber, 1950; *Back Home:* Glasgow, Wilson, 1932; *Choosing a Play: A Comedy of Community Drama:* Edinburgh, Porpoise Press, 1938 (first published 1935); *Old Music* in *North Light: Ten New One-Act Plays from the North*, compiled by Winifred Bannister: Glasgow, McLellan, 1947 (first published 1939); *Net Results:* London, Nelson, 1939; *Highland Pack:* London, Faber, 1949.
2   'In Search of Edwin Muir': B.B.C. Broadcast of 28th April 1964; p. 16 of script.

3   Gunn's early short story, 'The Sea', published in *Hidden Doors*, is rewritten and incorporated in *Morning Tide*.

4   *The White Hour*, pp. 28-32; pp. 51-7; pp. 128-42.

5   Ibid., pp. 65-8; pp. 274-85.

6   *Essays on Neil M. Gunn*, p. 23: Edited by David Morrison, Thurso, Caithness Books, 1971.

7   *The White Hour*, pp. 143-57.

8   Ibid., pp. 104-17.

9   Ibid., pp. 118-27.

10   Ibid., pp. 192-213.

11   Ibid., pp. 11-27; pp. 80-5.

12   *Hidden Doors*, pp. 116-32; pp. 170-5; pp. 176-90.

13   *The White Hour*, pp. 58-64.

14   Ibid., pp. 185-91; pp. 214-21; pp. 242-50; pp. 257-73.

15   See Chadwick, Nora: *The Celts*, pp. 204-6: Harmondsworth, Penguin Books, 1970.

16   *Saltire Review*, Vol. 5, Summer 1958, No. 15; Vol. 5, Autumn 1958, No. 16; Vol. 5, Winter 1958, No. 17; Vol. 6, Spring 1959, No. 18; Vol. 6, Autumn 1959, No. 19; Vol. 6, Winter 1961, No. 23.

17   Compare the archetypal Mrs Ross with Mrs Scott in Iain Crichton Smith's *Consider the Lilies*, and compare Gunn's symbolism of 'dead ash' with George Mackay Brown's poem, 'Dead Fires' in *Fishermen with Ploughs*.

18   Op. cit., p. 157.

19   Ibid., p. 187.

20   Ibid., p. 30.

21   Ibid., p. 218.

GENERAL

The Boy in the Stream :
The Development of Some Fundamental Concepts in the Work of Neil M. Gunn

J. B. PICK

Neil Gunn was born in Dunbeath on the craggy coast of Caithness into a community of crofters and fishermen at a time when this community was viable. Tom, 'the Philosopher', when reflecting on his own life in *The Serpent* (1943) shows the essential nature of the tradition in which Neil grew up.

> In my boyhood, I never actually remember seeing the laird in person, the owner of the land. . . . Once a year the men put on their Sunday suits and went to the place where the Factor was having his sitting for the collection of rents. They paid their pound or two, got their dram and came away. After that each man was his own master, worked his own land, having no boss or bureaucrat over him to drive or direct him. Accordingly in the community as a human or going concern, all were equal in social status, or rather the idea of class distinction among themselves could not arise, simply because it did not exist. The farther back you go the clearer this becomes because you recede more from the power of money. Then almost everything was, as we say, 'in kind'. Even what tribute was paid to the chief as leader was paid in kind. . . . But the crofting country, through long centuries, had reached beyond an active bureaucracy and leaders. True, the chief at intervals stirred up the clansmen to fight for some

power-scheme the chiefs had on hand, some dirty business or other, but actually for generations on end whole regions of the countryside lived in peace, cultivating the land and rearing their cattle and sheep. The individual bits of dirty business are remembered. History has so far been a remembering of the dirty business rather than an understanding of the arts and way of life of the peaceful generations. . . .

They naturally helped one another and at certain times—say, at the peat-cutting,—they voluntarily joined forces and worked in squads, and these were usually the happiest times of all. In short, you had a true balance between the maximum freedom of the individual and the common welfare of all, and at the same time . . . they had no bosses, no tyrants, no bureaucrats, no profit-drivers among themselves. . . .

And our minds quite naturally take the next step and say: if we could get our society today, *with* the machine, working after the old pattern . . . then once more the life of the folk would be warm and rich and thick. . . .

In *Butcher's Broom* (1934) Neil Gunn shows the crofting communities broken by the Clearances; in *The Silver Darlings* (1941) he shows the communities of crofter-fishermen building themselves on the wild and rocky coast. Continually he looks for the meaning of these events not in purely historical terms but in the sense: what has experience developed among these people that will stand up to the worst that time and circumstance can do to them? And his own experience of the community when it was full and alive sank deep into his consciousness a knowledge of the unyielding, canny accommodation his people made to the realities of the natural world. Land and sea were not enemies to be fought but dour, dangerous and rewarding partners within the rhythm of change. In subtle and essential ways this community made a unity of work and play. The work was hard and life frugal but play was *within the pattern*. The division of work as money-making toil from leisure as ' pleasure-seeking ' has been a loss to man's innate nature—a loss of health and unity. And it was recognition of this shared experience in the Chinese tradition which gave him such affection for the Ch'an formula: ' I draw water, I chop wood—miraculous deeds and acts of wonder! '

From his childhood he gained a faith in human nature which in fact remains the best basis for understanding it. The nature of man and of the Way proper to him are such that the awareness necessary for the acceptance of truth is achieved by following them.

Carl Rogers, the psychotherapist, approaching the matter from another direction, writes:

> When man . . . denies to awareness various aspects of his experience then we have all too often to fear him and his behaviour. . . . But when he is most fully man, when he is his complete organism, when awareness of experience . . . is most fully operative, then he is to be trusted, then his behaviour is constructive. . . . When a man's unique capacity of awareness is thus functioning freely and fully, we find that we have, not an animal whom we must fear . . . but an organism able to achieve, through the remarkable integrative capacity of its central nervous system, a balanced, realistic, self-enhanc- ing . . . behaviour.

To show how this community functioned even in decline let me describe its treatment of the ' idiot '. The hardware store in the Highland village near which I lived was kept by an elder of the Kirk known as Kennybuie. He did his best not to take money for his goods and survived because his customers conspired to defeat him. This was not easy for his customers because Kenny was a difficult man to argue with—he smiled so much and was so reluctant to commit himself to anything so definite as a denial.

He was a natural guardian for the idiot, though not related to him. The idiot was a round-faced man in his forties. He sat on an upturned herring box outside Kennybuie's store. It was his job to unload deliveries and his finest hour in each day came with the arrival of the mail bus. When it passed his herring box he set off at a lumbering trot until it stopped at the post office. Then he carried the newspapers from bus to shop with such dignity and self-importance that his tormentors, the kids of the village, scattered before him like hens before an elephant. On celebration day at the end of the war the village organised a procession led by a piper. At least the procession should have been led by a piper and the piper was certainly there piping vigorously but in front of the piper walked the idiot beaming with delight and waving his arms approximately in time to the music. Kennybuie provided him with a job and a status in the community, and the community as a whole accepted him as he was; in a city, having no family to look after him, he would have ended in an institution.

Neil Gunn's concentration upon this community in growth and decline in all its complexity (witness *The Key of the Chest*, 1945) had nothing to do with nostalgia. When he looks backward it is with an imaginative realism none the less realistic because it is imaginative. He was asked by *Chambers's Journal* for a series of short stories. *Chambers's* was a magazine with a limited market of a particular kind.

Neil hit upon the idea of stories dealing with the relationship of an old man and a small boy, and the adventures natural to them both. Such a framework would ensure that the taboos inevitable to *Chambers's Journal* could be safely forgotten, while at the same time the old man/small boy relationship was a real and familiar one in the Highland community, for those too old and those too young to do the full work of the place were inevitably companions. The result was published in book form as *Young Art and Old Hector* (1942).

Some time after the publication of this book Naomi Mitchison said to Neil that the stories seemed to her a touch over-gentle, and left out too much. Reflecting on this, and upon the appalling realities of the contemporary world—violence, tyranny, the destruction of human nature, concentration camps, purges—Neil decided to take young Art and old Hector and to show what their tradition has to say about such realities. The result was his imaginative and philosophical masterpiece *The Green Isle of the Great Deep* (1944) which deals with what human nature *is* and how it is distorted and destroyed by power, will and the analytic intellect.

The Gaelic paradise is visited by young Art and old Hector, who find it to be run scientifically by the methods of applied psychology. A man " if he is a physicist always has only one ultimate end in view: the discovery of the pattern of physical events. If he is a psychologist, the discovery of the pattern of mental events ". So says a student in the *Green Isle*. These discoveries are applied by the Questioner, whose function it is to lay open the unconscious and uproot the conscious mind. The separate, rootless consciousness is left, so that all men are shallow and obedient; they can no longer resist the efficiency of reason, and the Questioner is a trained reasoner. The Questioner probes all motives and the subconscious basis for any possible rebellion is revealed. His victims are impotent; released from their psychological burdens they grow flat and shadowless.* The Questioner remarks:

> "The later phase of life on Earth has tended to destroy the wholeness of the child mind at a very early stage. The intensive pursuit of what is called education has also tended to disintegrate the young mind. Where the young mind undergoes disintegration, its capacity for coherence and action are impaired. It can thus quickly be made amenable to those who can gather the parts together and suggest a saving line of action."

Such people as the Questioner

> live in their heads, where the knowledge of power gives to a good intention the edge of a sword. . . . The salmon of wisdom is caught in their net, and when the salmon is caught in the net of the law, its wisdom, which must be free, escapes through the mesh. . . . For love is the creation, and cruelty is that which destroys. In between there is no-man's-land, where men in their pride arrange clever things on the arid ground.

In all Neil Gunn's work there is awareness that if a man does not keep for himself an inner core of secret reality, he loses his birthright. Of what does this secret core consist? The clue lies in the fact that the woman Mary and the boy Art are alone able to resist the Questioner. Mary persuades her husband Robert to eat of the real, forbidden fruit which grows in the Green Isle, instead of eating only the

---

* Since the book was published brainwashing techniques have been used by governments everywhere, and most people know something about them.

de-energised gruel provided by the authorities. And Art
says to Hector, after having conversed with God:

" You see, first of all you get the knowledge. Then
you get wisdom. You follow that? "
" I follow."
" Then," said Art, another tone down, " you get
something else." And he looked at Hector who looked
at him.
" What? " asked Old Hector.
" The magic," said Art.

And a little later it is said: " For when knowledge
completes itself in wisdom, the magic is released."
What is the meaning of knowledge completing itself
in wisdom and releasing the magic?

Old Hector's eyes glimmered. " The ripe hazel
nuts of knowledge fell into the pool and the salmon
of wisdom ate them."
" And was made the wiser for the knowledge he ate.
It is the natural order. There is no other."
" And the pool— "
" The pool is everyman's pool of life."
" It is a beautiful legend," said Old Hector. " I
never saw it like that before."

But God answers him: " You saw it—but you had not
yet brought it into your head in order to puts words on it."
In *Morning Tide* (1931), *Highland River* (1937) and
again in *The Atom of Delight* (1956) Neil Gunn uses the boy
seeking in his river for that actual fish which is at once a
salmon for the pot, a forbidden treasure and the ancient
salmon of wisdom. In *The Atom of Delight* he describes
the boy sitting on a boulder staring downstream, cracking
and eating nuts.

The shallow river flowed around and past with its variety of lulling monotonous sounds; a soft wind, warmed by the sun, came upstream and murmured in my ears as it continually slipped from my face. . . .

Then the next thing happened, and happened, so far as I can remember, for the first time. I have tried but can find no simpler way of expressing what happened than by saying: *I came upon myself sitting there.*

Within the mood of content, as I have tried to recreate it, was this self and this self was me.

The state of content deepened wonderfully and everything around was embraced in it.

There was no ' losing ' of the self in the sense that there was a blank from which I awoke or came to. The self may have thinned away . . . it did—but so delightfully that it also remained at the centre in a continuous and perfectly natural way. And then within this amplitude the self as it were became aware of seeing itself, not as an ' I ' or an ' ego ' but rather as a stranger it had come upon and was even a little shy of.

The self which the boy came upon is not the *willing* self which seeks to dominate and control, but another self entirely, a hidden self which can only awaken while the will is asleep or occupied elsewhere. It is worth mentioning that this awakening can take place in action as well as in contemplation, for example in vocational work or in a game or sport when a man is fully ' in form '. To be ' in form ' is to move and act at once, without calculation, with no interruption between event and response. A man in form achieves what he does without strain. Nothing is forced. And within the self-loss that feels like self-fulfilment there are moments when an awareness of detached joy in unity comes upon him as if by surprise, a wondering realisation of existence which can be expressed: " So this is what the world is like, and here *I* am in it!" Both from his sitting on the boulder in the stream and from his pursuit of the salmon Neil gained the same insight.

Again and again in his books he indicates that we all search for the fulfilment of an experience in which the normal everyday self that insists and hopes and fears and desires and hates and agitates and worries is overcome, and the second self released. For example, the story told to Peter on page 62-3 of *The Well at the World's End* (1951) is a real story told to Neil by a real shepherd. It ends like this:

> "There had been a drying wind, too—not too cold. But now the wind had gone with the sun, and over the moor there was a fine light that went blue in the distance. I never before saw so—so beautiful a sight, so wide and—and beautiful. It came over me."
>
> Peter could neither move nor speak; he felt the boundary growing thin.
>
> "I am a married man," said the shepherd, "with three of a young family and though I say it myself I know when I'm well off. But—*I didn't want to go home.*"

Anyone who has experienced wonder knows that he must keep secret that inner core which actually *grows* with every such experience. If this inner core is probed, intellectualised, analysed, then the miracle will not happen and knowledge cannot complete itself in wisdom and set free the magic.

The value of a living community is that it serves to protect the inner core while making the life of work and struggle a form of *sharing*.

> A man could do what he liked with his own, whether croft or boat, and if he didn't do well he suffered. If bodily or other misfortune was the cause of

the suffering, then the others helped; as naturally, in fact, as a storm spread havoc or things grew in their season. (*The Atom of Delight.*)

In his thirteenth year Neil was sent away to relatives in Galloway for two years, where he was educated by a private tutor and found himself much alone. Community was broken. When he succeeded in passing the entrance examination for the Civil Service he was posted to London and initiated into the patterns and confusion of city life. What is essential in his reaction to such experience is not the loneliness and isolation he may have suffered but his continued recognition of the human struggle to create community and of the individual struggle to achieve spiritual independence, and that the two somehow go together—that if you have one without the other you have an insufficiency. He writes of himself and his fellows at this time, working during the day and cramming for exams at night:

> Now all this should have induced in the boys at least an anxiety neurosis. They should have scurried to the cramming college and had nightmares over essays in English composition. Suffering from malnutrition and introspection, they should have seen acres of mean streets as haunts of seedy sin. But nothing like this happened. Even the prospect of being thrown on the scrap-heap left them with a vague feeling of landing on their feet. (*The Atom of Delight.*)

Much later in his life, when Neil had passed his examinations for the middle reaches of the Civil Service, when his bachelor days were over and he had married Jessie Frew, he was sent to Wigan with the Customs and Excise department, and his reaction to this epitome of the industrial north of England was not one of dismay but recognition. Without the solidity of inner life which early growth in community gave him he might have felt threatened by this teeming alien urban life, but he did not. He recognised in the people a warmth of spirit which he had met before, a human reality he *knew*.

It is because his pilgrimage was in fact a series of recognitions of what he had already experienced in the community of his boyhood that the formula from the *Tao Te Ching*, ' Man follows Earth, Earth follows Heaven, Heaven follows the Way, the Way is what it is ', suits him so well. It is his unity with this formula that explains his understanding of the nature of freedom. ' So long as the second self remains whole,' he wrote, ' he will adventure, take a chance, cunningly avoid or evade, break the rules, spontaneously run his fantastic risks, until he comes to the stone in the river and cracks his nuts.' (*The Atom of Delight.*) Freedom lives in spontaneity, and one definition of freedom would be that state of mind for which spontaneous response is possible.

Throughout his life Neil Gunn has reacted with suspicion to all developments in society, government and literature which tend to split either individual or communal wholeness. Ludwig Klages in *The Science of Character* clearly states the dangers that Neil himself has seen and fought against for so long:

> . . . if we consider [the spiritual history] or Europe, it shows that horrible assault upon actuality which in a few centuries will have destroyed life completely on this planet. . . . Man completely deprived of soul and a pure machine of the will . . . a slave of a relatively small

minority of exploiters. This is the end of the ' ethical process ' of mankind.

As a young man in the Customs and Excise service, restored to the Highlands and continually in the company of that romantic, expansive and sensitive Irishman Maurice Walsh, he not only became one of the most subtle appreciators of whisky in Scotland but was able to give himself to the outdoor life which takes you to wild places where people are so few that they are always welcome, and where reality can change from sunny to threatening with a mere creeping of the clouds. The boyhood experience of hunting and fishing was revived and deepened, giving to all his books an underlying symbolism of hunt and quest—the physical hunt for food and the intellectual and spiritual hunt for meaning fused into an experience of wholeness which is its own reward. The search for the ' well at the world's end ' comes full circle to recognition that the end of the world is a familiar boulder in the middle of the stream where sits a small boy cracking nuts or a Chinese philosopher looking at the sky:

> How wonderful! How wonderful! There is no birth-and-death from which one has to escape, nor is there any supreme knowledge after which one has to strive. All the complications past and present are not worth the trouble of describing them.

Maurice Walsh's *The Key Above the Door* and Neil's *The Grey Coast* were published in the same year, 1926, and although it would be hard to find two books more different, either in method or intention, Neil and Maurice learned from one another. Maurice was always in the deepest difficulty over his plots, which became tenuous and convoluted because of over-anxiety, so that he applied frequently to Neil for suggestions. But the quality of his writing about the Highland countryside transcends his plots. I cannot resist quoting a few lines as witness:

> The sand was dry, and ran and crunched under his rope soles. The tide was barely moving. A small ripple lipped in, drew back, met another ripple, and made little wrinkles of commotion that cast shimmering reflections on the sunlit bottom. The ripple, the shimmer, the lovely translucent faint-green of the water were enticing.

To imagine a young man growing up in the Highlands of Scotland without confronting the realities of the Presbyterian Church is to imagine a blind and dumb impossibility. Neil Gunn's attitude to this confrontation has always been ambiguous. He feels his way back to an earlier pagan tradition of the Celtic peoples, seeing, for example, in the pilgrimage of Columba not so much the character and achievement of Columba himself as the character and achievement of those pagans who allowed Columba to convert them by the exercise of argument and reason. Not so barbaric, surely! This is one more reason why he recognised in the Taoist and Ch'an tradition of China a tradition close to his own, content to understand man without insisting upon putting the gods on an operating table.

Sun Circle, Neil's fourth novel, was published in 1933. In it the Druid says:

> " But inasmuch as ours is not a simple belief, but an intense and prolonged striving to get at the dividing of forces, with no gain and no loss, with no question of reward beyond the reward of being there, therefore we may feel that it possesses human loveliness in its naked form."

In a piece called ' Wells and Wishes ' in *Highland Pack* (1949) he writes:

> There is still a saying in the Gaelic north: *Tha e fox dhruidheachd,* which literally means: ' he is under druidism '—that is, he is bewitched; and another: *Tha e ri druidheachd*—' He is into druidism '—meaning that he is talking like a lewd pagan, for the time came when druidism was lewdness to Christian thought. What was in nature was the enemy of the Christian who considered himself born in sin.

But Neil did not consider himself born in sin. Although the greater part of his novel *The Serpent* is taken up with the conflict between Tom the atheist and his father, the Calvinist authoritarian, Neil himself did not need to depart from Christianity into atheism, for Christianity had never been his home. He was always aware that nature and man are not different in kind, that what is ' more ' in man is implicit in what he calls the ' psychic stuff' itself as the possibility of an oak tree lies in the acorn. He describes in *The Atom of Delight* how as a boy he was always ' as it were evasively careful ' to keep God outside his inner circle. God is a word that labels and so evades the mystery. What is necessary is not such a word but to understand reality and reality is a matter of experience.

It is in *Sun Circle* that he says: ' For one will often have a watchful malevolent loneliness, but two will live at the centre of the circle of perfection where thought has ceased and the moment achieves the eternal.' His wife Daisy, born Jessie Frew, gives meaning to this phrase.

While Neil talked—and it was an adventure he essayed on more than one occasion—Daisy was accustomed to sit easily silent with narrowed eyes, her chin lifted, looking far off into places where real flowers bloom and heather moves in the wind. Should he stray into countries too remote from the point of departure she would murmur, " You were talking about time." And he would laugh and return to the main road. For a while.

She was a gardener who touched everything with love and on occasion resented his antagonism, purposely exaggerated, to weeds and rabbits, which have their place in the scheme of things. Her solemnity sparkled and she smiled like a young girl for, as she said, " You're always young inside."

In *The Atom of Delight* Neil describes picking up a copy of L. H. Myers's *The Near and the Far* and finding pencil marks in the margin. By whom they were made he does not say, but they were made by Daisy. And he writes:

> As it happens, these are passages I might have marked myself, and I read them over again with the peculiar pleasure of discovery, the delight that momentarily withdraws from the book and enjoys itself. . . . To pick up by chance so rare a community of understanding!

It was with her enthusiastic consent that Neil gave up his job in the Civil Service when he was over forty, and devoted himself entirely to writing. The first thing they did was to go ' off in a boat ', an adventure described with characteristic vividness and evasiveness in the book of that name. For as long as Daisy lived they would in the same manner go ' off and away '—" I'm off! I'm away! Cheers! " as Neil says himself. But the ' off ' and the ' away ' were almost always penetrations into the Highland country and its gradations of light and shadow.

It is not surprising that Neil became politically a Nation-

alist.   Nor is it surprising that politics did not suit him.
He was energetic in the Nationalist movement and his
house was the centre of activity during campaigns in
Inverness in the early days.   His mind was always capable
of making the type of calculation required in any field of
activity.   But political calculation was tiring to him in a
way that affected the spirit.   And the more that writing
became his accepted vocation the more deeply did he find
it necessary to penetrate to the roots of that reality he wrote
about, which was a spiritual reality.

When a man becomes a writer in this sense he becomes
dedicated to the perception of truth.   He cannot help it.
To write anything other than truth is meaningless.   And
to be conscious that there are always visions over the hill is
to climb the hill and to go on farther and to reach the well
at the world's end.

The deeper Neil penetrated into the Highland landscape
of heart and mind the more his books implied that ' other
landscape ' which is seen so simply when the ' second self '
wakes up and looks at *this* world, alive in all its dimensions,
in all its depth and vividness.   For the ' other world ' is
' this world ' seen by one who is fully awake.   And it was
increasing familiarity with the ' other landscape ' which
made his recognition of Gurdjieff's vision inevitable when
he came upon Ouspensky's book *In Search of the Miraculous*
which deals with Gurdjieff's teaching.   He himself describes
the book like this:

> When I first read *In Search of the Miraculous* by
> P. D. Ouspensky, I was held as by a first-rate novel;
> continuously interesting, often exciting, always un-
> expected, and with the Bolshevik Revolution as back-
> ground.   Fundamentally it was—it is—a true tale of

adventure, a hunt through the forests of the human mind, following new psychological trails, discarding most of our modern ones, new—yet so old that at the start Ouspensky is heading for India in order to track down the ancient esoteric schools of the East. To his friends he said he was off to ' seek the miraculous '. Though unable to define ' miraculous ' it yet had for him a definite meaning, for he had " come to the conclusion a long time ago that there was no escape from the labyrinth of contradictions in which we live except by an entirely new road. . . . I already knew then as an undoubted fact that beyond this thin film of false reality there existed another reality from which, for some reason, something separated us. The ' miraculous ' was the way of penetration into this unknown reality."

Though he had some notable Eastern experiences, he failed to penetrate to his unknown reality; the secret was more deeply hidden than he had supposed. But then he had made it difficult for himself, because schools of a religious kind did not attract him (plenty of them in Russia), other schools with ' very nice ' people, of a slightly moral-philosophical type (sentimental with a shade of asceticism), did not possess ' real knowledge '; even ' Yogi schools ', complete with trance states, savoured of ' spiritualism ' and he could not trust them; and he was suspicious of what Orthodox mystics called ' beauty ' or allurement. In short, whatever a school was called—occult, esoteric or Yogi—he wanted it to exist on the ' ordinary earthly plane ', like any other kind of school. To think of schools on ' another plane ' was a sign of weakness, of dreams instead of real search, and such " dreams were one of the principle obstacles on our possible way to the miraculous."

Neil goes on to describe Ouspensky's meeting with Gurdjieff :

So they met and talked and Ouspensky records, in

English of a remarkable directness and clarity, G.'s answer to all his questions. Thus step by step the long journey began to what Ouspensky increasingly believed might be the unknown reality.

Those concepts of Gurdjieff's which most interested Neil were ' man as a machine '; the distinction G. makes between ' knowledge ' and ' being '; and ' self-remembering '. He writes:

> But to get the full impact of G.'s concept of mechanical man we must get some idea of the two lines along which man's development proceeds, the line of *knowledge* and the line of *being*. We can all understand that there are different levels of knowledge but we accept *being* as merely another name for existence. In our culture we put great value upon levels of man's knowledge, but normally ignore the level of his being. . . . It is only when the two interact in harmony that we have enrichment of *being* and an increase in its capacity to absorb ever more *knowledge* and to transmute it into *understanding*. When this does not happen man continues to live in *sleep*. When knowledge develops without being you have a ' weak Yogi ', when being develops without knowledge, a ' stupid saint '.

Farther on he deals with ' remembering yourself '.

> Applying this now to myself I realised that it was the word ' remember ' that blocked the line of communication to me. As I read on, however, I found that Ouspensky had been familiar with ' moments of self-remembering ' since childhood and while travelling in a new place had experienced a momentary sensation of strangeness in finding himself there. This sensation I perfectly understood. Often while on foot in the Highlands, in turning a corner, in opening out a vista, I had been stopped in breathless wonder at the scene before me. But this wonder was pervaded by the

wonder of finding myself there. This *I*—this *me*—here!
Certainly it had nothing to do with memory. On the
contrary it was as if you had found yourself for the first
time. Here is not the ordinary self of everyday, but a
new self, at once incredibly intimate and utterly demand-
ing, fresh as the first view of creation. Here at last is
the *conscious* self.

Neil continues, quoting Ouspensky: ' We " live and act
in deep sleep, not metaphorically but in absolute reality."
But " we can remember ourselves if we make sufficient
efforts, we *can* awaken ".'

In order to illustrate the concept of the ' second self ',
which is his own phrase, not Ouspensky's, Neil gives an
account of an experience he had while writing *The Well at
the World's End*.

The character involved in the novel had fallen down
a cliff in trying to save a lamb, but the lamb saved him
by getting squashed under his body in the final impact.
He had crawled to a cave . . . underwent crucial mental
experiences, and at last set out on a final hopeless crawl.
Perhaps it was because I knew the country that I began
to identify myself abnormally with my character. I
saw what he saw, became as it were the seeing person,
improvised his crutch, suffered what he suffered until
in one translated moment, in a look back at the mountain
slope, the swinging footbridge over the gorge, I saw
a face, larger than life size, looking down at me with an
expression of infinite understanding and compassion,
still, not doing anything, not going to do anything,
there. The effect upon me was one of an intimacy
I could never express, for the face was my own face.
. . . However, there is no need to complicate the
affair but merely to make my point that I had what
was for me a clear vision of my second self looking
down the few yards of sloping ground at my first self

L

prostrate in the heather and now held by an understanding and compassion that were infinite. Then the
infinite came elusively in and the second self became a
part, a manifestation, of a universal self or essence, a
part of, yet individual.

He then comments that the ' concern here is not with
academic considerations . . . but with man's development
from his present level of knowledge and being onto higher
levels; not analysis for learning's sake, not theorising, but
doing. Doing is one of his [Gurdjieff's] loaded words.
" Doing is magic," said G.' (' The Miraculous ' in *Point*
No. 4, Winter 1968-9.)

We are at once back with *The Green Isle of the Great
Deep*, published in 1944, four years before Ouspensky's
book was issued here: ' When knowledge completes itself
in wisdom, the magic is released.'

It has always interested me that many of those who most
admire the early novels such as *Morning Tide* and the
simpler books such as *Young Art and Old Hector* are most
irritable with what they describe as the ' mysticism ' of
later books such as *The Well at the World's End* or *The Other
Landscape*. If these books are read with that attention which
is an open-minded awareness of what is presented for
contemplation, and not a product of the will, it will be
found that they are propounding no doctrine, performing
no sleight of hand, but are dealing scrupulously and exactly
with experience. The word ' mystic ' derives from
Muein, to close the eyes or lips, and implies a turning inward.
Neil's experience of the second self was not the result of
turning inward but of an acceptance and realisation of the
world outside and the self within it, as witness his favourite
quotation from an Eastern text: ' Look lovingly on some

object. Do not go onto another object. Here in the middle of the object—the blessing.' (*112 Ways of Opening the Hidden Door to Consciousness.*) And since his books are an imaginative record of experience, if the reader trusts the experience described in *Morning Tide* he can also trust the experience described in *The Other Landscape*. Once this trust and attention are given it becomes startlingly obvious that the crucial experiences, such as that of the boy cracking nuts in the stream, had already occurred when the early books were written and that the later books are simply a further exploration of them.

There is a sense in which some readers do not *need*, say, *The Green Isle of the Great Deep*, for in a strange way the profundities of *The Green Isle* are implicit in the simplicity of *Young Art and Old Hector*. ' " You saw it—but you had not yet brought it into your head to put words on it." ' And they may prefer to avoid or to evade ' putting words on it ' in order to preserve for themselves that secret inner core which will ' sense ' without making knowledge explicit. What Neil is trying to do in the later books is to complete knowledge in wisdom and so release the magic. And to me there is in the *Green Isle* a simplicity quite as pure as that of *Young Art and Old Hector*, and at a level where the transmutation of intellectual complexities into spiritual simplicity certainly has the quality of magic. ' If water thus achieves lucidity from stillness, how much more the faculties of the mind.' (*Chwang Tzu.*)

The implicit presence in the early books of the material which also forms the later ones makes clear the way in which the work forms a whole which has many dimensions, just as the life forms a whole and the writer himself forms a whole, because knowledge and being have grown together.

Neil Gunn's Animistic Vision

KURT WITTIG

On the surface, Neil Gunn's novels seem chiefly or even exclusively concerned to mirror the way of life followed by crofting and fishing communities in Caithness and Sutherland. So a reader might wonder what relevance Gunn has to our modern life, or what makes his novels outstanding works of art that are a concern of all humanity. But Gunn is not satisfied with what meets the eye; those crofting and fishing communities are his personal experience that he has to probe to reach the source of his being and ours. He is well aware that each individual lives his life on many different levels at the same time. In all his novels we seem to be moving on many different 'planes of being', in apparently self-sufficient circles which yet have innumerable points of contact with one another. There is the landscape and 'the other landscape which the delight inhabits', a 'secret world within the ordinary world' that may be haunting you 'like something forgotten'. When these planes 'tilt' or 'the landscapes interpenetrate',[1] that momentary contact of different circles allows us to glimpse beneath the surface and to gain insight into the deeper meaning of life.

Consider Gunn's dialogue. Often it is not merely a communication, an exchange of opinions and information, but the words are only the ripple on the surface which betrays thoughts or feelings that lie beneath; and there is much 'searching innuendo', much stealthy manœuvring,

as each of the speakers probes the other's mind, and tries
first to draw him on and ultimately to drive him into a
blind corner.[2] A speaker may not be unlike a fisherman
fighting and outwitting his salmon: 'Lachlan might now
have been playing *him* on the end of the line, trussing him
up '; or he may ' use talk like a weapon ' or like a game of
chess where the ' verbal pieces ' can be lifted from the
board one by one.[3] Doubtless this reflects an essential
feature of Scots conversation, with its laconic remarks and
the metaphysical deliberation with which it chooses each
individual word. And it also gives dramatic quality to the
silence between the words, where the real conflict on a
deeper level is going on: ' But in these few moments of
silence between them awareness became acute.'[4] ' So
behind the words another silent conversation must have
been going on, " the other conversation ", that for each is
the important one.' ' There is always, however, the
implication behind such talk and it can be more elusive
than a serpent.' ' The implication is the terrible thing that
is not spoken. But it is remembered.'[5] Gunn can paint
the force of the silence through which one cannot break,
when one just cannot find a word no matter how much
depends upon it; a silence that one experiences as a force, a
black madness choking one. In *The Grey Coast*, the boy
' could not as yet bring himself to the point of considering
any action in its bearing on Maggie. He could not do it. . . .'[6]

Consequently the real life is that which is lived inside
the mind. This life gets its vivid signals through all the
senses—and Gunn's writing is full of wonderfully poetic
impressions of the outside world, such as ' the hiss-hiss of
the milk muffled now by the froth coming through the
silence '.[7] The magic of the senses is a constant fascination:

' Scent, taste, hearing and seeing—how rich the body in
what so miraculously is! The fifth, the sense of feeling, the
fingers touching—the boy's hand on a rabbit's back, on a
bird's closed wings . . . with its fine claws now digging
into his skin, its beak having a real sharp peck at him, so
that he cries out in a sharpened delight. . . .' [8] But these
innumerable minute impressions have no objective value,
they are the highly personal elements out of which the
mind creates its own reality. Gunn does not give us sense-
impressions as such, but the vivid signals that eye, ear, nose,
tongue, feet, hands of a given character receive, signals that
are flashed to the mind where they trigger the reflexes.
Follow Kenn, in *Highland River*, stalking up the strath with
his friends:

> Eyes flash to earth to guide feet. Primroses, anemones,
> delicate green leaves of the wood-sorrel. Bite the
> leaves; chew them. Cuckoo's spit. Red bells of the
> blaeberry. A good crop. Dead bracken. Violets.
> Living bracken with bowed heads. Dandelions. A
> trickle of water. Orchis and marsh-mallows. Grey
> grass. Broken sticks and stones. Hazel-shoots—for
> rabbit-snares. Green grass. Young rabbits. Galloping
> little rabbits. A black rabbit!
>   " A BLACK RABBIT! "
> And back along the wood the answering yell:
> " WHERE? "
> The sun comes through. [9]

Here everything is measured against the boy's immediate
experience; we see, hear, smell, taste, breathe with his
heightened senses. We feel with his small, frail, warm
body, both the electrifying spark of seeing a black rabbit—
and the dark and intangible fears that seem to lurk around
him: ' At the sound, as at a signal in a weird fairy tale, the

whole world changed. . . . Fear had him by the throat.'[10]
Compare with this the more rationalised sense-life of an
adult:

> Something of this can be experienced in daylight, but
> in darkness, in a cave, there is touch, deliberate conscious
> touch, a hand grips, even the inside of the head *feels*
> the near approach of solid mass; while ears hear what is
> lost in the light and nostrils discriminate a smell into
> its sources lest there be one dangerous source. It is an
> elemental traffic which cannot be carried much farther.
> It generates in time the cold glow of a thin fine delight.
> That was his first insight.[11]

Gunn, we see, does not merely enumerate the impressions
flashed to the mind; he follows them into the mind and
registers the picture they evoke there. It may still be a
fairly objective comparison when a character says, ' There
were smaller clouds coming up out of the east after it,
puff-cheeked like the angels of an old master ';[12] but
mostly these images or projections go far beyond comparisons and are highly subjective, as when Gunn says of
the rising rage within a boy, ' The surge boiled up inside,
the surge that could hardly contain the wet spindrift of
rage.'[13] Who does not know the fleeting impression that
a voice, in a special light, seems to be disembodied or
separated from the speaker: ' His voice and himself disappeared in the glimmering night ' ?[14]

This penetration into the mind is not only a dominant
trait in Neil Gunn's own style—as it is in so much of
Scottish literature; with their keen observation based on
their vivid sense-impressions, his characters, too, are
endowed with this faculty. By sheer subjective intensity
his characters visualise their objects inside their mind: ' So

vividly in the dark could Kenn see a rabbit or a fox that he could put his hand on it.' ' Unless Kenn saw a thing he could never with certainty remember it.' [15] ' So vivid was the visualisation that Ivor's fingers closed involuntarily on a stone.' Frequently Gunn's characters watch themselves mentally: ' The picture became very vivid.   He saw himself. . . .' [16]   The picture created within the mind is just as real as that perceived by the senses. When Urquhart, in *The Other Landscape*, notices the implication of a threat, ' the sunlight darkened in front of me and I had the sensation of hounds on the hunt. It was almost visual '. Such a mental picture can be projected into another person's mind:

> When I said earlier that Annabel stood in the doorway of my mind, I saw my mind like an inner room and Annabel standing in its doorway with one hand against the jamb, arrested. Much as if she had come into the doorway of this room and stood looking at us.
>
> If she appeared it was in the room of my mind, not in the room of the house. It may be that in his search he could visualise Annabel so acutely that I was affected by his projection of her.
>
> Then I suddenly saw Annabel in my mind, but I couldn't look at her.[17]

Often the picture thus created is evoked by the Highlander's way of speaking in just such pictures: ' I asked her questions and she answered in pictures that I saw.' [18]   A character can identify so completely with another character he knows that he seems to be right inside the other, knowing what the other is doing or going to do without even seeing him: ' She saw what was passing in the old man's mind by the very set of his head to his shoulders.' ' But his eyes did not see ould Jeems. . . .   She was out there. . . .' [19]

In all these examples we see that in moments of heightened sensitiveness the reality created inside the mind has a life of its own:

> One can see mute things with an extraordinary clarity. Then a touch, just a touch, of clairvoyance seems to come out of the listening and the mind grows abnormally sensitive. The slow movement of the water, its mounting rhythm, the crash, the recession . . . all in miniature, like the memory of a full theme. . . . I broke the hypnotic effect by getting up.[20]

Neil Gunn knows the feelings of a boy in the strath ' with every sense heightened to that pitch where even familiar bends or trees or boulders took on a look of extraordinary stillness or expectancy '.[21] Here the object is no longer a dead thing, but a living creation: the ' thing itself ' is alive. This intensity of vision is essentially animistic: Gunn, and his characters, hold a thing within arm's length and regard it with ' the eyes and the mind fastened upon it ', and in this intensity of vision the thing assumes its own life. It may just be a conventional metaphor to speak of ' the eyes of the night ',[22] but we are right inside the mind of a character when we read of ' watching tree-trunks ',[23] ' an invisible power, animated within itself ' coming out of the night,[24] and even more so when, in *Highland River*, Kenn feels ' the tin pail that the tinkers had made watched with bright face '.[25] To the boy (Neil Gunn himself) who has just won his fight with the salmon, the world takes a strange air of expectancy:

> Perhaps the incredible in the true puts him a little beside himself, for as he walks back towards the pool and his clothes a delicious langour assails his body, and nature gets translated, too, so that the sunlight, the leaves,

L 2

the pink roses of a wild briar—particularly the wide-open pink roses—seem to stop and look in a strange un-forgettable way as he goes by, the shyness of adoration upon him.

A black lump in the darkness had the air of *waiting*, and a bush seen in the starlight, a bush that *hadn't been there before*, was now standing watching on the outer fringe of the trees.[26]

A thing may be 'too white for argument',[27] mocking interest 'crawl like the worm', anger 'curl in on itself',[28] or the wood of a chair may react like a living being: '... then [he] rammed himself back in his chair till the wood protested and ground the stone floor'.[29]

This animism—'beatings of the heart in moments of vivid life'[30]—gains its deepest intensity when vivid mental images or impressions from two different levels of life are suddenly flashed together and, for a split second, give us an insight into a deeper meaning, often a momentary glimpse of the underlying ritual of life. This may some-times do no more than establish the matter-of-course kinship of a boy with the animate and inanimate world around him: 'When the potatoes elbowed their way through their skins, Kenn and his brothers said they were laughing.'[31] As a rule, this flashing-together reaches deeper levels of our being, as in *Butcher's Broom* when we hear of the pipe, 'Its notes bubbled in their blood'; or, in *The Other Landscape*, 'Tension gets drawn out until it is time that is drawn out, so thin, so fine, that its range becomes enormous.' Thus the abstract world, too, is suddenly highlighted by this intensity of vision. 'The thought mushroomed up until it was the dome of the sky.'[32] 'His spirit crept out again, its tender feelers searching the

desk beside him.' ³³ Doesn't it make you see the spirit,
like a snail, finding its way with its feelers, ready in its
sensitiveness and shyness, to withdraw into its shell at the
slightest disturbing sound or movement? Doesn't the world
seem peopled by strange beings when we hear ' The silence
became so audible that Jeems heard the chuckle that was
Tullach's dark smile '? No wonder a woman may have
' a merging sense of oneness with the elements about her '.³⁴

Let us follow one example of an image, sharp in itself,
that suddenly touches a different plane of existence and for
a moment gives us an insight into the ultimate unity behind
the apparent complexity, in the same way as one suddenly
sees the face in a puzzle picture; the same kind of unity
that Einstein envisaged in the four-dimensional space-time
continuum.³⁵ In the first chapter of *The Other Landscape*
the narrator is watching sea-gulls from the cliffs:

> Then a bird rose quite close to me, banked and went
> down, on outstretched wings that never flapped. The
> fulmar, I thought, and started back.

One page later, the motionless flight of the bird suggests
a mental picture:

> The fulmar in its apparently blind weaving had startled
> me more than a bit.

And then, in the latter part of the novel, after Einstein's
space-time continuum has been scrutinised, the two different
levels are flashed together in a new insight:

> And down he came, the fulmar, in the loveliest of
> curves and up and over . . . and down, without a single
> wing-beat. Carved out of wood, he seemed, hypnotised
> and hypnotising, a flying shuttle of the continuum,
> weaving a spell which held the cliffs to silence. Beyond

the spell, cliff and ear listened, and perhaps some ear heard'.[36]

Neil Gunn is well aware that this animism traces back to an ancient pagan phase in the history of man:

> The first or earliest phase has got the name of *animism* because things in nature were then reckoned to be animated by spirits and demonic powers. . . . Actually, in the living of life today all three phases get mixed up in an extraordinary manner. Of the three, the earliest, the animistic, was most exhaustive and complete. As a way of life, a system of beliefs, it covered everything. This gave it its enormous penetrative power. In fact it is in this phase, says Freud, that myths have their sure foundation. And what the myth now means in our art and poetry . . . continues to astonish many, who see them as throw-backs to the primitive.[37]

It is especially the landscape that appears like a living force shaping the fate of man. Anybody who has seen the northern Highlands will not only understand, but *feel* a sentence like ' the moor waited, silent and flat '.[38] Indeed, when I first saw the far north, Caithness and Sutherland, where the strange mountains rise so abruptly out of the lonely moors, lying there like waiting animals watching you, I could not escape the premonition of the presence of primordial powers, of a living agent. This feeling is everywhere in Neil Gunn, yet there is nothing romantic or sentimental about it: to his Highlanders, the environment is more than the background before which their lives unfold themselves: ' In how much was affection a manifestation, a necessity, of environment—of sea and glen, of struggle and resource, of self-dependence and endurance? ' What emerges is 'the positiveness of the affection itself and its lasting effect on the communal life '.[39]   From this it is only a short step to the seeing of life in terms of an allegory:

> In the centre of this gloom was the fire, and sitting round it, their knees drawn together, their heads stooped, were the old woman, like fate, the young woman, like love, and the small boy with the swallow of life in his hand.[40]

The small boy with the swallow of life in his hand.

Neil Gunn is well aware that this animism has distinctly Gaelic undertones and proceeds straight from Gaelic speech. The Gaelic basis of his style is apparent in the rhythms, sentence-structure and idioms of the dialogue, but also, though less obviously, of the narrative.   There has always been a pervading impressionistic quality in Gaelic (and Celtic) speech: its substantial approach (' he put sharpness on it' instead of ' he sharpened it') and its paratactic sentence-structure, which prefers a sequence of clauses linked merely by *agus* ' and ' to one of clauses subordinated by means of other conjunctions, inevitably give rise to a string of pictures or impressions.   But this seeming uniformity of clause strung after clause gains in subtlety and diversity by the strongly modal and conditional approach [41] which enables a writer or speaker to catch the most transient images in a swift series of phrases powerfully suggestive of light and movement: a shaft of sunlight ' bright as a dash of lime ', the ' foam-white rowing ', a glittering pool, and even the quick shimmer of trout jumping, when for a split second we see flashing scales and spots.[42]   In Gaelic, the poet is not satisfied with these numerous miniature sense-impressions, he also gives us the image which they create in his own mind: the notes from MacCrimmon's pipe chanter are as numerous as the midges around a roe-buck in summer-time, and his fingering on the chanter suggests wicker-work.[43]

Neil Gunn is no native speaker of Gaelic, nor am I sure that he knows the works of the Scottish Gaelic poets of the eighteenth century. But many of the quotations from his works fall exactly into line with the examples just given, and a simile like ' the haze on the mountains was like the smoke-bloom on ripe blaeberries '[44] is clearly of Gaelic derivation: the way of dividing the spectrum that lies behind the colour-adjectives used in Gaelic requires, for exactness, some such comparison: ' More than that, for colour here may be vivid but also it is deep. In her native tongue [Gaelic] the colour adjectives suggest this depth, and translating them into English literally translates them from a deep to a surface manifestation. . . . Yet never with anything merely vague in the soft and deep.'[45] Gunn's father could speak Gaelic, and four of the five fishermen in his boat for the summer fishing were Islanders from the West who used to speak Gaelic among themselves. So, from an early age on, Neil Gunn was accustomed to the sound of the old tongue. But above all, Gunn is aware of the Gaelic substratum in the speech of the Highlanders, which distinctly colours their way of expression even though the words are English. This is unmistakable in Gunn's use of prepositions, and in sentences like ' You are so ', ' after all the rain there's been in it ',[46] ' I have heard him tell that story in a way that would take half the night and you interested and laughing '. Gaelic is for Gunn the unique expression of the working of his people's mind. It is ' a tongue and a rhythm that were not merely countless centuries old, but had been born out of the earth on which they starved and feasted '.[47] It has ' phrases that snare the heart with a hair ', names that evoke ' each kind of man with an astonishing, almost laughable magic '.[48] A man may say in greeting ' " It's the fine day that's in it ", as though he were setting the day in the hollow of the world so that they might with courteous detachment regard it '.[49] Here is the root of Neil Gunn's animism. There is nothing vaguely sentimental about Gunn's attitude to the old tongue. In describing a *ceilidh* he shows how an almost poetic way of expression is handed down together with all the traditional lore and wisdom, and in his account of a proverb-match we can recognise the essence of his own dialogue. The speech of his people is full of imaginative comparisons; and if, before reciting a poem, there are seemingly endless arguments, that only serves to tune the minds, for the variations are often more important than the subject. His people

> revelled in this sort of invention, for it was born naturally out of their love of the ancient tales of their race, of proverbs, of impromptu satirical verses, of song-choruses, of witty sayings and divinations. They relished the finer turns with a far keener appreciation than they relished differences in food or drink and shelter.[50]

Interesting though Neil Gunn's style may be—his sense-impressions, his animism, the flashing together of images, the Gaelic substratum—it is no end in itself, but serves a deeper artistic purpose. The various levels at which man lives his life are not simply a personal, private experience; the flash of insight that we have when the different circles of life suddenly touch is meant to highlight an experience deeper than chance happenings picked out at random. Gunn takes us beyond the accidental; he is looking for the pattern of life, the underlying ritual, the myth, ' the design that never changed '.[51] In itself, the experience of the individual is of little interest, unless it has a relevance for all life, for the life of the race, so that the writer can say ' This is it! ' [52] ' Here is destiny! ' When, at the end of *Butcher's Broom*, dark Mhairi, the old knowing woman, comes back to gather herbs near the burnt-out home from which she and hers have been evicted in the Clearances, Gunn sees in her

> the human mother carrying on her ancient solitary busi-
> ness with the earth, talking good and familiar sense with
> boulder and flower and rock, and now and then follow-
> ing a root below the surface; in easy accord, the
> communion sensible and so full of natural understanding
> that silence might extend into external silence, for wind
> and sun to play upon.[53]

The Clearances, which form the background to this novel, mark the central tragedy of Highland history; but *Butcher's Broom* is not an historical or political novel. Gunn approaches the Clearances as the buried root of contemp-orary Highland difficulties, and as the immediate cause of the crofting problem that the present generation is desper-ately trying to solve; if you have seen the Highlands dotted with the burnt-out shells of houses and heard the submerged violence in a Highlander's voice when he speaks of the Clearances you will understand that this tragedy is not a thing of the past. History is here regarded as the matrix of the present. But to have this importance, history must be the history of the folk, not history as contained in schoolbooks. Neil Gunn is not interested in the exploits and achievements of kings and generals and statesmen, but in folk-life and folk-history. 'The people *before his time*, in the straths, on the moor, by the sea. The nameless folk who went back into time. The sensation of half seeing them without trying to was sometimes quite strong, and a moment's concentration could shape a few figures moving here and there. . . . A thousand years made no difference. . . . This is the well from which the human tribe must drink or it will perish.'[54]   The other landscape behind the physical one can become a haunting idea to Gunn:

> However, the track finished at the tumbled ruins of two cottages in a shallow hollow. The trunk of an old tree, with one stunted branch outthrust like a withered arm, had at one time been used as a post for fencing wire. I recognised it as the rowan or mountain ash, grown to keep evil spirits away. This brought back so much of my own boyhood that I stood looking and listening until my mouth went dry. . . .
>
> I went on, then looked back over my shoulder and saw what were once the little cultivated fields, could hear what cries I wished to hear, young running feet, the woman singing in the byre's deep dusk as she milked the cow . . . and I saw the dismembered rowan tree, the tragic gesture of its solitary arm against the sky. . . .
>
> For example, when I looked back over my shoulder at the little landscape of the two ruins and saw finally the dismembered rowan tree with its one arm thrust against the sky, I had a feeling of turning away from a landscape behind the physical one I looked at.[55]

There is nothing vague or general here; to Gunn, the past is the history of folk-experience, of all those communal developments and revolutions that have a direct impact on the daily life of our own generation. Nor is this merely another instance of the modern tendency to see history from the social and economic side. Neil Gunn makes himself the spokesman of the old Gaelic way of life, a strongly communal way of life in the polity of the clan. The history of his own folk has taught him that whenever a man of genius of 'humble origin', a man of the folk, aspired to a background more propitious to 'the free exercise of their finer gifts of recognition', he not only failed, but was bound to fail 'because the greater the genius the more certain the failure of finding the desired background where it was looked for'. 'If kings and nobles and millionaires did not especially attract Kenn, he believed it was because he had no particular need of them, not out of pride, inverted or otherwise, but simply because all the more subtle elements of human intuitions, the sap and health of life, came naturally out of his heritage from the folk.' And similarly: ' " You have the folk idea strong in you." " That may come out of our past, for we were a fairly communal folk until we were thoroughly debauched by predatory chiefs and the like. A feeling lingers that the poor have always been wronged. It goes pretty deep. . . ." ' [56]

Again we see the paramount importance of the Gaelic experience in Gunn's writings: in this experience he can find the *rhythm and pattern of life*. This is in no way nostalgic or romantic: Gunn is aware how profoundly man is affected by his environment—and how profoundly he affects it. He knows, too, how close man can grow to the things by which he is surrounded: that is what made the Clearances so tragic. Fortunately for us, Gunn grew up in a surrounding and at a time that were breathing with the rhythm of life itself; what he says of Kenn in *Highland River* is equally true of Neil Gunn himself: ' Ultimately

the sheiling meant food, the river fish, and the peat bank
fire. The contacts were direct and the results were seen.
There was thus about the most ordinary labour some of the
excitement of the creation.' [57] And above the river near
Gunn's birthplace stands one of those brochs, whose
history is shrouded in mystery, which gave rise in the boy
to the search for the past of his race. Gunn feels that man
is at one with all his ancestors, he carries his racial past in
him. The old folk-customs, songs, poems, proverbs,
ceilidhs are not incidental features in the lives of his people,
but an integral part of their basic existence. Thus a smoor-
ing song, or simply the humming of a traditional air, bring
out the ritual of life to which both they and their ancestors
were subjected.[58] So does the primordial thrill of the hunt.
' The subject has interested me ever since as a boy in the
Highlands I hunted and fished as naturally as any primitive
man or otter. I confess it is one of my ambitions to write
something of the mind of the primitive hunter, with
special reference to the interaction between that mind and
the hunting background, particularly at the most vivid
moments when a certain kind of communion or integration
takes place.' [59] This is not a romantic notion,[60] but another
signpost, a pointer on the way in the history of the race.

Frequently Gunn takes a boy, or a woman, as the
central figure: in them the myth of life with its primordial
urges and racial heritage is strongest. A boy still preserves
his wholeness, is integrated in himself; with his rich
sense-life and animistic responses he is ' more than half-way
between the savage and modern man '.[61] And in a woman,
Gunn feels, ' all the history of her people is writ on her
face '. Women minister to the needs of life in an eternal
ritual:

Sometimes, too, he would hear the two women talking away.   Occasionally his mother's voice would lift and crack, but his granny's voice was always so sensible and calm.   It's not that his granny's voice was humouring his mother's fancies.   It was more than that, and it was the ' more ' that searched him out.   She was the mother talking to her child, hardly listening at times because her hands were busy; chiding now and then, but prepared to explain over and over.   There was something so normal about this, so assured, that it gave Iain a conception of women that he never afterwards forgot.

At the beginning of life and at its end, they were there, handling the unbearable with competent hands, doing little things with knowledge in their eyes, moving about, silent or speaking as the need demanded.   They were there, with the awful progression of minutes on their hands.[62]

There are movements in a woman older than time itself; [63] she is so absolute in her certainty that she is the one force that cannot be subdued by outward powers such as a corporate state.[64]   Frequently Gunn sees woman as the quiet, self-assured presence dominating a circle, the circle of life's experience: ' She was the starting point of a circle that finished in her.   Within that circle were their faces.   The paraffin lamp, which was now on the mantelshelf, shone down on them its soft light.' [65]

If a woman finds her natural symbol in the shape of the circle, a boy seems to find his in a river and the quest for its source: [66]   in *Highland River*, even in hunting the salmon as it pursues its pilgrimage between light and darkness back to the source of its life, Kenn is making a similar journey back to the source of his own life: ' From that day, the river became the river of life for Kenn '; and, when Kenn has returned to his native village in the maturity of his life,

' the river ran through him with all its ancient potency '.[67]

But where is this source? What is the law, the ritual, the driving force by which man is governed in tracing the pattern of his life? This is the key question of modern literature. In America, with its severed strands of history, Ernest Hemingway finds this force by going back to the elemental, primitive, instinctive values within the individual. In Scotland, with its strong roots in Gaeldom, Neil Gunn answers this question in terms of man's ancestral past, and in terms of the nameless ages before the dawn of history. Gunn's mind quickens when he stands before the traces of his real ancestors, who left the brochs behind them: ' If he could recapture this he would recapture . . . the old primordial goodness of life . . . its moments of absolute ecstasy.' Therefore man must find his source: ' It is a far cry to the golden age, to the blue smoke of the heather fire and the scent of the primrose! Our river took a wrong turning somewhere. But we haven't forgotten the source. Why blame me for trying to escape to it? Who knows what's waiting me there?' [68] His mind wanders back to the Culdees, the Druids—and before? Who peered for salmon then?

As he broods on the old dark potent ways, Gunn sees man as in the last analysis a product of the processes that went to the making of the race itself, and ' ancestral ' is sometimes almost identical with ' atavistic '. Why does the heart beat higher in hunting, in fishing? Isn't it everywhere in Scottish literature? Why is the soul searched by the cry of the peewit and curlew? What is it that allures us in the scent of the heather fire of the primrose, if not some ancestral instinct? The frenzy a boy feels when burning dry whin in spring is an age-old tribal urge, and darkness, 'mythic night', holds man with primordial powers: ' In this darkness of the world identity is lost and time becomes one with the monstrous beginnings of life, which legend recreates in such beings as centaur or water kelpie.' [69]   And beyond that is the sea, a mystic and cleansing force, the uncertain sea, older than myth itself.

'The monstrous beginnings of life.' The 'blind' instinctive urges that drive us on, that make us act as we do, are older even than our ancestors, they trace back to man's pre-human heritage, to the very beginnings of life. When Kenn, in *Highland River*, muses on his fight with the huge salmon, he ' was inclined to fall into a state of abstraction, where story and meaning ran into a silver glimmer, or dropped out of sight altogether, dropped, perhaps, upon some "continental ledge" of the mind, whence, through aeons back beyond reckoning, it had emerged upon the beaches, the rivers, and finally upon the dry land '.[70]

Frequently in Gunn's novels some picture of our life is flashed together with some image arising from the past to give us a momentary glimpse of the unchanging pattern of life. But this is not done by an abstraction on the side of the writer; Neil Gunn does not teach or preach: to Kenn, in *Highland River*, a birch after a May shower has ' not properly a sensuous scent, it has the tang of life and growth '.[71] The glimpse reaches farther back into timelessness in *The Silver Bough*:

> All at once he saw old Fachie by the sheltered gable of his house, his left arm outstretched and his dog rushing low to the earth to round up a cow or a stirk that had got into the young corn. There were no other figures to be seen and in a moment the little drama with the old bent figure might have been of any age back to Neolithic

times. Grant stood looking from his little window as from a newer kind of earth-house. For a miraculous moment the cat appeared on the garden wall. A blackbird whistled and was gone. Between the bursts he heard the pounding thunder of the sea.[72]

For that 'miraculous moment' an impression of the senses flashlights an image in the mind, and for a split second we seem to see our place in the universe. But Gunn does not merely hark back; he always strives to relate this historic or primeval, pre-human past to the present, and in doing so he uses the patterns of the past to express the contemporary issues with which he is ultimately concerned, from culture, science, and Einstein to brain-washing, totalitariansim, and Marxism. ' In fact if a Scot is interested in dialectical materialism of proletarian humanism, it seems to me he should study the old system in order to find out how the new system would be likely to work amongst his kind. It might help him at least to get rid of his more idealistic wind.' [73]

My own favourite among Neil Gunn's novels is *Highland River*, which, to my mind, contains Gunn's style and vision at their best. Outwardly the plot is simply the story of Kenn's search for the source of the Highland river where he was born; but, as Neil Gunn says in the dedication, ' some ancestral instinct, at first glimpse of the river, must have taken control '. Thus the action is only a gateway to Gunn's interpretation of life, of the modern world, of the heritage of man.

The Highland river becomes the river of life to Kenn at the age of nine, when, one early dawn, he discovers an enormous salmon in the pool. Irrational, primal fear comes upon him: ' Out of that noiseless world in the grey of the morning all his ancestors came at him', and he simply must catch this salmon. Man ancestral has met man modern. The mysterious force that makes the fish seek the source of the river enters Kenn's breast, and he too feels a compulsion to follow the traces of his ancestors. First, he makes the lower part of the river, the realm of man, his own; then he conquers the middle part, the strath with its darkness and ancestral memories. And finally, after the war and a career as a scientist, Kenn finds the way from the habitation of man by the sea to the source in the moor, where he discovers what man has lost. But this is only a framework, and only beginning and end have their fixed place in time. At any moment, the shadow of the dim past may fall across Kenn's path, or the hand reach for the stars. This novel—or is it a prose poem?—comprises the whole complexity of life: science, Shakespeare, Nietzsche, Kepler—but mirrored in a perfect crystal. We divine the real history of mankind and the myth of life, from men of daring, from fishers and explorers to the modern scientist, while politicians, clerks, generals are what the river carries with it.

Let us, finally, bind up the circle of this essay by going back to the first question: how can Neil Gunn, who on the surface seems to mirror the way of life followed by crofting and fishing communities in Caithness and Sutherland, have relevance to all modern life? His novels are wonderfully observed stories of specific given characters, whom we acknowledge as real and true; their adventures and experiences are highly personal and local. But what makes them reach our own innermost experience is that they are ultimately based on a fundamental pattern to be found in life everywhere; we glimpse this pattern in a kind of vision that seems to be our own.

' The only way I know of testing whether an intimate memorable experience can be communicated to others is by finding out whether others have had an experience of a sufficiently comparable kind. . . . There can be no question here, at least, of projecting a state of mind into another mind and then finding it there *unless* the other mind has a capacity however latent for entertaining it. All literature, it seems to me, consists precisely in a communication that touches off an innate capacity for its acceptance and so induces an immediate response.' [74] All Gunn's strength, his vision, his style come from his people, from the Scottish tradition, from the Gaelic past, but he applies them to the crucial questions of our time. What he has to say is a concern of all men. Let me finish with a paragraph from the last page of Neil Gunn's last novel, *The Other Landscape*:

> Scraps of the talk came back which we had had in the white house, but in a moment they were like some ogham script, scrawled on stones, about something beyond what could be said, something other. And though nothing of this other might be known, or nothing that could be conveyed, yet equal to it and indeed in some mysterious way going beyond it was the sheer wonder of man's being on its quest. For of that now I had no doubt.

APPENDIX

Much though Neil Gunn enlarges the scope of Scottish fiction, it must be pointed out that his style and vision rise straight out of Scottish soil. Animism, and its constituent

parts of impressionism, flashing together of images, penetration into the mind, or pan-demonism of landscape, are
to be found in writers both of the Highlands and the
Lowlands (as also in Anglo-Welsh and Anglo-Irish literature).
Among the former, mention must be made of Neil Munro's
novels with their detailed mosaic of intimate observation of
localities and people in close personal relation,[75] and of
J. MacDougall Hay's *Gillespie* (1914) with its theme and
variations in different consciousnesses.[76]   In Lowland
literature, one can follow them all the way from Henryson's
and Dunbar's quick flashes and comparisons through
Alexander Hume's *Day Estivall*, James Hogg with his
uncanny penetration into another's mind and uncomfortable
dualism of objective and subjective reality in *The Private
Memoirs and Confessions of a Justified Sinner* (1824),[77] R. L.
Stevenson's *Weir of Hermiston* (1896) with its landscape
alive with meaning, to Eric Linklater [78] and ' Lewis Grassic
Gibbon ' (James Leslie Mitchell).   But we must a little more
at length dwell on one writer who not only gave a definition
of this style but also claimed it as specifically Scottish:
George Douglas Brown in his landmark of Scottish fiction,
The House with the Green Shutters (1901).

In this Scottish tragedy, the catastrophe of old Gourlay
is precipitated by young John Gourlay, a weakling, ' cursed
with an imagination in excess of his brains ', and ' with
impressions which he couldn't intellectualise '.   Old
Gourlay despises him; but stung by the malice of the
' bodies ', that chorus of leading men at Barbie, and not
to be outdone by his successful rival, he decides to send him
to secondary school and to college.   It is no mere question
of an oversensitive boy brought up in uncongenial surroundings, in a society without culture.   John lives by impressions,

they spring to life in his mind, and the pictures they create are his reality. We are given the key to this phenomenon in Chapter XVII, in which young John's Edinburgh friends discuss the strange Scots knack of phrase-making. Though Englishmen think that Carlyle was unique in this respect, ' every other Scots peasant has the gift '. As a case in point, one of them repeats a sentence he once heard said: ' The thumb-mark of his Maker was wet in the clay of him.' Another wonders ' What's the cause of that extraordinary vividness in the speech of the Scotch peasantry '; and John's answer is that " It comes from a power of seeing things vividly inside your mind . . . seeing them so vivid that you can see the likeness between them. When Bauldy Johnston said ' the thumb-mark of his Maker was wet in the clay of him ', he *saw* the print of a thumb in wet clay, and he *saw* the Almighty making a man out of mud . . . —so Bauldy flashed the two ideas together and the metaphor sprang! " [79] In a letter Brown remarks that the peasants of his country ' not merely see what they say, they *say* it so that you see it also '.[80] In the novel, old Gourlay coins many such phrases, and young John escapes into a world of vivid mental pictures which he can only express when drink loosens his inhibitions. In a lucky moment this wins him the class essay prize, but his professor warns him that this gift, if uncontrolled, may be a curse. With its ' gaspy little sentences ', all joined together by *and*, just ' as if a number of impressions had seized the writer's mind ', in Gaelic language and literature. In this way Brown is able to enter into the minds of old Gourlay and his son and lets them reveal themselves so that they are seen both from outside and in. The resulting subjective picture built up of numerous apparently objective details has an intense reality of its own, which makes possible scenes of great dramatic intensity and is itself alive, changing, taking part in the action as if possessed by so many demons: ' What he saw, it possessed him, not he it.'

NOTES ON REFERENCES

1   *The Other Landscape,* pp. 241, 157, 169, 318, 68.
2   See esp. *The Grey Coast,* pp. 22ff. and *The Other Landscape.*
3   *The Other Landscape,* pp. 16, 64, 24.
4   *The Grey Coast,* p. 7.
5   *The Other Landscape,* pp. 68, 70, 111.
6   *The Grey Coast,* p. 34.
7   *The Grey Coast,* p. 24.
8   *The Atom of Delight,* p. 150.
9   *Highland River,* p. 238
10   *Highland River,* p. 10.
11   *The Other Landscape,* p. 235. Neil Gunn's autobiographical *The Atom of Delight* is full of delights conveyed by the senses, a magic world that is richest in the life of a boy: see esp. p. 148 ' But for boys. . . .'
12   *The Other Landscape,* p. 44.
13   *The Atom of Delight,* p. 108.
14   *Butcher's Broom.*
15   *Highland River,* p. 42.
16   *The Grey Coast,* p. 16; see also *The Atom of Delight,* pp. 29f., 36.
17   *The Other Landscape,* pp. 141, 101, 163 (similarly 274), 192.
18   *The Other Landscape,* p. 272.
19   *The Grey Coast,* pp. 8, 16f.
20   *The Other Landscape,* p. 32.
21   *The Atom of Delight,* p. 36.
22   *The Grey Coast.*
23   *Sun Circle.*
24   *The Atom of Delight,* p. 62.
25   *Highland River,* p. 16.

26 *The Atom of Delight*, pp. 48, 65; similarly p. 284: 'not to mention the way a rosebush looked at the boy when he had landed his fish'.
27 *The Grey Coast*, p. 36.
28 *The Other Landscape*, pp. 198, 16.
29 *The Grey Coast*.
30 *The Atom of Delight*, p. 65.
31 *Highland River*, p. 100.
32 *The Other Landscape*, pp. 13, 56.
33 *Highland River*, p. 41.
34 *The Grey Coast*, pp. 259, 127.
35 *The Other Landscape*, pp. 202, 204; 201f.; *The Atom of Delight*, pp. 21f.
36 *The Other Landscape*, pp. 9, 10, 222.
37 *The Atom of Delight*, p. 63.
38 *Sun Circle*, p. 73. The idea of waiting, of expectancy is frequent in Gunn's work: 'After that I took things easy and wandered up into and through and round places I had never seen before, the places that are always at the back of beyond, waiting. This strangely familiar air I simply accepted, this stillness of waiting.' (*The Other Landscape*, p. 134; cf. above quotations from *The Atom of Delight*, pp. 65, 36.)
39 *Highland River*, p. 104.
40 *Butcher's Broom*, p. 31.
41 Thus the potential mood is often used to make a positive statement polite: 'B'e mo chomhairle dhuit sin a dheanamh.' I.e. 'It were my advice to you to do it.' On the other hand a statement may for emphasis be put in the form of a conditional sentence: 'Chunnaic e tigh beag fada uaidhe, agus ma b'fhada uaidhe, cha b'fhada esan ga ruigheachd.' I.e. 'He saw a little house a long way off, and if it would be a long way off, he would not be long reaching it.' (From J. F. Campbell's *West Highland Tales*.)
42 Examples taken from eighteenth-century Scottish Gaelic poetry.
43 In Gunn's *The Grey Coast* a woman's knitting fingers with their indifference 'trap' an important suitor into helplessness; cp. also above quotation of the 'fulmar in its apparently blind weaving'. (*The Other Landscape*, p. 10.)
44 *Butcher's Broom*, p. 350; see also the boy's delights in

gathering hazelnuts and blaeberries in *The Atom of Delight,*
pp. 26f.

45   *The Other Landscape,* p. 77.
46   A translation of Gaelic *ann*; cp. *Scottish National Dictionary*
      in IB 4 (6), *in* (i) *t* 'there, present, available'. 'With all
      the smoke that was in it.' 'And so there would be that in
      it: the question of Lachlan's employment and pay as a
      gillie.' (*The Other Landscape,* pp. 218, 48.)
47   *Butcher's Broom,* p. 293.
48   Many such descriptions were taken over into Scots, but the
      underlying structure of the name with its etymology is
      lost to a non-Gaelic ear and only the general idea remains;
      see *S.N.D. grawbach, groick, gow, grannach, gyacher, loogan,*
      lupikin, moosk and many others.
49   *Butcher's Broom,* p. 13.
50   *Butcher's Broom,* p. 278.
51   *The Serpent.*
52   *The Atom of Delight,* p. 8.
53   *Butcher's Broom,* p. 426.
54   *The Atom of Delight,* pp. 182f.
55   *The Other Landscape,* pp. 8, 57, 67f.
56   *Highland River,* pp. 297, 310.
57   Of his own boyhood, Gunn says: 'But in the simple
      economic picture there were a few basic safeguards. The
      cow meant milk, butter and crowdie or cream cheese.
      The stack of peats provided fuel for a year as the potato-pit
      potatoes. . . . Fresh white fish, hens and eggs were always
      around. Rabbits were never far off. . . .' (*The Atom of*
      Delight, p. 121.)
58   *Butcher's Broom; The Other Landscape,* p. 190.
59   *The Other Landscape,* p. 10; Urquhart, the narrator of this
      novel, is an anthropologist.
60   '. . . it must have been in the blood out of an immense
      ancestry. It was, of course. If man has been on this earth
      for about a million years, only the last six thousand or so
      have been what we call civilized. For a stretch of time
      inconceivable to the mind he was a hunter. That this has
      conditioned the cells in his body and most of them in his
      head may be taken as biologically reasonable. Out of his
      hunting came the first arts and crafts. . . .' (*The Atom*
      of Delight, p. 32.)

61   *The Atom of Delight*, pp. 262, 65.

62   *The Drinking Well.*

63   *Sun Circle.*

64   *The Green Isle of the Great Deep.*

65   *Morning Tide;* cp. also above ' In the centre of the gloom . . .', and the preceding quotation where women seem to bind up a circle; the same idea is to be found in *The Other Landscape*, p. 106.

66   In *The Atom of Delight*, the circle occurs in the life of a boy as a protective circle put around the second self (e.g. p. 88).

67   *Highland River*, p. 323.

68   *Highland River*, p. 168.

69   *Butcher's Broom*, pp. 297f.

70   *Highland River*, p. 42.

71   *Highland River*, p. 237

72   There is a similar evocation of timelessness in *The Atom of Delight* of a woman taking her cow to the bull: ' Then the original pattern reasserts itself, the woman leading, bent forward slightly, followed by the cow on the rope, like figures on an archaic frieze ' (p. 151).

73   *Highland River*, p. 311.

74   *The Atom of Delight*, p. 75.

75   ' I put myself in his place, and felt the skin of myself in his place, and felt the skin of my back pimpling ' (*John Splendid*, 1898); poking the fire ' made the boy and the man and the timbers and bunks dance and shake in the world between light and shadow' (*Gilian the Dreamer*, 1899); ' his body [in shooting] . . . —all but an eye and a shoulder ' (*John Splendid*).

76   The sea ' watching with fixed glassy eyes '; ' in the heart of the glowing sky pain was seated '.

77   ' If you and I believe that we see a person, why, we do see him.'

78   Whose characters ' played chess with words for queens and bishops, and ideas for common pawns ' (*White-Maa's Saga*, 1929).

79   Op. cit., pp. 182f.

80   See J. Veitch, *George Douglas Brown* (1952), pp. 94f.

Neil Gunn's Mysticism

ALEXANDER REID

At the end of the day the writers who mean most to us are those who speak most directly ' to our own condition '; who have confronted and overcome problems in which we are still involved.

Neil M. Gunn was such a writer for me in my early twenties when I was overwhelmed by his *Wild Geese Overhead*, and more than thirty years later he remains such a writer. Even in his earliest works I can still find perceptions and insights the full significance of which had escaped me at earlier readings, because I lacked the apparatus of response. Gunn in short is one of those very rare authors with whom the reader can grow. He is not only an exceptionally fine literary artist. He is a prophetic writer in the sense that William Blake (with whom Gunn has much in common) used these words, and it is with Gunn the explorer of the conditions of the evolution of consciousness that I am concerned here. My excuse (if any is needed) is that this approach enables me to demonstrate something about Neil Gunn's achievement which has not, so far as I know, been noticed before by critics—that though each of his novels can be read with pleasure in isolation from the rest, all, without exception, take on a larger significance if they are viewed as contributory volumes to a single work which might awkwardly but fairly accurately be entitled ' A Scottish Mystic's Search for the Conditions of Human Fulfilment '.

This larger work was not of course planned. It grew with its author as the fictionalised projection of his personal life experience, and if the work in the end has shape, it is because Gunn's personal life has shape—a shape which was determined by an experience in his early boyhood, when sitting chewing hazel nuts on a stone in that Highland River which he evokes so lovingly in many of his novels. In *The Atom of Delight* he recalls his experience as follows:

As I sat on that boulder, staring downstream, my automatic jaws, in action so like a cud-chewing cow's, induced a state of content, which, far-sighted like the cow's, saw nothing, and, if meditative, meditated on nothing. The shallow river flowed around and past with its variety of lulling monotonous sounds; a soft wind, warmed by the sun, came upstream and murmured in my ears as it continuously slipped from my face. As I say, how I got there I do not remember. I do not even remember whether anyone had been with me on that expedition, much less what anxieties might have to be resolved with ' excuses ' when I got home. I was just there.

Then the next thing happened, and happened so far as I can remember, for the first time. I have tried hard but can find no simpler way of expressing what happened than by saying: *I came upon myself sitting there.*

Within the mood of content, as I have tried to recreate it, was this self and this self was me.

The state of content deepened wonderfully and everything around was embraced in it.

There was no ' losing ' of the self in the sense that was a blank from which I awoke and came to. The self may have thinned away—it did—but so delightfully that it also remained at the centre in a continuous and perfectly natural way. And then, within this amplitude the self as it were became aware of seeing itself, not as

M

an 'I' or an 'ego', but rather as a stranger it had come upon and was even a little shy of.

Transitory, evanescent—no doubt, but the scene comes back across half a century, vivid to the crack in the boulder that held the nut.

In *The Atom of Delight* Gunn says of such experiences that they are 'both an end and a beginning'.

They are an end for the reasons he gives in the passage above; because, to quote the most famous of Western mystical philosophers, 'They are a further than which there is no further'—a state of consciousness in which if we could wish while it persisted (though in truth we do not wish, having already all that we wish) the only conceivable wish would be that the state of being out of which this consciousness arises should go on for ever. They are a beginning because when the experience has passed, when we are again identified with what Gunn calls our 'first selfs', our nostalgia for the Edenic state from which we have been exiled gives rise to a desire to return to it which *may* result in a revolutionary change in the life pattern of the individuals concerned. I stress the word *may* in the above sentence because, though mystical experiences of varying degrees of intensity are not uncommon, the present state of the world makes it evident that though many are called only a few choose, practically, to respond. Neil Gunn is well aware of this and in *The Well at the World's End*, which on one of its three levels is explicitly concerned with mystical experience, he gives examples of both positive and negative responses. The shepherd, Alastair, who, after a hard day on the hill, was 'carried away' in contemplation of an unusually beautiful sunset and realised (though he considered himself lucky in life) that he 'didn't want to go home', responds positively. His behaviour in a later part of the novel when he tries 'to take on himself' the suffering of a young man, for which he feels responsible, is utterly irrational in terms of the currently accepted theory of the relationship between individual and individual, but by no means irrational if we believe as both Eastern and Western mystics in all ages have maintained that we are in a quite literal sense of the words ' members of one another' . . . Alick, the highly intellectual whisky smuggler in the same novel for whom ' time stopped ' one morning as he looked down from a window on a Spanish garden, on the other hand responds negatively. He can neither ' accept ' his experience as a basis for action, because it seems to him too much at odds with his accepted frame of reference, nor can he dismiss his recollection of it. In consequence the recollection of the experience acts like a psychological irritant, and unable to commit himself wholeheartedly either to the world of ' getting and spending ' or to the very different world at which his vision hinted, he lives in obeyance, as it were, like the tramps in Beckett's *Waiting for Godot*.

Though the minute detail in which he recalls the incident—' the scene comes back across half a century, vivid to the crack in the boulder that held the nut '—shows how deep an impression it made on him, Gunn, as a child, seems at first simply to accept his first draught from the well at the world's end as what Christian philosophers call a ' gratuitous grace '; as one wonder in a world that was full of wonders. And in view of his age and his happy childhood this was natural. Though it was delightful to discover that he and the world were even more interesting than he had imagined, if Eden was so close to Dunbeath, then Eden could wait. He could explore Eden later. Meanwhile there were more urgent matters to attend to—mussels to gather, salmon to be captured.

A recollection of the experience, as part of the general context of his happy childhood, had *something* to do with his bid for economic independence as a fifteen-year-old civil servant in London, and a great deal to do with his rapid rejection of London for a post in Edinburgh, and, after some years in Edinburgh, for another in his native Caithness.

But the Neil Gunn who returned to the Highlands was very different from the carefree boy of *Morning Tide* for whom the upper pools of a nearby river were the ends of the earth. In the interval there had been a World War and in London and in Edinburgh he had seen the appalling conditions in which the mass of the people lived; heard the socially damned shrieking in agony in the ' black traps ' of crumbling slum tenements. And the Highlands too were changed, their economy in ruins; the fishing harbours silted up; the boats that remained rotting on the beaches. Did Gunn expect it to be different? Intellectually he was certainly aware of the situation. Nevertheless both the extent and the human effects of this Highland poverty seemed to have come as a shock to him—a shock that is reflected in the concern of his first novel, *The Grey Coast*. This is the saddest of all Gunn's novels and it could not be otherwise, for its whole theme is the life-frustrating effect of sheer want—not the lurid melodramatic poverty of the city slum dwellers but the quiet uncomplaining poverty of a proud people who had turned down the lamp of life to a flickering peep to ward off the total darkness of destitution as long as possible. What Gunn recognised in writing this novel was that there is no life which is not subject to material conditions and that unless man has faith in the security of at least his bare existence, he will feel impelled to weigh and measure every action. In such circumstances, even so apparently trivial a surrender to her feelings as that of the heroine Maggie when she waves her apron from the cliffs to her fisherlad lover, is dangerous.

Some readers have looked on *The Grey Coast* as a false start to Gunn's career as a novelist—an apprentice work before he found his true vein in depicting the heroic world of *Morning Tide*, the novel which followed five years later. But, if we look at Gunn's novels as contributory volumes to a single work, this is clearly not so. On the contrary, when considered in this larger perspective, it is evident that *The Grey Coast* and *The Lost Glen*, the third of the novels, are together the anti-thesis of which *Morning Tide* is the thesis. They have the same relationship to *Morning Tide* as Blake's *Songs of Experience* to his *Songs of Innocence*. *Morning Tide* is the promise of happiness which in *The Grey Coast* and *The Lost Glen* is so bleakly denied by the workings of an economic system which takes no regard for the individual life; a system in which the peoples of the Highlands are involved, but over which they have no control. As Ewan (the tormented ex-student returned to the Highlands and now a gillie) sees in a flash of self-transcendence, he and his tormentor Colonel Hicks are ' chance figures ' in a larger drama ' that affected the very earth beneath their feet '. All he (like Maggie in *The Grey Coast*) can do in their situations is keep faithful in the secret worlds of their thoughts and dreams, into which Tullochs and Colonel Hicks cannot enter, to the values of ' the lost glen ' of innocence, in the hope that in some future time the life pattern of these values will again be realised.

But what if the ' terrible times' endure so long that the memory of ' the glen of innocence' is lost? May not the end of the human story be a universalisation of the situation at the end of *The Lost Glen* where Ewan, provoked too far—provoked to the point of despair—turns on and destroys his destroyer, but in doing so commits himself to death? Gunn does not believe that this will happen. Though he foresees a very long dark night of suffering for the Maggies and Ewans of the world, he is convinced that this night will not last for ever. The three novels which follow mark stages in his search for grounds for this belief—for at least a long-term optimism.

Sun Circle, the first of the three, is set in ninth-century Caithness, in that shadowy era when Christianity and the pagan religions of the Picts and the Norsemen were in conflict—a conflict personalised in the novel in a love triangle involving Aniel, a young Druid, and two women: Nessa, the daughter of a Christianised Pictish Chief, who in the course of the action betrays her own people as a result of her passion for Haakon the young leader of the Viking invaders; and Breeta, the ' eternal' Celtic woman, who while consciously a Christian has not wholly broken away from the old nature religion, as her love for Aniel (about which she feels guilty) makes clear.

Sun Circle is one of Gunn's most difficult novels because he has used it as a vehicle for so many—perhaps too many!—ideas. Some though not all of its difficulties disappear, however, if one views it not so much as a historical tale but as a dramatisation of the psychological conflict which results when an individual adopts an attitude to life which involves the exclusion from consciousness of any important aspect of his being. Still alive in the unconscious of the individual concerned, the repressed fragment then becomes an internal and hidden enemy of the ' conscious self'; given the opportunity to become the ally of any external aggressor—as Nessa becomes the ally of Haakon.

That the symbol of ' wholeness ' in this novel is the mandala-like ' Sun Circle ' of the Druids indicates very clearly that as Gunn sees it at this time, the ancient ' religion of nature ' is more favourable to the development and retention of an integrated personality than the Christian faith which supplanted it. Christianity (Gunn is, of course, talking of Christianity as preached by the churches in Scotland) by exalting certain human attributes and degrading others provokes that irresolvable conflict between ' the law in the mind ' and ' the law in the members ' which St Paul lamented.

Though, in his later novels, Gunn takes a kindlier view of Christianity than he does here, he never retracted on this basic criticism. In his view nothing that is truly a part of the man should be denied expression. ' Man must for ever move, like a liberator through his own unconsciousness.'

In *Sun Circle* Gunn's central concern is with the concept of the ' whole ' individual, with what promotes and what threatens the integration of the individual. In *Butcher's Broom*, the novel which followed, and which tells the tragic story of the Sutherland ' Clearances ' when the clansfolk were driven from their ancestral lands by a traitor ' Chief ' who discovered she could make more money from sheep than from rents, the centre of interest is the community.

It has been held against Gunn's treatment of the Clear-ances in this deeply moving novel that he lays too much emphasis on life in Kildonan village *before* the Clearances rather than on the Clearances themselves. But this is to mistake his purpose in a novel which he was almost certainly already contemplating while writing *Sun Circle*. (The Countess who betrays her people, and Dark Mairi, whose charity is all-embracing, in *Butcher's Broom*, have obvious affinities with the treacherous Nessa and the gentle Breeta in the earlier novel.)

What then *was* Gunn's purpose in writing this tale of the great betrayal? It was, I suggest, to *use* the sad story of the Clearances as an opportunity to evoke a functioning genuinely human society—that is, a society in which the price of the joys and benefits of association is not the subordination of the associated individuals to a predetermined pattern which is destructive of that individual wholeness essential to happiness. Whether he was justified (though his account clings close to the record) in identifying the ideal 'Innocent society' with the historical pre-Clearances Highland village community is of course debatable. (It is significant, for example, that though Dark Mairi, who is doubtfully Christian, and Elie, the gentle, unmarried mother to whom she gives shelter, are not excluded from the community, they are only partially integrated with it). Nevertheless even if he *does* glamorise life of the pre-Clearance community a little this does negate his argument that the kind of society he pictures in *Butcher's Broom* is nearer to the 'heart's desire' than the cohesive societies which have replaced it.

On this reading of the novel, incidentally, Gunn's view of the Clearances as a tragedy and not one of the long list of atrocities which make up history can be seen as profoundly right. For what laid the folk of Kildonan open to destruction was their trust. And yet, without trust, Innocence is already lost!

If, as I have suggested, Gunn's first three novels can be equated with William Blake's *Songs of Innocence* and *Songs of Experience*, his fifth novel, *Highland River*, can be equated with Blake's *Marriage of Heaven and Hell*. *Highland River* is not only remarkable for its beautiful evocation of the Highland scene and its subtle interpretation of Highland character. It has a special importance among his novels because it marks the successful conclusion of his search for a reconciliation between the world of everyday experience and the visionary world into which he had entered in his ' second self ' experiences. Gunn does not expound in the book on the means by which he achieved this reconciliation. Instead he leaves it to the reader to infer its nature from the standpoint from which the novel is written, which to my knowledge is unique in literature.

What justifies this large claim?

On the face of it *Highland River* seems simple enough. It is a fictionalised autobiography in which ' though there is no individual autobiography . . . every incident may have its double ' in Gunn's own past. But there is a catch in this. Gunn does not tell the life story of his thirty-seven-year-old scientist, Ken, in the usual time order. Instead chapters about Ken's adventures as a child and as a youth (in a world which is recognisably the same as that of *Morning Tide*) are intermixed in what seems a quite arbitrary way with chapters about much later periods of Ken's life—as a student, as a soldier in the First World War, as a working scientist.

What is the explanation of this order, and, equally puzzling, why is the *main* ' centre ' from which Ken's past history is reflected upon set so near to the end of the book?

The usual explanation of these structural oddities is that Gunn's aim is to show that all the past events of a life

M 2

are coincident in *memory*, but Gunn's aim is, I suggest, much more ambitious than this. As I understand it, the aim of *Highland River* is nothing less than to picture the world of the four-dimensional self which J. W. Dunne* postulates as a necessary ground for the everyday self if we are to find a rational explanation for precognition, telepathy, mystical experiences, etc.

Whether Gunn arrived at a conception of the self and its relationship to the world which is close to Dunne's as a result of his independent thinking, or whether he accepted the theory from Dunne—with whose work he was familiar —is unimportant. What is important is that from *Highland River* onwards a theory of a temporal transcendent self is basic to all Gunn's novels. He had located the lost Eden. It was neither in the past nor in the future. Like the Kingdom of Heaven, it was within, and it could not be lost because it was the source of our being. But he also knew that although this ' source ' could be talked about, its essence escapes verbal communication.

Up until *Highland River* the subject of Gunn's writings had been rooted in his personal search. Thereafter he is turned towards ' the world ', to interpret the world in the light of his findings. If one compares the novels written before and after *Highland River* as groups, it is at once evident that Gunn's view of the world in later books is in general more objective and also that he sees the events he is treating within a much wider frame of reference. It is as if the writer had taken two steps back from his subject matter.

The increase in objectivity is particularly evident in Gunn's later treatment of specifically Highland matters.

* See *An Experiment with Time*, Faber, 1927, and *The New Immortality*, Faber, 1936. Also Gunn's own *Second Sight*, Faber, 1940.

In the early novels, and particularly in *Sun Circle* and *Butcher's Broom*, there is a certain amount of what Lévy-Bruhl calls ' participation mystique ' in Gunn's vision. He is looking to the Highlands and to the Highland tradition for an affirmation of his personal values and in some part finding it because he is putting it there. He is in love with the Highlands and the Highland tradition in the same way that his professor errant Peter Munro is in love, for a time, with Peggy in the *Well at the World's End*. When Peter sees Peggy for the first time, he imagines that she is all the lost good he has been looking for: ' The lost paradise was in her eyes . . . the light that lit the way to the well at the world's end. She was the Tao's acolyte. She was what he sought but she did not know it yet and he did not know it yet, for when he tried to know it he stopped and everything stopped. . . .' Peter's illusions about Peggy, however, do not last. In a flash of self-understanding he realises that it is not Peggy he has ' fallen in love with '. It is the same ' anima image ' which had enchanted him before when he encountered it attached to his wife Fand, when Fand was a girl of Peggy's age. With this recognition Peter falls out of love as quickly as he has fallen into it. But he does not lose by this. In compensation he now meets the real Peggy for the first time and Peggy is well worth meeting in her own right. Though she is not, as he can now see, ' the answer to all his longings ', she is a beautiful and charming young girl in whom he can enjoy a ' detached ' delight. ' Detached, more or less, that is,' as Peter reflects, for something of the magic with which he has invested her is still working.

A ' detached delight ' is a perfect description of Gunn's later attitude towards the Highlands and the people who live there. Though the Highlands remain in a very special sense ' his place ' and the people who live there ' his people ', he has no longer any need to see them as different from what they are. In the post-*Highland River* novels the Celt or Highlander is no longer *by birthright* a superior being to the common run of humanity. He is subject to the same weaknesses as everyone else but has two advantages over those who are trapped in industrial society. He has before him the ' innocent ' pattern of nature and some of its innocence rubs off on him, and he is the lucky inheritor of a cultural tradition which gives priority to encouraging the development of ' whole ' human beings and not to the pursuit of ' technological progress ', ' the increase of the gross national product ', and the other abstractions for which, in the ' modern world ', the present good of life is so often sacrificed.

Gunn's ' detachment ' is also reflected in a change in his prose style. On the whole the style of his later books is at once simpler and more profound than that of the ' search novels '. Gunn is no longer trying to argue either himself or the reader into a preferred vision of the world. Like the singing girl at the *ceilidh* he lets this story tell itself and ' leaves it ' with the reader. The result, when he is writing at the height of his powers in books like *The Green Isle of the Great Deep* and the last two-thirds of *The Silver Darlings*, is a vision of the world in which everything seems to be seen *sub specie eternatis*—as in this passage from *The Silver Darlings*:

> The *Seafoam* had now a very complicated motion of pitch and roll. Their voices were tired from being raised to carry. Steering was a more delicate art than ever and Roddie's head seemed to get a curious swinging

motion from the cross seas that bore down on them. For ever he had to be watchful, with stem or stern ready, and when they rose at a slant over a shoulder Finn could see the backs of the seas, herds of slate-blue backs, racing over an endless wilderness, a sweep of wind round their mighty flanks, like brutes of ocean, hurrying to some far ultimate congregation. But always from the lowest swinging trough, rising to out-top them, was the boat's stem, steadfast in its wooden dream.

Why is this prose so beautiful? That the rhythm of the writing mirrors so perfectly the movement of a small sailing-boat in a heavy sea and that the three unexpected words 'congregation' and 'wooden dream' are placed so rightly is not, surely, a sufficient explanation. Is the secret of the passage not this: that because Gunn is 'nowhere in particular' in the scene he is describing, it is possible for him to be everywhere? He is *with* Roddy as Roddy sways watchfully at the rudder. He is *with* Finn seeing over his shoulder the backs of the waves. He is *with* and away with the hurrying waves. He is not in but *with* the boat as, true to its own nature, it lifts out of the trough 'steadfast in its wooden dream'.

That there is a consistent world-view implicit in all the novels from *Highland River* to *The Other Landscape* is evident, and I would suggest that this world-view could be put in the following sentence. *There is only one eternal and infinite Being and all individual beings are forms of this One.*

I will not attempt to 'prove' by analysing Gunn's value judgements in any particular later novel, that this is the way Gunn now *sees* the world, for to do so I would have to write at book length. If the reader will follow the adventures of Gunn's characters in the later 'problem' novels I think they will agree that these characters fare well or badly in direct relation to whether or not their lives are in accord with the conception of the nature of the Cosmos and the nature of the individual as postulated above. Gunn's characters (Will in *Wild Geese Overhead* and Nan in *The Shadow* are examples) in these books always come to grief for the same reason. In the pursuit of some goal or ideal, they commit themselves to *courses of action* which their reasoning suggests are necessary means to desired ends, but which in practice are irreconcilable with the ' laws ' of the non-rational levels of the self. In consequence (to borrow Jung's language) their ' conscious selfs ' become alienated at once from their origins (in the unconscious) and, at the same time, from ' the world '. Up to this point Gunn's psychology is identical with Jung's, but Gunn goes further than Jung.* In Gunn if the self is reintegrated ' the recovery of the world ' is almost always marked by a mystical experience in which the individual feels a sense of atonement with an underlying reality which is presumably the common basis both of his own nature and of nature in general. The psychology may be close to that of Jung but the metaphysics are those of Buddhism and of William Blake.

In praising Gunn's novels as the greatest achievement in the field of fiction of the Scottish Renaissance writers, Kurt Wittig in *The Scottish Tradition in Literature* wrote that Neil Gunn is not interested ' in chance happenings; he is looking for the pattern of life '. In this essay I have tried to trace first the movement of Gunn's mind in the search for this pattern and also to suggest the rough outline of the pattern to which his later writings by implication point. I have

---

* See *The Secret of the Golden Flower*, Kegan Paul, 1945.

adopted this approach because many critics who recognise the importance of Gunn's achievement in other respects, tend to 'write off' his 'mysticism' as an inessential and even slightly irritating element in his work; whereas, as I see it, it is the formative influence behind his writings. If he had not been a mystic he might and indeed probably would have written novels, but he would not have written the novels we know. That he has pursued his personal search for 'the Well at the World's End' in terms of the history and present life of our own people is for readers in Scotland a happy accident. But it *is* in a sense an accident. Gunn could have pursued the same search anywhere in the world. His novels are a posing and his personal answers to what are in the end the only important questions: *Who are we?* and *What shall we do with our lives?* So long as the values of innocence and the facts of experience remain in contradiction men will continue to ask these questions and Gunn's novels will continue to find readers among those who go to literature for something more than distraction from what so often seems to be only 'sound and fury, signifying nothing'.

Neil Gunn and the Scottish Renaissance

HUGH MacDIARMID

Forty-six years ago, acclaiming Neil Gunn's first novel, *The Grey Coast*, I expressed my belief that Gunn was ' the only Scottish prose writer of promise . . . in relation to that which is distinctively Scottish rather than tributary to the " vast engulfing sea " of English literature '. But Edwin Muir had already pointed out that I was more concerned with the potential than with the actual, and I was declaring elsewhere that ' no revival of Scottish literature can be of consequence to a literary aspirant worthy of his salt unless it is so aligned with contemporary tendencies in European thought and expression that it has with it the possibility of eventually carrying Scottish work once more into the mainstream of European literature '. In the close on half a century that has elapsed, has Gunn made good the promise I discerned in him? It is not quite a fair question and I put it with reluctance. For in those early days of the 'twenties, when the ideas of a Scottish Literary Renaissance were first being canvassed, there was no one in Scotland with whom I was in closer touch. He used to come down from Inverness to Montrose and we would talk together from supper-time to breakfast-time, thus, to our great delight, controverting the widely accepted image of the Scot as largely anti-social and inarticulate. In those all-night talks, as Gunn himself has put it, ' there was hardly a place or institution where the enemy wasn't, particularly in the small hours of high discussion, as I have reason to remember. Getting the

Gaelic aristocratic idea into Lallans harness, or attaining the terrible sobriety of *A Drunk Man*, or mounting any high-mettled paradox for a raid across any border, has been of the essence. . . .' Gunn and I seemed to have a great deal in common and it was certainly impossible then to imagine that we were to follow very different courses in literature, politics and philosophy of life. In a broadcast in 1961, I said of these early days: ' I was already in touch with several young Scottish writers, but immediately I found in Neil Gunn the only one up to then who shared my—admittedly nascent—ideas on how Scottish literature might be manœuvered back into an independent status based on its old traditions but moving forward to cope with the requirements of twentieth-century life.'

Scotland has never had what could be written about as ' The Scottish Novel ' in anything like the way that England has had, and still has, the English novel, written about *ad nauseam* in books and essays. It was, I think, a profoundly Scottish feeling that Cecil Gray expressed when he said: ' Even today the whole hierarchy of the English novelists from Fielding and Smollett, through Dickens and Meredith means precisely nothing to me. I simply cannot read them. I have tried hard. I have read several books of each. I have given them all a fair trial, but it is no use.' I think he would have expressed his disgusted disinterest even more strongly if he had been confronted with the monstrous broadcast serialisation of Galsworthy's *Forsyte Saga* and Hugh Walpole's *Herries Chronicle*. It is significant that Joyce's *Ulysses* and *Finnegan's Wake* came not from England but from Ireland. Why has Scotland not produced something as remote from the common novel? The answer is that there has been a sequence of novels utterly different from any of the schools of English fiction.

The best essay on this is Mr J. D. Scott's on ' R. L. Stevenson and G. D. Brown; The Myth of Lord Braxfield ', which appeared in *Horizon*, May 1946.

Francis Jeffrey, in a review of Galt's novels in the *Edinburgh Review*, noted—' The author of the Parish Annals seems to have sought chiefly to rival the humorous and less dignified parts of his original . . . with traits of sly and sarcastic sagacity, and occasionally softened and relieved by touches of unexpected tenderness and simple pathos.' How well the reader of Galt learns to know these touches, and how he winces from them; they are what prevent a serious comparison of *The Entail* with, shall we say, *César Birotteau*. Yet *The Entail* is a considerable novel, the rather terrible story of an old man's obsession about money and land, with its streak of genuine and moving fantasy, and its *genre*, its picture of a kind of life which had good qualities, and which no longer exists. We see the same picture in Scott, but in all Galt's novels except *The Entail* it is obscured by the ' touches ', and after 1832 the national inspiration failed altogether. For more than sixty years, sixty years that saw the publication of *Les Fleurs du Mal* and *L'Education Sentimentale*, of *Middlemarch* and *Erewhon*, of *On the Eve* and *The Idiot*, of *Leaves of Grass* and *Daisy Miller*, and of the *Origin of Species* and *Das Kapital*, no Scottish writer attempted to forge in the smithy of his soul the uncreated conscience of his race. The country of Dunbar and Burns was silent. It was not until the end of the century that the silence was broken. It was in 1893 that Stevenson's last unfinished novel, *Weir of Hermiston*, was published. Eight years later George Douglas Brown, a young Scot living as a journalist in London, published *The House with the Green Shutters*. A year later, he too was dead.

Asserting that these two novels, *Weir of Hermiston* and *The House with the Green Shutters*, have certain claims to greatness, Mr Scott proceeds to examine the nature and the strength of these claims. He points out that they are both historical novels, and goes on by looking behind the character of Hermiston at the original upon which Stevenson modelled him, at the archetypal figure of Lord Justice Clerk Braxfield. Mr Scott retells several of the well-known stories illustrative of Braxfield's brutality or, as Cockburn called it, his ' cherished coarseness '. For the roots of the Braxfield stories are deep in the soil of Scotland.

> To put the matter briefly, it is the reaction of a Scot to these stories which is the equivalent of what an Englishman calls his sense of humour. . . . In analysing the national character of which these stories are a reflection there are certain elementary facts which must be borne in mind. The geographical situation of Scotland is such that life is a harder struggle, than, for instance, in Dorset or the valley of the Seine. The life that is lived there is the hard life of all inhospitable northern lands, and we need look no further for the origin of the dour thrawn quality which is commonly supposed to be predominant. There is also, however, present in this character—I do not seek to explain it—perhaps it is Highland—a quality which is gay, vain, gracious and fantastical. No one would pretend, of course, that this quality either is peculiarly Scottish, although it does occasionally occur in some purity. Stevenson's Alan Breck Stewart is an example of one aspect of it, the sweet maturedness of it appears in Scott himself, and another aspect appeared in Sir Thomas Urquhart of Cromartie, the translator of Rabelais, who died in a fit of laughter on hearing of the restoration of Charles II. What is, I think, to some extent peculiar to Scotland is the presence of these two very different qualities in what we call ' one person '.

It is a fusion, or it might be more accurate to say, a clash between them, which is at the root of the Braxfield touch. . . . He was decidedly *not* one of the things that 'blooms in our kailyard', and there was no place for him in the Scotland which was coming into being in the years following his death (1799), the Scotland in which Stevenson was born and grew up. This was a very fine specimen, a laboratory specimen, of bourgeois society, and Mr Edwin Muir, in a brilliant essay, has indicated its effects on Stevenson. Such a society, passionate in its suppression of truth, can hardly permit the existence of a serious writer, but it is prepared to allow certain writers, those whose conception of themselves as light entertainers precludes any unfortunate preoccupations with reality, to exist under licence.

After dealing with some of the faults of *The House with the Green Shutters* (which nevertheless, as he says, leaves us with the impression that its author has produced an important novel) and asserting that like *Weir* ' both novels may be considered as attempts to realise the demoniac quality of the national character, to unfasten the bonds of religion, respectability, sentimentality and success, which lived it down ', but ' Stevenson made a better job of it, more explicit and never irrelevant, his is the novel of the demoniac in action, the release of the authentic and suppressed ', Mr Scott goes on to say:

> Compared to this, Brown fumbles. He is writing simultaneously about Scotland *embourgeosié*—Presbyterian, respectable, back-biting, full of ability and success, and the Scotland of Braxfield, the repressed, forgotten, demoniac Scotland. . . . The Braxfield type lacks the essential hypocrisy of the nineteenth-century Scotland. That Brown fails to make clear the historical nature of this process of suppression is, I think, the

fundamental defect of his novel. . . . It is not the sordidness which I think Brown fails to balance, but the emotionalism. And, as I suggest, this failure arises from his inability to see the full implications of the suppression of Braxfield's Scotland.

Mr Scott ends his invaluable essay, saying:

We are not all Scottish: but the *House*, which is, like *Weir*, ' pretty Scotch, ' is not parochial. Indeed, when it is most Scottish it is almost universal. And if we look from the novel itself to the man who wrote it and the circumstances in which it was written, we find that the forces which are hostile to art are universal too. . . . If we are successful in delivering ourselves from the man who reached for his revolver when he heard the word culture, we must still keep an eye on the weapons for which the bourgeoisie reach when they become aware of creative talent. If these weapons are more subtle and less dangerous than the revolver, the literary careers of Scott, Galt, Brown and Stevenson [and, I would add, Gunn, MacColla, and Lewis Grassic Gibbon] show that they can be very dangerous indeed.

I have written elsewhere that after the sixty years' silence was broken by *Weir of Hermiston*, then *The House with the Green Shutters*, there came in this sequence Lewis Grassic Gibbon's *A Scots Quair*. We may add to that tiny tally some Tobias Smollett and the best of Eric Linklater. Fionn MacColla's *The Albannach*, belonging, however, to Gaelic Scotland, also deserves mention alongside these, and so, more conspicuously, does Sydney Goodsir Smith's *Carotid Cornucopius*. They all, in some measure, link up with the best of the Makars and of Fergusson and Burns and with Sir Thomas Urquhart's translation of Rabelais. If it is objected that this is a Lowland Scots tradition, and not a Highland one, it must be replied that it is the only distinctive tradition of the novel in Scottish literature, and that Gaelic literature has no tradition of the novel at all.

I should not write about the novel because, though Gunn and the memory of our days together forty-odd years ago are very dear to me, I have never been able to see the novel as an art form and agree with what J. M. Cohen says in his *A History of Western Literature*, namely, that ' the novel is only the youngest of artistic forms, and it is easy to imagine that even its commercial varieties may decay in the next fifty years, destroyed by the competition of television and the televised film. . . . In poetry, therefore, remains the hope for Literature's survival. . . . That there is some new poetry, concerned on the whole with the serious subject of man's isolation, with his need of a myth by which to understand the universe, and of some change in his own states of mind, is the most hopeful sign at this mid-century '. Poetry of this kind in Scotland is mostly to be found not in volumes of verse but in novels, and in Gibbon's *Scots Quair* it is abundant and expresses fully the three concerns Mr Cohen indicates in the above passage. Gunn's novels are even more full of it, and in a higher quality. Still, in so far as they are novels and not volumes of poetry, Dr David Craig is right when he says they are flawed and split by a backward-looking agrarian provincialism, and they are far enough from that species of writing which Compton Mackenzie discerned years ago must come in this age of speed and unprecedented change and which would make the expression of modern man as far removed from that of the average mind as from that of Neolithic man. Sir Compton has not however taken his adjuration to himself, and neither has any other Scottish (or English) author.

I think the real criticism of Gunn's work as a whole is that he perpetuates the myth of Highland and Island spiritual superiority and does not realise the truth of what the late Dr Anna Ramsay said in her *Challenge to the Highlands* (1933):

> There is a popular belief in Scotland, which has long been carefully fostered, that a sharp differentiation has always existed between the two parts of Scotland, the Highlands and the Lowlands, and the character of their inhabitants; and the Highlander, a dreamer and a poet, a mystic and a romantic, is contrasted with the shrewd, keen, pushing, practical Lowlander. In reading Scottish history I have been continually struck by the strange unreality of this conception. Nothing could be more remote from the facts of everyday life, as it appeared in the pages of history. The Highlander has never produced any great poetry or any great art to speak of; and far from being given to dreams, he seemed to be entirely concerned with the more practical aspects of life; money and the ownership of land appeared to be his dominant passions. It has been pointed out, and with perfect truth, that almost every Highland feud took its rise originally from a quarrel about the possession of land. The Highlander excelled in practical work; he made a good colonist, pioneer, soldier, scientist, engineer. *But* for poetry, romance, idealism one must go to the Lowlands.

Neil Gunn has given us a wonderful body of work—greater than Gibbon's, and therefore the greatest achievement of its kind in modern Scottish literature, and since Sir Walter Scott; and, if like Scott's, it has its political and other flaws, and is based on unreal conceptions, it has nevertheless splendid qualities. Dr Kurt Wittig, however, was wrong, when he said that Gunn more clearly that anyone 'embodies the aims of the Scottish Renaissance'. Dr Wittig forgets that one of the three or four stated aims of the Renaissance Movement was 'to break out of confinement to mere earthly eudaemonism with Christian nuances, that pseudo-religious mental climate which keeps the harmonies and solutions of our writers on so contemptibly shallower a level than the conflicts and tragedies which encompass our lives'.

Gunn's animism—and his personalism, his love of his fellows, his fine human qualities, are all derivative from Christianity. That will not do, as George Steiner says in *In Bluebeard's Castle*—by far the best analysis of the present condition and future of literature known to me—'In our current barbarism an extinct theology is at work, a body of transcendent reference whose slow, incomplete death has produced surrogate, parodistic forms. . . . The "poetry of facts" and realisation of the miraculous delicacies of perception in contemporary science, already informs literature at those nerve-points where it is both disciplined and under the stress of the future.'

I am afraid that is wholly lacking from Gunn's work, and the work of all other Scottish writers. As Francis Grierson—one of the many Scottish writers who have been thrust into oblivion by their inferior successors—said in his essay, 'The Celtic Temperament' (1913):

> The Celt speaks of Nature with a kind of mystical authority. The Celtic mind, at its best, becomes identified with Nature. It becomes one with the modes, conditions, and symbols of natural things. Other minds recognise the beauties and the forces of Nature, but rarely penetrate to the core of the thing seen; they

depict the outward appearance of trees, meadows, rivers and mountains; the Celt speaks for them, interprets the appearance, turns the material form into a spiritual atmosphere, explains the mystery of shapes and shadows, light and darkness, sensation and sound. To the ordinary mind the four seasons mean nothing more than change in health or variation in the conditions of bodily comfort; to the Celtic mind every day, every month, every season has its soul as well as its visible atmosphere.

He might have been describing in anticipation the writings of Neil Gunn. Alas, the survival value of such thoughts or feelings is another matter, not the principal issue today, perhaps, but certainly tomorrow or next day.

The questions I have raised in this essay regarding the significance, present and future of Neil Gunn's work are not questions I could raise with regard to any other living Scottish fictionist. That is Gunn's value. All the others— Robin Jenkins, Nigel Tranter, Alan Sharpe, William McIlvanney—are not discussable in these or any other serious terms. In short, no matter how far we have got away from each other in the forty-odd years that have elapsed since those happy night-long discussions we had in Montrose, Gunn and I in our very different ways have opened up the question of Scottish literature in a fashion that enables such issues to be raised, and there are perhaps no other Scottish writers today of whom that can be said.

Neil Gunn and Scottish Fiction

JAMES B. CAIRD

Neil Gunn's earliest novel, *The Grey Coast*, was published in 1926, the year when MacDiarmid's masterpiece, *A Drunk Man Looks at the Thistle*, appeared. Can it be that, on the strength of these two important works, one in the sphere of poetry, the other in that of prose fiction, 1926 was an *annus mirabilis* in Scottish letters, as 1922 had been in European letters, with the appearance of *The Waste Land*, *Ulysses* and the concluding volumes of *À La Recherche du Temps Perdu*? Certainly both works signalled an important advance, Gunn's rather less so than MacDiarmid's.

In his stimulating, if occasionally over-indulgent *Contemporary Scottish Studies*, which appeared in the same year, C. M. Grieve—MacDiarmid's *alter ego*—was enthusiastic in his welcome of Gunn's novel. Up till then Gunn had been a busy excise officer—like Burns before him—and his literary output had consisted of short sketches and short stories contributed to *The Glasgow Herald*, *Chambers's Journal*, *The Cornhill* and other periodicals. Grieve stated that, even in those ephemeral writings, there were 'sudden breakings through into dimensions' unknown to the editors of those publications. He referred to *The Grey Coast* as representing something new and big in Scottish literature, but qualified this judgement by saying that Gunn 'has not wholly found himself nor has Scotland re-acquired entire autonomy in his consciousness'. (Is this, one wonders, a literary or a political comment?) Grieve continued by saying that

> his work remains unequal . . . now falling into a Kailyard rut, now tinged with the Celtic twilight. Above these levels it manifests a point of view not dissimilar to George Douglas Brown's, but more humane, more *divers et ondoyant* than his, but, at the same time, less organic. . . . If he can rid himself of his remaining inequalities—sustain himself wholly at the pitch of the best elements in this book—and bring the method by which he encompassed them to full maturity, he will rapidly take rank as the foremost of living Scottish novelists—a George Douglas Brown come to magnanimity and endowed with all the knowledge psychology has acquired since Brown's day.

Considering the period at which it was written, and that Gunn had produced comparatively little evidence of his future importance as a novelist, this is a remarkably perceptive and prescient piece of criticism. Gunn certainly ranks among the foremost living Scottish writters of fiction; indeed according to Kurt Wittig he is Scotland's greatest twentieth-century novelist. He has certainly displayed more ' humanity and magnanimity ' than Brown: it would be difficult not to. Influenced to a certain extent by Proust but, more organically, urged by the need to forge a suitable medium for the expression of a subtler, more complex personality than Brown's, he writes in a more *divers et ondoyant* style than the author of *The House with the Green Shutters*. He has, too, been profoundly influenced by ' all the knowledge psychology has acquired since Brown's day ', not by Behaviourism, which is anathema to him, but by Freud and, like so many other creative artists, by Jung. The concept of the ' collective unconscious ' (Yeats's ' Great Memory '), plays an important part in his work. Other discernible influences are Zen Buddhism (*The Well at the World's End*), Celtic mythology (*passim* but particularly in *Young Art and Old Hector*), and the discoveries of anthropologists and archaeologists (in particular *Sun Circle* and *The Silver Bough*, but there are references throughout the novels, in *Highland River* and *The Well at the World's End* for instance).

Grieve's comparison with Brown and his reference to the Kailyard are, however, rather misleading. Kailyardism involves a sickly sentimentality, a 'fiddling of harmonics on the strings of sensation', a distortion, a dishonest—sometimes, as in Barrie, a cynical—caricature of humble Scottish life. It is essentially a 'decadent' phenomenon, a morbid exaggeration and over-emphasis of something that in itself is not necessarily bad. (Some strands of it may be traced to Galt and to the Burns of 'The Cotter's Saturday Night'.) The choice of humble life in itself, or the celebration of domestic 'piety' (in an undenominational sense) that we find in Gunn's *Morning Tide* is not Kailyard. It might be said with partial truth that Lewis Grassic Gibbon's trilogy, *A Scots Quair*, effects a synthesis of the Kailyard and Green Shutters traditions; that is to say if one is given to the application of the Marxist dialectic to literary history. Certainly in reading *Sunset Song* and *Cloud Howe* (*Grey Granite* is different in that, with all its imperfections, it is the first serious Marxist novel about city life to have appeared in Britain), we are constantly reminded of the sharply opposed presentations of rural and small-town life in the works of the Kailyarders and George Douglas Brown respectively. In reading Gunn we forget that either existed. On a superficial level this may be due to the fact that his stories are set either in the Highlands or on the Caithness coast.

What substance is there in Grieve's comment that Gunn's work is occasionally 'tinged with the Celtic twilight'? The phrase 'Celtic twilight' is often used imprecisely. Almost any novelist who deals with a Highland theme—unless like Compton Mackenzie in a vein of caricature—is liable to be accused loosely and inaccurately of Celtic twilightism. The 'Celtic twilight' is a mixture of degenerate pre-Raphaelism with MacPherson's *Ossian*, and is found at its most flagrant in the work of 'Fiona Macleod' (William Sharp, who corresponded with Yeats and was for a time taken seriously by him, since the early Yeats was slightly tarred with the same brush). The main characteristics of the 'Celtic twilight' are a vague, generally spurious, mysticism and an enervating nostalgia. Sharp, for instance, refers to 'the remote life of a doomed and passing race', and usually expresses himself in a misty crepuscular style with echoes of MacPherson. The following passage from his dedication to *The Sin Eaters* pointedly illustrates these characteristics:

'Tha mi Dubhachas'—'I have the gloom'. Ah, that saying! How often have I heard it in the remote isles! 'The Gloom'. It is not grief, nor any common sorrow, nor that deep despondency of weariness that comes of accomplished things, too soon, too literally fulfilled. But it is akin to each of these, and involves each. It is, rather, the unconscious knowledge of the lamentation of a race, the unknowing surety of an inheritance of woe. On the lips of the children of what people, save in the last despoiled sanctuaries of the Gael, could be heard these all too significant sayings; 'Tha mi Dubhachas—I have the gloom'; 'Ma tha sin an Dan—If that be ordained, If it be Destiny'? (*The Sin Eater*, London, Heinemann, edition of 1927.)

It is unfortunate that Sharp should have repeated the phrase 'Tha Mi Dubhachas', since, as Gaelic, it is as spurious as the whole passage. Literally translated it reads, 'I *am* the Gloom', which is nonsense. The correct form is 'Tha Dubhachas orm'—'The gloom is on me'.

The emergence of the Celtic twilight with its defeatism and self-luxuriating resignation is perhaps an understandable phenomenon in view of the development of both Irish and Highland history in the eighteenth and nineteenth centuries, but one cannot equate Celticism with this subdued crepuscular note. Although a nostalgic note is struck in many eighteenth- and nineteenth-century songs, gloom is not characteristic of Celtic literature in general. It is not vague, diffuse and consistently melancholy, but sharp, concrete and much of it joyous. When one thinks of Celtic poetry, early Irish nature verse comes to mind, ringing with birdsong and redolent of blossom, or the witty ribaldry of Brian Merriman's 'The Midnight Court'. Or take the 'Tain Bo Cuailgne'! Its action was sparked off not, as in *The Iliad*, by the seizure of a beautiful woman, but, characteristically, of a bull. Or if one looks for examples from Scottish Gaelic, there are the taunting satirical verses of Iain Lom, the heroic pitting of man against wave in Alexander MacDonald's 'Birlinn of Clanranald', or Duncan Ban Macintyre's enthusiastically detailed and 'physical' 'Praise of Ben Dorain'. Nor is there any twilight nostalgia in the poems of Sorley Maclean and George Campbell Hay. There is anger and regret at the condition of the modern Highlands and at the historical forces that brought it about—anglicisation, the Clearances, emigration, economic neglect—and this is true of the novels of Gunn from *The Grey Coast* onwards. (Sometimes, as in

The Lost Glen, indignation becomes uncontrolled and leads to caricature.) Only very occasionally does his writing become vague and imprecise in the manner of the Celtic twilight. The following phrase from *The Well at the World's End* is a case in point: ' figures caught into silence into an immortal hour in a poetic play by a long-dead Gaelic poet ', which is worthy of William Sharp himself. But this happens very rarely; the author of *The Silver Darlings* and *The Drinking Well* is by no means an escapist basking in the fading splendour of a Celtic twilight and drugging himself with dreams of Tir nan Og.

The role played by the Highlands in the Scottish novel has been relatively unimportant until comparatively recently. They form the background to a few of the Waverley novels, to *Waverley, Rob Roy, The Fair Maid of Perth* and *A Legend of Montrose,* but here it is the old wild picturesque survivals—clan feuds and antique notions of honour and loyalty—that are involved. The settings, too, are for the most part the southern Highlands, Perthshire and parts of Argyll and Lochaber. Apart from his creation of Rob Roy, Evan Dhu in *Waverley* and Robin Oig in *The Two Drovers,* Scott did not show the intimate knowledge and understanding of the Highlands and of the Highland character that he had of the Borders and the Central Lowlands. There is an element of pasteboard about, for example, Fergus Macivor, a stagy unreal quality that corresponds to the over-romanticised scenery against which some of the action takes place. If Galt fathered the Kailyarders, Scott was equally the worthy progenitor of a series of unworthy popular romances about the Highlands. Not that one would include Stevenson's novels in that category, although he too is not quite convincing in his portrayal of Highland character, as opposed to landscape, in *Kidnapped* and *Catriona*. Neither Alan Breck Stewart nor Catriona Drummond is quite credible: they are both too literary, too much manufactured from a prescription of what constitutes the Highland character. That prolific Victorian best-seller, William Black, set many of his popular romances in the Highlands, *e.g. A Princess of Thule* (1873), or *Macleod of Dare* (1878). His West Highland sunsets were notorious, but he is read now only by research students. He achieved relatively greater artistic as opposed to popular success with his short stories that reflect the life of shepherds and keepers in the Stronelarig area of the Monadliath Mountains where he spent many successive summers.

None of these novelists was himself a Highlander. It was not until the present century that a serious attempt was made by Highlanders themselves to convey the character and problems of their area in fiction. Neil Munro was a disciple of Stevenson—with a difference. He had a profounder understanding of the psychology and the thought and speech rhythms of the Highlander, and he is a better and more subtle writer than he has often been given credit for, but much of his work is warped by nostalgia of the 'ochone, the brave days that are gone' type. MacDiarmid has accused him, with some justification, of evading reality (' He turned a blind eye on all vital issues '—article in *The Modern Scot*, Autumn 1931). Munro nowhere came to grips with the situation of the Highlands in his own day, but remained wilfully anachronistic in his values and allegiances. John MacDougall Hay's titanic novel, *Gillespie* (1914), has for its locale a Highland fishing community based on Tarbert, Loch Fyne. It is much more than an imitation of *The House with the Green Shutters*, although the central situation of the two novels is parallel. Both are in a sense historical novels, dealing with periods anterior to the novelist's own, and both are concerned not only with the ruin engendered by the personalities of their protagonists, but also with the interplay of these protagonists with the communities they try to dominate and that finally reject them. Neither is the product of a desire to escape from unpleasant spiritual or economic reality. Both are relevant to the Scotland of their days and ours. A later Highland novelist of some promise was the late Ian Macpherson. His most important book, *Land of Our Fathers*, was published in 1933. It is set against the background of the aftermath of the Clearances. Its theme is the conflict between the Gaelic-speaking crofters and the rising sheepmen on Speyside with, in turn, the partial suppression of the new pastoral economy by deer forests. The evocation of the natural setting, the pasture lands around Nethy Bridge and the drove road over Drumochter, is moving and effective.

But undoubtedly the most distinguished Highland novelists of the century are Fionn MacColla and Neil Gunn. MacColla (T. D. MacDonald), a Gaelic speaker of Highland origin, although reared in Montrose, published his first novel, *The Albannach*, in 1932 (originally published by Heritage, it has recently—1971—been reprinted by the Reprographia Press in Edinburgh). It is a satirical and lyrical picture, written in a prose of tough sweetness and incorporating Gaelic rhythms and idiom, of an area in Wester Ross poisoned by sectarian fanaticism and ' naysaying '. The community is threatened by cultural and linguistic disintegration, yet it contains within itself the germ of a possible renaissance along its original line of

N

development. *The Albannach* is an uneven work, yet it has a vigour, pungency and intensity that more than make up for its defects. MacColla's other novel, *And the Cock Crew*, appeared in 1945. Like Gunn's *Butcher's Broom*, it is concerned with the Clearances, but MacColla approaches the theme more subjectively than does Gunn. He stresses the impact of this traumatic development on the mind of his protagonist, Maighstir Sachari, a Church of Scotland minister in a Sutherland strath, who cannot at first make up his mind whether the Clearances are a judgement of God on the people for their sins, as so many of his brethren, anxious to safeguard their position with those in authority, have preached, or whether they are due to the wickedness and greed of men. This part of the novel is a subtle analysis of the Calvinistic outlook presented, not scornfully nor contemptuously as in *The Albannach*, but with real insight. The opposing point of view, secular and political, and urging the need to resist, is presented by Fearchar, the old bard, who expounds the cultural, spiritual and political dangers of anglicisation. The dialogue between these two is one of the most intellectually exciting passages in twentieth-century Scottish fiction.

MacColla, however, has published only two novels. He has neither the volume nor the range of Gunn, who has twenty novels to his credit, ranging from *The Grey Coast* of 1926 to *The Other Landscape* of 1954. Inevitably there are inequalities in Gunn's work, as there are in that of any important novelist with a prolific output. But few Scottish novelists, with the exceptions of Scott, Galt and, in our own day, Eric Linklater, have produced such a body of consistently good work. (The output, as distinct from the quality, of Brown, Hay, Gibbon and MacColla, has been comparatively tenuous.) The initial promise of *The Grey Coast* was more than sustained by the appearance in the nineteen-thirties—Gunn's most creative period—of such novels as *Morning Tide* (his greatest popular success, since it was chosen by the Book of the Month panel), *Highland River, Sun Circle, Butcher's Broom* and *The Silver Darlings*. The works of this period may conveniently be classified into personal, semi-autobiographical and historical novels. Those belonging to the first group are concerned mainly with the development of a sensitive individual living in a crofting and fishing community and deeply affected both by his environment of sea, cliff, moor and strath and by atavistic intimations of the life of older and earlier inhabitants of the area—a kind of intuitive perception and investigation of temporal strata. To this category belong *Morning Tide* and the very much more personal, complex and subtle *Highland River*, which is an exploration in time and space of the deepest roots of the protagonist's and the author's being. The river, in its course from the sparse cold world of the moorland to the sea, is divided, like the life of man, into three parts. In his autobiographical *The Atom of Delight*—in many ways rather an evasive and reticent work—he describes his following, in childhood, Dunbeath Water to its source. This was to be the apparent theme of *Highland River*. In *The Atom of Delight*, too, he pays tribute to the writers with whom he felt a particular kinship, to Yeats, to the Wordsworth of ' The Prelude ' and, above all, to Proust whom he acknowledges as his master in the craft of novel-writing. He draws an interesting contrast and parallel between the way of life of ' the boy at Combray ' and that of himself, ' the boy of the strath '. In a sense much of Gunn's work might be described as ' *La*

Recherche du Temps Perdu '. (It is unfortunate that Scott-Moncrieff's excellent translation should have for its title ' *Remembrance* of Things Past '. ' *Recherche* ' is much more positive, active and conative than ' remembrance '.) This *recherche* in Gunn's case is directed not only to his personal past, but also to the past of the community in which he was brought up. The following passage, from *Highland River*, illustrates the point:

> On one side of the harbour mouth the place-name was Gaelic, on the other side it was Norse. Where the lower valley broadened out to flat fertile land the name was Norse, but the braes behind it were Gaelic. A mile up the river where the main stream was joined by its first real tributary, the promontory overlooking the meeting of the waters was crowned by the ruins of a broch that must have been the principal stronghold of the glen when the Picts, or perhaps some earlier people, were in their heyday. And all these elements of race still existed, along the banks of the river, not only visibly in the appearance of the folk themselves, but invisibly in the stones and earth. The ' influence ' continued sometimes so subtly that Kenn had more than once been surprised into a quick heart-beat by the very stillness of certain ancient spots as though the spots had absorbed in some mysterious way not only the thought but the very being of the dark men of pre-history.

The other category, that of historical novels, is represented by *Sun Circle, Butcher's Broom* and *The Silver Darlings*, ranging in time from the ninth century to the early nineteenth. There is a sense, of course, in which all of Gunn's novels might be described as ' historical ', since in them we are constantly made aware of the anthropological

and archaeological background. This is certainly true of
The Silver Bough, where the principal character is an
archaeologist, and of the later *The Well at the World's End*,
where he is a professor of Ancient History. The latter work
is set, for the most part, in a landscape of dark moor with
hills in the distance, and the traces of abandoned home-
steads and farmsteads—traces, too, of the habitations of
the Picts and, stretching even further back in time, of the
megalithic people. Munro, the protagonist, is ever conscious of this background, and it modifies his thoughts and
his actions. Even in *The Key of the Chest*, which is a kind of
superior thriller, he has his commentator, the Anglo-Welsh
scholar, Gwynn, refer on more than one occasion to ' the
integrated imaginative life of the primitive world '. Gwynn
describes the church in this particular West Highland
community at the turn of the century as acting in a ' widder-
shins ' direction in its attempt to crush the ' superstition '
that stands for a whole way of life:

> And what is he [the minister] offering in its place? Not
> a new way of life, here and now, on earth in relation
> to sea and land, with the natural happiness and mirth
> which come out of a wholeness of living, magic,
> imagination, all the emotions and desires in the one
> integrated pattern—not that, but a quite other thing,
> namely the salvation of the soul in a *future* life. . . .
> ' Thou shalt not ' is the commandment.

The three specifically historical novels are all set in the
north-east corner of the Highlands, and are concerned with
the lives of communities in that area at different periods of
ferment and crisis. For Gunn history is not a matter of
kings and dynasties, of warfare or political manœuvre. He
would never have contemplated a novel dealing yet once

N 2

more with one of that all too popular pair, Mary Queen of Scots or Bonnie Prince Charlie. For him it is the life of the people that matters, and political, economic or ecclesiastical decisions, whether they be made in London, Edinburgh, Dunrobin Castle, Rome or Iona, acquire importance only because of their impact on the dwellers in the straths or by the seaboard. In this sense Gunn might be described as a Marxist novelist, however remote his own political or social tenets may be from Marxism. What Lukacs said of Scott (*The Historical Novel*, London, Merlin Press, 1962) may be applied to Gunn: ' for him it means that certain crises in the personal destinies of a number of human beings coincide and interweave within the determining contexts of an historical crisis '. Like Scott, too, he ' portrays the great transformations of history as transformations of popular life '. Yet, although Gunn is in one of his aspects an important historical novelist, and hence concerned with the impact of time on human destiny, paradoxically, in the more personal novels, above all in *Highland River*, he is preoccupied with the illusory nature of time. Kenn, the boy, Kenn, the adolescent and Kenn, the mature man are all one; they appear to coexist, and this principle of coexistence applies to the race as well as to the individual. The Pict, the broch builder of the Dark Ages, is one with the crofter-fishermen who now dwells in the strath.

The moments of crisis that he has chosen for his historical novels are: (1) in *Sun Circle* the conflict in the ninth century between paganism and Christianity in the northeast Highlands (a theme that looks forward to later times, just as his contemporary themes look backwards), (2) in *Butcher's Broom* the impact of the Clearances at the beginning of the nineteenth century on the life of the people in a

Sutherland strath, and (3) in *The Silver Darlings* the movement of some of the people from the strath down to the seaboard, and the building of the Caithness fishing industry. In a sense his earliest novel, *The Grey Coast*, is a continuation of the story, since it is set on the Caithness sea-coast in the nineteen-twenties when the fishing had gone into decline and poverty and emigration were rife.

In preparation for these works, particularly for *The Silver Darlings*, Gunn did a considerable amount of research, but what resulted was not a lifelessly accurate and over-documented historical reconstruction like George Eliot's *Romola* or Flaubert's *Salammbô*. All three of Gunn's novels are infused with sympathy and imagination. It has sometimes been said of Gunn that his novels lack action, that he is over given to meditation, contemplation, the evocation of ' the particular moment, the arrested scene, that holds a significance difficult to define ' (*The Atom of Delight*). This is true particularly of the later novels like *The Well at the World's End*, which is a kind of spiritual picaresque novel, but where the story does not really begin until after the tenth chapter. The pace is often slow: much of what happens happens below the surface and emerges in a glance, an imperceptible movement, a nuance in conversation. There is a great deal of fencing in the attitudes of his characters to one another; words are used more often to conceal than to reveal intention: the unspoken, as in the encounters between Maggie and Tullach in *The Grey Coast*, is highly important. Occasionally things build up carefully and slowly to a climax involving action, but the action itself is sometimes sustained like a note in music held for a perceptibly long time. There is some resemblance between Gunn's art and the art behind a pibroch.

He seems to benefit from the discipline imposed by a definite story line, and he is often most successful when the meditative strain is balanced by action, when, for instance, he is precipitated into narrative by a historical theme, as in *Butcher's Broom* and *The Silver Darlings*. In these cases documentation, instead of being an inhibiting force, may actually be a liberating one. (His relative lack of success in this respect in *Sun Circle* may be due to the fact that historical guide-lines for this period are tenuous and that Gunn has been tempted occasionally into Lawrentian evocations of the dark gods and the bloodstream.) Francis Russell Hart has pointed out, however, in his essay, ' Beyond History and Tragedy, Neil Gunn's Early Fiction ' (*Essays on Neil M. Gunn*, Caithness Books, 1971), that Gunn in *The Silver Darlings* resisted the temptation to make the book a period piece in the manner of Neil Paterson's *Behold Thy Daughter*. In *The Atom of Delight* Gunn attacks this kind of verisimilitude in terms not unlike those used by Virginia Woolf in her critique of the novels of Bennett, Wells and Galsworthy.

Since Gunn stopped writing, the Scottish novel has moved in new directions. Having for so long ignored the impact of industrialism and contemporary urban life (with the striking exception of Gibbon's *Grey Granite*) it has now, with the work of such writers as Robin Jenkins (although he shows an untypical versatility and ranges spatially as widely as Linklater), Alan Sharp, Archie Hinde, William MacIlvanney and others, made good this deficiency. But there is a tendency in some quarters to regard industrial squalor and urban *malaise* as the only ' real ' Scotland, and to consider novelists who do not confine their attention to such themes as escapists. (Hence much of the indiscriminate hurling of clichés like ' Kailyarder ' or ' Celtic

Twilight '.) This is to ignore the fact that life in a Border glen, a Highland strath, on a Buchan farm, in one of the many small towns that provided material for Scottish novelists in the past, or in one of the northern or western islands is every bit as ' real ' and significant as life in the Central Belt. The novels and short stories of Iain Crichton Smith and of George Mackay Brown, with their sharply observed yet compassionate presentation of life in the remoter Celtic and Scandinavian regions of Scotland, amply illustrate the truth of this statement. It is significant that both are fine poets as well as prose artists. In a sense, although they are both highly individual and original writers, and by no means conscious imitators of Gunn, they may be said to perpetuate his tradition.

What in effect is Gunn's principal contribution to the Scottish novel? He stands quite apart from the Green Shutters tradition. The loose allegation of Kailyardism cannot be sustained. He has too strong a grasp of economic and social reality and is too precise a delineator of psychic, almost mystical experience, those ' moments of penetration ' he refers to in *The Well at the World's End*, to be daubed with the smear of Celtic Twilightism. But he is too sensitive an artist to provide, even in his most strongly documented work, a mere ' slice of life ', a commonplace transcript of reality. He has brought to his work outstanding qualities of delicacy, subtlety, psychological penetration and insight, and a poetic apprehension and presentation of experience. His emphasis on such virtues as loyalty and courage links him with Conrad, as does his interpretation of the relationship between man and the sea. In his insistence on the need for ' integration ' in the life of the individual and the community, he stands with Edwin Muir as one of the sanest and sagest forces in modern Scottish literature. (Muir's *Autobiography* and Gunn's *Highland River* are two of the most exquisite Scottish prose works of the century.) He has been the most successful novelist so far to have chosen life in the Highlands as his main theme (or rather the two-way traffic of the interaction between the individual or community and the phsyical and spiritual environment of the area). But he is far more than a regional novelist of the type of the Limousin Charles Silvestre, the Breton Alphonse de Chateaubriant or the Shropshire Mary Webb. Like Hardy and Lewis Grassic Gibbon he transcends regionalism and acquires universality.

BIBLIOGRAPHICAL

Neil M. Gunn : A Bibliography

W. R. AITKEN

In 1926, on the evidence of his first novel, *The Grey Coast*, and the handful of short stories and sketches that had preceded it, C. M. Grieve suggested that Neil Gunn was likely to ' take rank as the foremost of living Scottish novelists '. More than thirty years later, when Gunn had behind him a considerable body of work throughout which he had maintained a consistently high standard, Kurt Wittig could write: ' It seems to me, however, that modern Scottish fiction reaches its highest peak in the novels of Neil M. Gunn.' Others share Kurt Wittig's opinion and recognise that Grieve's prophecy has been fulfilled.

If the propagandists of the Scottish literary renaissance sometimes find it a little difficult to ' place ' Neil Gunn in the movement, his allegiance to what William Power called ' the literary " idea " of Scotland ' has never been questioned, and it is worth mentioning that his first novel, published in the year of *Penny Wheep* and the *Drunk Man*, carried on its title-page a poem by Hugh MacDiarmid.

Neil Gunn has made his reputation as a novelist and prose writer, but he first appeared in MacDiarmid's *Scottish Chapbook* as a poet, and he is the author of several plays. Four one-act plays are listed below, and his unpublished three-act play, *The Ancient Fire*, was warmly received when it was produced by the Scottish National Players a generation ago.

The bibliography of Neil Gunn has few complexities.

Two of his novels were published in the United States under other titles: *Butcher's Broom* as *Highland Night*, and *The Serpent* as *Man Goes Alone*. Some copies of the first edition of *Morning Tide* are dated 1930, although publication was delayed until January 1931, when the novel was the Book Society Choice for that month, and *The Drinking Well* is dated 1946, although apparently the book was not published until February 1947, when a second impression was required, on its selection as a Book Society Recommendation. *Highland River* was awarded the James Tait Black Memorial Prize for 1937, and was selected as the *Evening Standard* Book of the Month and recommended by the Book Society in June 1937, recommended by the Junior Book Club in July 1937, and also commended by the Saltire Society.

Only one novel displays textual variants, although the author made minor revisions in reprinting some of the stories from *Hidden Doors* (1929) in *The White Hour* (1950). When his first novel, *The Grey Coast*, was reissued in April 1931 by The Porpoise Press, following the success of *Morning Tide* and some five years after its first publication by Jonathan Cape, the author carefully revised the text, making alterations throughout the book on more than one hundred and sixty of its three hundred and thirteen pages. These changes range from the mere addition or deletion of a comma to a quite substantial rewriting of the text, including the correction of a few misprints—'proprieties' for 'properties', 'born' for 'borne'. The changes are mainly in the interest of simplicity, directness and precision; in particular, the adjective 'subtle' and the adverb 'subtly', gravely overworked in the first version, are frequently deleted or replaced. In view of the author's careful revision of this novel it is unfortunate that the reprint of 1965 sponsored by the London and Home Counties Branch of the Library Association should have reproduced and so given a wider circulation to the un-revised text.

The bibliography which follows has been developed from the check list the compiler published in *The Bibliotheck* in 1961; it includes, as far as is known, all Neil Gunn's books published in English, whether at home or abroad, and the translations the compiler has been able to identify. A selected list of critical references is appended. Bio-graphical and bibliographical notes on Neil Gunn are to be found in a number of encyclopedias, biographical diction-aries and reference books, and in *Twentieth Century Authors* (1942) and its first supplement (1955) the novelist has provided a brief autobiographical sketch.

For help in tracing foreign translations of Neil Gunn's work the compiler is indebted to colleagues in the National Library of Scotland, and in particular to Mr Stanley M. Simpson, and he would also acknowledge with thanks the helpful interest of Mrs Cruickshank of the Archives Depart-ment of Faber & Faber Ltd, Neil Gunn's publishers, and Miss Dickson of the Scottish Library in Edinburgh Public Library.

BOOKS

1a   *The Grey Coast.* London: Jonathan Cape, 1926.
      Reprinted by Cedric Chivers Ltd, Bath, at the
      request of the London and Home Counties Branch of
      the Library Association [1965].
 b   ——— Boston: Little, Brown, 1926.
 c   *The Grey Coast.* Edinburgh: The Porpoise Press, 1931.
      Reissued after the success of *Morning Tide.*
2   *Hidden Doors.* [short stories] Edinburgh: The Porpoise
      Press, 1929.
      Acknowledgements are made to the editors of *The
      Dublin Magazine, The Scottish Nation, The Northern
      Review, The Scots Magazine* and *The Cornhill.* Seven
      of the fifteen stories were reprinted in *The White Hour,
      and Other Stories* (1950).
3a   *Morning Tide.* Edinburgh: The Porpoise Press, 1931.
      Later impressions give the date of first publication as
      January 1931, and this is confirmed by the *English
      Catalogue,* but there are some copies of the first edition
      in which the imprint date is 1930. My theory is that
      publication was planned for late 1930 and printing
      began with that imprint date, but when the novel was
      selected as the Book Society Choice for January
      1931, publication was postponed and the imprint
      date was amended while the first edition was in the
      press.
 b   ——— Illustrated by Maitland de Gogorza. New
      York: Harcourt, Brace, 1931.
 c   ——— London: Faber & Faber, 1932. *The Faber
      Library,* 7.
 d   ——— London: Penguin Books, 1936. *Penguin
      Books,* 51.
 e   ——— Berlin: Tauchnitz, 1938.
 f   ——— London: Faber & Faber, 1953. New edition,
      reset.
4   *Back Home: A Play in One Act.* Glasgow: W.Wilson,
      1932. *Scottish National Plays Series,* 9.
      Reprinted in *The Best One-Act Plays of* 1931, ed. J. W.
      Marriott (London: Harrap, 1932).

5   *The Lost Glen.* Edinburgh: The Porpoise Press, 1932.
6   *Sun Circle.* Edinburgh: The Porpoise Press, 1933.
7a   *Butcher's Broom.* Edinburgh: The Porpoise Press, 1934.
     Reprinted by Cedric Chivers Ltd, Bath, at the request
     of the London and Home Counties Branch of the
     Library Association [1965].
 b   With title: *Highland Night.* Illustrated by Freda Bone.
     New York: Harcourt, Brace, 1935.
 c   With title: *Exiles From Their Father's Land.* Auswahl
     aus dem Roman *Butcher's Broom.* Bearbeitet von W.
     Frerichs. Braunschweig: Westermann, 1939.
8   *Whisky & Scotland: A Practical and Spiritual Survey.*
     London: George Routledge & Sons, 1935. *The
     Voice of Scotland Series.*
9a   *Highland River.* Edinburgh: The Porpoise Press, 1937.
     Awarded the James Tait Black Memorial Prize for
     1937.
 b   ———— Philadelphia: Lippincott, 1937.
 c   ———— Berlin: Tauchnitz, 1937.
 d   ———— London: Faber & Faber, 1942. New edition,
     reset.
 e   ———— London: Faber & Faber, 1943. ' Q ' Series.
 f   ———— Arrow Books, 1960. *Grey Arrow Series.*
10   *Choosing a Play: A Comedy of Community Drama.* Edin-
     burgh: The Porpoise Press [1938].
     A reissue of pp. 117-40 of *Scottish One-Act Plays*, ed.
     John Macnair Reid (Edinburgh: The Porpoise
     Press, 1935).
11   *Off in a Boat.* London: Faber & Faber, 1938.
     Written ' For the crew [his wife], this simple record of
     a holiday in a boat, bought in ignorance and navigated
     by faith and a defective engine '.
12   *Old Music.* London: Nelson [1939]. *Nelson's Plays for
     Amateurs*, 2.
     Reprinted in *North Light: Ten New One-Act Plays
     from the North*, compiled by Winifred Bannister
     (Glasgow: Maclellan, 1947).
13   *Net Results.* London: Nelson [1939]. *Nelson's Plays for
     Amateurs*, 11.
14   *Wild Geese Overhead.* London: Faber & Faber, 1939.
15   *Second Sight.* London: Faber & Faber, 1940.

16a   *The Silver Darlings.* London: Faber & Faber, 1941.
       Reprinted, London: Faber & Faber, 1969.
  b   ———— New York: G. W. Stewart, 1945.
17a   *Young Art and Old Hector.* London: Faber & Faber, 1942.
  b   ———— New York: G. W. Stewart, 1944.
18   *Storm and Precipice, and Other Pieces.* [selected extracts]
       London: Faber & Faber, 1942. *Sesame Books.*
19a   *The Serpent.* London: Faber & Faber, 1943.
  b   With title: *Man Goes Alone.* New York: G. W.
       Stewart, 1944.
  c   *The Serpent.* Inverness: Club Leabhar, 1969.
20   *The Green Isle of the Great Deep.* London: Faber &
       Faber, 1944.
21a   *The Key of the Chest.* London: Faber & Faber, 1945.
       Reprinted 1966 by Cedric Chivers Ltd, Bath, at the
       request of the London and Home Counties Branch
       of the Library Association.
  b   ———— New York: G. W. Stewart, 1946.
22a   *The Drinking Well.* London: Faber & Faber, 1946.
       Although the imprint date is 1946, it would appear
       that publication was delayed until early in 1947.
       Whitaker gives the publication date as February 1947,
       and the Library of Congress Catalog, more exactly,
       as 21 February 1947.
  b   ———— New York: G. W. Stewart, 1947.
23   *The Shadow.* London: Faber & Faber, 1948.
24   *The Silver Bough.* London: Faber & Faber, 1948.
25   *The Lost Chart.* London: Faber & Faber, 1949.
26   *Highland Pack.* With drawings by Keith Henderson.
       London: Faber & Faber, 1949.
       ' Most of these notes on country life appeared under a
       pseudonym in the pages of *The Scots Magazine* during
       the early years of the last war.' (Foreword)
       Acknowledgements are also made to *The Glasgow
       Herald*, the *S.M.T.* (now *Scotland's*) *Magazine* and
       Chambers's Journal.
27   *The White Hour, and Other Stories.* London: Faber &
       Faber, 1950.
       ' The majority of these stories appeared in the *Scots
       Magazine* over a period of many years; others in
       Chambers's Journal, The Cornhill, Dublin Magazine,

Scotland's Magazine, Scottish Field, Spectator; a few have been taken from a collection called *Hidden Doors* (1929) now long out of print. . . . Some that might have been included are omitted because at least their substance was incorporated in novels. Minor revisions have been made.' (Author's note) Of the twenty-six stories in this volume seven had appeared in *Hidden Doors*: ' Symbolical ', ' Blaeberries ', ' Such Stuff as Dreams ', ' Down to the Sea ', ' Half-Light ', ' The Moor ', and the title story, ' The White Hour '.

28   *The Well at the World's End.* London: Faber & Faber, 1951.

Reprinted 1968 by Cedric Chivers Ltd, Bath, at the request of the London and Home Counties Branch of the Library Association.

29   *Bloodhunt.* London: Faber & Faber, 1952.

30   *The Other Landscape.* London: Faber & Faber, 1954.

31   *The Atom of Delight.* [autobiographical] London: Faber & Faber, 1956.

TRANSLATIONS

CZECH
[*Morning Tide* (1931)]
Ranní Příliv. Praha: Nakladatelské Družstvo Máje, 1947. *Standard Library. Anglo-Americka Knihovna.*

FRENCH
[*The Drinking Well* (1946)]
La source d'eau vive. Traduit de l'anglais par A. Vaillant et J. Brousse. Paris: Editions ' Je sers ' (Neuchâtel: Delachaux et Niestlé), 1949.

GERMAN
[*Morning Tide* (1931)]
Frühflut: Roman. Berechtigte Übersetzung aus dem Englischen von Fritz Wölcken. München: Langen & Muller, 1938.

[*Butcher's Broom* (1934)]
Das verlorene Leben: Roman. Berechtigte Übersetzung aus dem
Englischen von F. Lennox. München: Langen & Muller,
1937.
[*The Green Isle of the Great Deep* (1944)]
Felsen der Herrschaft: Roman. Berechtigte Übersetzung aus dem
Englischen von Fritz Wölcken. München: Nymphenberger
Verlagshandlung, 1949.
[*The Well at the World's End* (1951)]
Der Quell am Ende der Welt: Roman. Berechtigte Übersetzung
aus dem Englischen von Sophie Angermann. München:
Nymphenberger Verlagshandlung, 1955.

SPANISH

[*Morning Tide* (1931)]
Marea de la mañana. Traducción del ingéls por Francisco Pina.
Madrid: Imp. Diana, Editorial Dédalo, 1933. *Selección
Literaria.*
———— Barcelona: Tipografía La Académica, Ediciones
Lauro, 1942. *Colección Aretusa,* 13.
———— Madrid: Imprenta Diana, 1946. *Novelas y Cuentos.*

SOME CRITICAL STUDIES

GRIEVE, C. M. *Contemporary Scottish Studies: First Series.*
London: Leonard Parsons, 1926. Chapter 33, 'Neil M.
Gunn', pp. 268-73.
GIBBON, LEWIS GRASSIC. 'Literary Lights.' In GIBBON, LEWIS
GRASSIC, and MACDIARMID, HUGH. *Scottish Scene, or The
Intelligent Man's Guide to Albyn.* London: Jarrolds, 1934.
(Reprinted in GIBBON, LEWIS GRASSIC. *A Scots Hairst: Essays
and Short Stories.* Ed. by Ian S. Munro. London: Hutchin-
son, 1967.)
GRAHAM, JOHN. 'The Novels of Neil Gunn.' *Jabberwock,*
Edinburgh University Review, 2 (2) May 1948, pp. 9-12.

ANGUS, STEWART [pseud. of Matthew Moulton]. 'The Novels of Neil M. Gunn.' *Scottish Periodical*, I (2) Summer 1948, pp. 94-103.

LECLAIRE, LUCIEN. *Le roman régionaliste dans les îles Britanniques, 1800-1950.* Paris: Société d'édition 'Les Belles Lettres', 1954. pp. 185-6.

————— *A general analytical bibliography of the regional novelists of the British Isles, 1800-1950.* Paris: Société d'édition 'Les Belles Lettres', 1954. pp. 312-13.

WITTIG, KURT. *The Scottish Tradition in Literature.* Edinburgh: Oliver & Boyd, 1958. pp. 333-9.

NAKAMURA, TOKASABURO. *Neil M. Gunn: A Study.* Tokyo: The University of Tokyo Press, 1962. *Proceedings of the Department of Foreign Languages and Literatures, College of General Education, University of Tokyo,* vol. 10, no. 1.

HART, FRANCIS R. 'The Hunter and the Circle: Neil Gunn's Fiction of Violence.' *Studies in Scottish Literature*, I (1963-4), pp. 65-82.

CAIRD, J. B. *Neil M. Gunn: Novelist of the North.* [Caithness County Council, 1964.]

BRUCE, GEORGE. 'Neil Miller Gunn.' In *Two Essays* ('Neil Miller Gunn' by George Bruce and 'James Leslie Mitchell, Lewis Grassic Gibbon' by Ian S. Munro). Edinburgh: National Library of Scotland, 1971.

MORRISON, DAVID, ed. *Essays on Neil M. Gunn.* Thurso: Caithness Books, 1971.

The essays are: 'The Novels of Neil M. Gunn' (John L. Broom); 'Neil M. Gunn, Recorder and Interpreter' (Francis Thompson); 'Neil M. Gunn, Novelist of the North' (J. B. Caird)—largely a reprint of Caird's 1964 essay; 'Beyond History and Tragedy, Neil Gunn's Early Fiction' (Francis Russell Hart). There is an introduction by the editor and a check list of Neil Gunn's British and American editions by the present compiler.

GIFFORD, DOUGLAS. 'Neil M. Gunn's Fiction of Delight.' *Scottish International Review*, 5(5) May 1972, pp. 25-7.

Contributors

George Mackay Brown: Orcadian poet, short-story writer, dramatist, novelist and essayist.

Francis Russell Hart: Professor of English in the University of Massachusetts at Boston; author of critical studies of Scottish writers.

Neil Paterson: Scottish novelist and scriptwriter, and chairman of the Literature Committee of the Scottish Arts Council.

John Ross: Lecturer in English in the University of Glasgow.

Marie-Hélène Rescanières: Graduate of the University of Toulouse, and presently engaged in research on Gunn.

Douglas Gifford: Lecturer in English in the University of Strathclyde, and editor and critic.

Alexander Scott: Head of the Department of Scottish Literature in the University of Glasgow, and poet, dramatist, short-story writer, critic, biographer and editor.

Donald Campbell: poet and critic; author of *Rhymes 'n Reasons* (1972).

Gillian Shepherd: research student on Modern Scottish Fiction in the University of Strathclyde.

Andrew Noble: Lecturer in English in the University of Strathclyde; Ph.D. from the University of Sussex on Modern American Fiction.

George Bruce: poet, critic, and Fellow in Creative Writing in the University of Glasgow.

Stewart Conn: poet and playwright; Producer in charge of Drama for radio in Scottish B.B.C., where he has produced numerous adaptations of Gunn's novels.

James Aitchison: poet and short-story writer; teacher of English in Telford Technical College; Ph.D. from the University of Strathclyde on Edwin Muir.

J. B. Pick: novelist, scriptwriter, critic and editor.

Kurt Wittig: Professor of English in the University of Freiburg; author of *The Scottish Tradition in Literature* (1958).

Alexander Reid: dramatist and critic who has adapted a number of Gunn's novels for radio.

Hugh MacDiarmid: the greatest living Scottish poet.

James B. Caird: H.M. Inspector of Schools in Ross and Cromarty; author of critical studies in Scottish Literature.

W. R. Aitken: Senior Lecturer in Librarianship in the University of Strathclyde; Ph.D. from the University of Edinburgh on the history of Library Movement in Scotland.